BRUMBACK LIBRARY
3 3045 00188 0919

D1295111

# THE GREATEST MAN WHO EVER LIVED

## THE SUPREME BUDDHA

**AUTHOR**
**VEN. WERAGODA SARADA MAHA THERO**

**EDITOR:**
**EDWIN ARIYADASA**

*ADAPTED FROM THE MATERIAL IN "**bUDU HĀMUDURUVO***
*BY LATE **VEN. PANDIT GANEGAMA SARANANKARA MAHA THERO,***
*WITH A SENSE OF RESPECT AND GRATITUDE*

**PUBLISHED BY**
**SINGAPORE BUDDHIST MEDITATION CENTRE**
No. 1, Jalan Mas Puteh, Singapore 128607.
Tel: (05) 7783330 Fax: (65) 7730150

**AUTHOR**
Ven. Weragoda Sarada Maha Thero

**EDITOR**
Edwin Ariyadasa

**ILLUSTRATOR**
P. Wickramanayake

**GRAPHICS CONCEPT**
Piyaratna Hewabatage
**Assistants**
Saman Siriwardana
Lalith Rohana Liyanage
Ashoka Kamalasiri

**COMPUTER GRAPHICS & DESKTOP PUBLISHING**
Mdm. Ang Lian Swee (Sita)
Ven. W. Sunanda
E. Surawansa
K. M. Maithri
Mahinda Kumara Tilakarathna

**COMPUTER CONSULTANT**
Ong Hua Siong
Ven. W. Sunanda

**First Published**
10th May 1998

**Printed in Singapore**
ISBN: 981-04-0282-1



**Ven. Weragoda Sarada Maha Thero**
**Singapore Buddhist Meditation Centre**
**No. 1, Jalan Mas Puteh, Singapore 128607.**
**Tel: (65) 7783330 Fax: (65) 7730150**

Reprinted for free distribution by
**The Corporate Body of the Buddha Educational Foundation**
11F., 55 Hang Chow South Road Sec 1, Taipei, Taiwan, R.O.C.
Tel: 886-2-23951198 , Fax: 886-2-23913415
Email: overseas@budaedu.org
Website: http://www.budaedu.org

# THE GREATEST MAN WHO EVER LIVED

## THE SUPREME BUDDHA


**AUTHOR:**

VEN. WERAGODA SARADA MAHA THERO



**EDITOR:**
Edwin Ariyadasa

**ILLUSTRATOR:**
P. Wickramanayake

**GRAPHIC CONCEPTS:**
Piyaratna Hewabatage

*Do not believe in anything (simply)*
*because you have heard it.*
*Do not believe in traditions because they*
*have been handed down for many generations.*
*Do not believe in anything because it is*
*spoken and rumoured by many.*
*Do not believe in anything (simply) because*
*it is found written in your religious books.*
*Do not believe in anything merely on the authority*
*of your teachers and elders.*
*But after observation and analysis,*
*when you find that anything agrees with reason*
*and is conducive to the good and benefit of one and all*
*then accept it and live up to it.*

*BUDDHA*
*(Anguttara Nikaya, Vol. I, 188-193 P. T. S. Ed.)*

# INTRODUCTION

## VEN. WERAGODA SARADA MAHA THERO

The rich and fertile history of mankind has yielded several human treasures that are for all time, and for all places. These universal beings have etched themselves in the collective memory of humanity by their victories, triumphs and conquests of peace, love and affection They stand out vividly, leagues above those so-called conquerors who waded through oceans of tears to reach thrones of blood for one passing moment in history's eternity.

The great men of mankind, who epitomize the positive and wholesome urges of life, are venerated as leaders of religious systems, saints, sages, seers, philosophers, men of letters, artists and scientists, who have illuminated the path of mankind's progress out of the morass of ignorance, into enlightened thinking in variegated fields. Of all those human beings who assisted the world of men and women to win the upper reaches of spiritual experience, discarding the gross and the grotesque, only a handful stand out as the greatest in terms of their service to man.

From among this limited and restricted coterie of such great personalities, who adorned the annals of man so far, who is the greatest man who ever lived? To anyone whose vision is not clouded by prejudices, and whose capacity for objective thinking is not impaired even slightly, there just cannot be any ambiguity about responding to this question. The greatest man who ever lived in this world of ours, dominating the whole of human history by his boundless compassion and unrestricted loving-kindness, is no other than the **Supreme Buddha**.

No other being in the whole of mankind has ever made such sacrifices as He has done in order to achieve liberation for Himself and for all men and women. The luxury He discarded in His unswerving quest for Truth, in His search for the ending of human suffering, is rarely paralleled, to say the least. Giving up even a trivial possession may prove an intensely troubling ordeal for ordinary men and women. But, what Prince Siddhartha turned his back on, was a golden cocoon of luxury that had been carefully choreographed by a fond royal father who would have gone to any extent to prevent the intrusion of life's sordid realities on his privileged son's pristine mind.

He renounced all that, and accepted an austere, ascetic way of life by choice. He tortured His body in a totally committed episode of intense self-mortification that lasted six gruelling years. His mission of forty-five years was an era of unprecedented challenge in the whole of man's spiritual progress.

The profile of the Supreme Buddha's life has been chartered in millions of books and other creative works. But, the subtleties and significant details of the events, incidents, episodes and encounters that make up his life as the Supreme Buddha, have been recorded at book-length only very rarely.

The present work has succeeded in delving deep into some very unlikely places in the Tipitaka (the Three Baskets) to explore aspects of the life of the Supreme Buddha that most of those spiritual chroniclers tend to miss. As a result of this sustained exercise this book has been able to reveal details that will, without any doubt, surprise most readers who had been persuading themselves that they knew everything that was to be known about the life of the Supreme Buddha.

The present work is inspired largely by the assiduous research done by late **Ven. Pandit Ganegama Saranankara Maha Thero** who, with his unmitigated devotion, viewed the life of the Buddha with an entirely fresh vision. Those who will recall this work will invariably experience an unusual spiritual joy when they explore this work with an ever sharpening sense of discovery. When the material mustered here is studied by the moderns, they will begin to appreciate that the Supreme Buddha is the greatest man who ever lived.

The views and concepts generated by the Supreme Buddha have an unfailing capacity to stand the test of time. They possess the potentiality to provide the proper responses to the challenges that emerge in each passing era. As is our publications habit we have illustrated the present work, too, with especially commissioned art-works. These illustrations visualize some of the stories, episodes and events in the life of the Buddha, with such vividness that these incidents come alive to those devotees who study this work.

Along with the main offering, which is "**The Greatest Man Who Ever Lived - The Supreme Buddha**" we offer in this work additional material of equal significance. One of the special segments of the present publication is the story of the Buddha's sacred relics. Since the epic of the dissemination of the Buddha's relics, through the length and the breadth of the Buddhist world, had its historical beginning in the Great Demise, we have included in this work a brief segment the **Mahā Parinibbāna Sutta** (the Discourse on the Great Demise of the Enlightened One).

The story of the Buddha's relics is a narration of the annals of the bodily relics of the Enlightened One. The immediate reason for the printing of this segment on the relics is the unprecedented Exposition of the Buddha's relics from India and Sri Lanka, at Phor Kark See Buddhist Temple, Bright Hill, Singapore. This Exposition is jointly sponsored by The Singapore Buddhist Meditation Centre and the Phor Kark See Buddhist Temple.

The primary intention in bringing out this book is to give a totally new vision of the life of the Buddha as "**The Greatest Man Who Ever Lived**". This book will establish beyond doubt, that the Supreme Buddha is truly a universal Man who is unchallenged and unparalleled in this stature. In our publications programme we have always had a special consideration for the younger generation or readers. Here, too, the illustrations, done on a very lavish scale, will attract the young ones, enabling them to take a lively interest in the life of the Buddha, as a personality who stands out as a universal spiritual Victor.

A work of this kind of complexity has inevitably to be the outcome of sustained team effort. As the author of this important publication, I have been blessed with the rare privilege of receiving the dedicated and committed assistance of outstanding individuals and groups. Of those, I must make special mention of Mr. Edwin Ariyadasa, the well-known Media Expert of Sri Lanka who has been an integral part of our Institution as the Editor of our publications.

Equally important is the contribution of Mr. P. Wickramanayaka, eminent Sri Lankan Artist, who has consistently elevated the quality of our publications by his unique illustrations. My special sense of gratitude to Mr. Piyaratne Hewabatage has to be recorded here. His graphics and illustrations, for SBMC publications have given them a distinguished personality. The present work is partly an adjunct to the Relics Exposition Ceremony, organized by The Singapore Buddhist Meditation Centre in collaboration with Phor Kark See Temple, Bright Hill, Singapore.

I must acknowledge here the closest collaboration I was able to receive from the Phor Kark See Temple, for the publication of this significant work. It was their sponsorship that enabled this publication to be brought out as part of the Relics Exposition ceremony. While acknowledging the contribution made by Ven.Sik Kwang Sheng, chief administrator of Phor Kark See Temple. I must extend my thanks to young Mr. Shen Shi An of, Phor Kark See Temple, for his tireless coordinating effort.

As always, Mr. Sito Woon Chee, President and members of the Singapore Buddhist Meditation Centre have cooperated on this publication effort, with their usual enthusiasm and understanding.

**Among numerous supporters, who have made this a successful project, some names stand out. The total text was made print-ready by Ms. Ang Lian Swee (Sita), challenging the insistent imperatives of time. Sacrificing vast segments of her leisure, Ms. Ang Lian Swee saw to it that the text was available on time to the Author-Editor team for their scrutiny.**

Rev. Sunanda, kept urging everyone on, with an alert eye on all aspects of the progress of the work. A dynamic trio of female lay devotees, made up of Ms. Yeo Lee Choo, Ms. Tan Jiak Koon Janet and Ms.Terene Seow always found the time to attend to significant details that needed looking into. Ven. Wandurambe Sangharatana, assisted us with the proof of this publication. May much merit accrue to him, for that service to the Dhamma. To all those, who contributed towards the fulfillment of this Dhamma project, I wish happiness, good health and prosperity.

Metta Cittena

**Ven. Weragoda Sarada Maha Thero**
Chief Monk
Singapore Buddhist Meditation Centre
No. 1, Jalan Mas Puteh
Singapore 128607
8th May 1998.

# FOREWORD

## VEN. DR. K. SRI DHAMMANANDA MAHA NAYAKA THERO

The publications effort of Ven. Weragoda Sarada , seems to possess the power of an elemental force. It is irresistible and overpowering. It keeps on moving onwards, with an undiminished vigour. His current work, takes him to the very source of it all- The Life of The Supreme Buddha. Ven. Weragoda Sarada's present publication titled **"The Greatest Man Who Ever Lived - The Supreme Buddha,"** projects a totally fresh vision of the Buddha, even to those who are quite familiar with the story of the Enlightened One. The unique feature of the work is that, it enables a modern reader, to see the Supreme Buddha, as a contemporary, who meets the challenges of life, in our day. Ven. Sarada, has introduced a new concept to publishing, through his new, voluminous works. Usually he prints many books together. His idea of the multiple-book has made the present volume a collection of several works within the covers of one publication.

Though his main presentation here is **"The Greatest Man Who Ever Lived - The Supreme Buddha"**, he has added a few more works to his principal Book. One of these is the story of the Buddha's Bodily Relics. To my mind, this is perhaps the first time that the story of the Buddha's relics, has been told in an inter-connected version. It is axiomatic, that the story of the Buddha's Relics should begin at the logical beginning - which is **Mahā Parinibbāna Sutta**. (The Discourse on the Great Demise- the passing away of the Buddha.) The present work prints a version of the **Mahā Parinibbāna Sutta** as well. The inevitable hall-mark of Ven. Sarada's publications is the illustration-aspect. True to the tradition, he himself has initiated, the present work is replete with especially commissioned illustrations in colour, that make their point eloquently and tellingly.

As one of his ardent well-wishers, I feel it my duty to congratulate Ven. Weragado Sarada for an extremely satisfying publication that will keep the readers engrossed. While marvelling at his irrepressible publishing vigour, we will await his next work, which I am sure will arrive right on the heels of the present. My best wishes and high blessings are always with Ven. Weragoda Sarada. May he continue from success to greater sucess.

Metta Cittena

**Ven. Dr. K. Sri Dhammananda Maha Nayaka Thero, Ph.D., D. Litt.**
Chief Prelate, Singapore, Malaysia.
8th May 1998.

# MESSAGE

**VEN. SIK KWANG SHENG**

May I begin my message, with Greetings to all those whose dedication and devo tion have made this historical Exposition of the Buddha's holy relics, an act of great merit. With this unique Exposition of the Buddha's Holy Relics and the celebration of Vesak 1998, we display our utmost gratitude to the **"Greatest Man Who Ever Lived - Supreme Buddha.** The Supremely Enlightened Being illuminated a path for the whole of mankind to reach the Eternal bliss of **Nibbāna**.

His life story and his noble spiritual mission that continued for 45 years, and is continuing even today more than two-thousand five -hundred years after his Demise, provide the whole of mankind the spiritual goal we should all yearn to reach. At this holy moment when we convert Phor Kark See Temple into a Gandha Kuti (Fragrant chamber) for the sacred relics of Sakyamuni Buddha, I feel a deep sense of obligation to venerate the memory of my master Late Ven. Sik Hong Choon, who still inspires us, though he is not among us today physically.

May the merit that accrues from this act of veneration ensure the Bliss of **Nibbāna** to late Ven. Sik Hong Choon. I consider it proper to express my gratitude to Ven. Weragoda Sarada Maha Thero, Chief Monk, Singapore Buddhist Meditation Centre, whose substantial support made it possible for Phor Kark See Temple to participate in this historical and sacred Relics Exposition at Phor Kark See Temple.

This unprecedented Relics Exposition contributes extensively towards the strengthening of the close and intimate ties that already exist among Buddhist communities right round the globe. I must congratulate Ven. Weragoda Sarada Maha Thero, once again, for so thoughtfully publishing this valuable Book on the Life of the Supreme Buddha, tracing, in addition, the glorious story of the bodily Relics of the Enlightened One.

May all beings be happy.

Metta Cittena,

**VEN. SIK KWANG SHENG,**
Chief Administrator Phor Kark See Temple, Singapore.
8th May 1998.

# MESSAGE

**SITO WOON CHEE**

While the world is fast approaching the year 2000, the publications programme of the Singapore Buddhist Meditation Centre, is moving rapidly towards its 200th title. This, therefore, is a oment of justifiable pride to SBMC. Our current publication and the events with which we are presently associated, tend to add a new dimension to SBMC services. The present book titled "**The Greatest Man Who Ever Lived - the Supreme Buddha**" has become more significant than just being our latest publication. This work has assumed the status of a literary monument, as it were, to an event of far reaching significance in which the SBMC is a collaborating partner.

The sacred occasion is the Exposition of the Supreme Buddha's holy relics at Phor Kark See Temple, at Bright Hill Road, Singapore in joint collaboration with Singapore Buddhist Meditation Centre. To reflect this collaboration, the present publication prints a substantial segment of the history of the Bodily Relics of the Supremely Enlightened One.

In effect, the present book is a memento of this unprecedented religious event, preserving the memory of this unique Relics Exposition for generations to come.

As always, on this occasion too, the total achievement is the product of the fertile mind of our unfailing spiritual guide and preceptor Ven. Weragoda Sarada Maha Thero, Chief Monk, Singapore Buddhist Meditation Centre. We at the SBMC are perpetually aware that we can pursue a project to high success, because we are always blessed with the practical and pragmatic approach, that is adopted by Ven. Weragoda Sarada Maha Thero.

I deem it my duty to express the gratitude of us all, to Ven. Weragoda Sarada Maha Thero for his substantial service to the SBMC, and through it, to the whole world of Buddhist learning.

As President, I must offer my grateful thanks to all members of the SBMC and to all supporters and well-wishers for being with us in our endeavours to spread the word of the Buddha, right round the globe.

Metta Cittena

**SITO WOON CHEE**
President, Singapore Buddhist Meditation Centre

8th May 1998.

# CONTENTS

## A great battle

*The whole universe is a vast field of battle. Everywhere there is fighting. Existence is nothing but a vain struggle against germs of dreadful diseases, molecules against molecules, atoms against atoms, and electrons against electrons. Mind is still more a scene of battle. Forms, sounds, tastes etc. are resultants of counteracting and belligerent forces. The very existence of war proves that there is a state of Perfect Peace. It is what we call Nibbana.*

***Ven. Narada Thera, "The Bodhisatta Ideal"***

CHAPTER 1

## THE BUDDHA IS NOT A GOD. HE IS A GREAT HUMAN BEING

Those who do not know the Buddha properly, consider Him a God. The Buddha never esteemed such unnecessary glory, praise or honour. Nor did He expect such things.

> "O Bhikkhus, gains, offerings, glory, praise are all harsh and fierce.They are a danger preventing the achievement of the highest bliss of liberation." **(Dāruno Bhikkhave lābha sakkāra siloko kaṭuko, pharuso antarāyiko, anuttarassa yogakkhemassa adhigamāya.")**
>
> *(Saṃyutta Nikāya - Lābha Sakkāra Saṃyutta)*

The Buddha appeared among men solely to make people see their ignorance, lack of awareness, wrong views, fallacies, and wrong actions. Such a great man will never expect limitless deference, praise or honour from the people.

One day, the Buddha walked along the road from the city of **Ukkaṭṭhā** to the city of **Setavyā**. A Brahmin named Drona, travelling along the same road after the Buddha, saw His footprints. He looked at them and thought, "These can never be the footprints of a human being." The Buddha stepped aside from the road and sat under a tree. Brahmin Drona walked up to the Buddha, whose demeanour was exceedingly calm and serene, and questioned Him thus:

**Brahmin:** "Are you a God?"

**The Buddha:** "Brahmin, I am not a God."

**Brahmin:** "Are you a **Gandhabba** (divine musician)?"

**The Buddha:** "Brahmin, I am not a **Gandhabba**."

**Brahmin:** "Are you a **Yakkha**?"

**The Buddha:** "Brahmin, I am not a **Yakkha**."

**Brahmin:** "Are you a human being?"

**The Buddha:** "Brahmin, I am not a human being, either."

**Brahmin:** "When I ask you whether you are a God, you say "No, I am not a God." When I ask you whether you are a **Gandhabba**, a **Yakkha** or a human being, you say "No." If that were so, who are you?"

**The Buddha:** "O Brahmin, if I am a god, I must have those sense-desires. But, I have eradicated sense-desires fully. Therefore, I am not a God.

If I am a **Gandhabba**, I must have sense-desires. But, I have eradicated those fully. Therefore, I am not a **Gandhabba**.

O Brahmin, if I am a **Yakkha**, I must have the sense-desires that a **Yakkha** should have. But, I eradicated all that fully. Therefore, I am not a **Yakkha,** either.

O Brahmin, if I am an ordinary human being, I must have the sense-desires of ordinary men. But, I have totally eradicated those. Therefore, I am not a human being like other human beings. **O Brahmin, a blue lotus, red lotus or white lotus is born in the water. It grows in the water. But, it remains uncontaminated and untouched by water. I, too, am like that. I was born among men of this world.** I grew up among men in this world. But, I have risen above the world and ordinary men and women. I am not attached to the world. Therefore, O Brahmin, I am a superior human being who has destroyed all the weaknesses of ordinary human beings (**uttara manusso**). In short, **I am a Buddha. The best way to describe me is 'Buddha'. O Brahmin, please call me 'Buddha'."**

***(Anguttara Nikāya - Catukka Nipāta - Donāloka Sutta)***

The above dialogue between a Brahmin and the Buddha establishes that the word 'human being' used to denote an ordinary person full of defilements and blemishes, should be used for the Buddha only when we have to indicate such varieties of beings as **Sura**, **Asura**, **nara,** and **nāga**. The life of the Buddha has two separate segments. From the time He was born as Prince **Siddhārtha** until He attained supreme Enlightenment, He was an ordinary human being - an Aspirant Buddha.

Since He eradicated all such blemishes as lust (**rāga**) immediately on His attainment of Enlightenment, He is a superior human being. He is, to-date, the greatest human being in the whole of humankind. He can be compared not to a human being, but to a Buddha. As there is no one to whom He can be compared, He is described as 'incomparable'. He is described also as 'comparable to only himself - the Buddha'.

He is a strange human being among human beings - an unusual human being. He is a strange person among persons. He is an equally strange human being among beings. Since two such persons cannot be seen at one time, He is also described as the 'unique being'.

**Prince Siddhārtha was born to human parents. He was born with a human form. He lived as a Buddha and He lived for a human life span, and passed away as a superior human being.** Such blemishes as lust, anger, ignorance, egotism, pride, jealousy and hatred, that are found in all human beings, were not seen in Him. What were seen in Him were such great human qualities as loving-kindness, compassion, altruistic joy, equanimity, morality, concentration, and insight, which are rarely found in other human beings.

The Buddha spoke a language that was current in His day. He spoke in a simple idiom that anyone could understand. He took such food and drink as other human beings consumed. There are many places in His Words that reflect human qualities well. In one place He speaks thus:

"I am an old man now. I have only a brief time left to live. I will pass away, leaving you. I have done my duty by you."

These words are similar in style to the last words of an aged father to his children gathered round his death bed. Here, the Buddha is seen clearly as a human being speaking to human beings.

"O **Ānanda**, now I am decrepit, advanced in years, grown old. I am now eighty years old. Just as an old creaking chariot is kept going by binding pieces together, my body, too, is kept going now, bound together by my saintly powers."

***A Brahmin named Drona, travelling along the same road after the Buddha, saw His footprints. He looked at them and thought, "These can never be the footprints of a human being."***

*see page 1*

**(Ahamkho pana Ānanda, etarahi jinno, vuḍḍho, mahallako, addhagato vayo anuppato, āsitiko me vayo vattati, seyyathāpi Ananda jajjara sakataṃ vedha missakena yāpeti, eva meva kho Ānanda vedha missakena maññe tathagatassa kāyoyāpeti.**"

*(Mahā Parinibbāna Sutta)*

(An eighty-year-old is seen through these words.)

After He took the meal offered by **Cunda Kammāra Putta**, the Buddha was afflicted with a serious illness. He requested **Ven. Ānanda** three times this way:

"**Ananda, I am very thirsty. Fetch some water for me quickly.**"

Through the words He used, we can discern a sick person who is exceedingly thirsty.

**Vakkali**, who was fascinated by the Buddha's incomparable physical beauty, became a **bhikkhu** (monk) only to keep on looking at Him.

Once, the Buddha asked **Ven. Vakkali,**

"**Vakkali,** what profit do you get from this impure body?" (**Kim te Vakkali iminā pūtikāyena**?)

**This shows that His body is a human body full of thirty-two varieties of impurities.**

Once, the Buddha said,

"O monks, give up just one thing because of my Word. If you give it up, I promise, I guarantee that you will win the state of 'Non-Returner'. The only thing you should give up is 'craving'."(**"Ekadhammamaṃ bhikkhave pajahatha. Ahaṃ vo pāṭibhogo anāgamikāya. Katamamaṃ ekadhammamaṃ:Lobhaṃ Bhikkhave ekadhammamaṃ."**)

**In the Buddha's Words 'I promise. I guarantee', an ordinary human ring can be heard.** All persons do not always say 'I promise. I guarantee.' These are the words of a person who possesses a strong self-confidence acquired through seeing, through experiencing and through experimenting.

On His death bed, the Buddha addressed the monks this way:

**"O Bhikkhus, if any monk present here has any doubt whatsoever, either about me, or the Dhamma, or the Sangha, or the Path, or the rules, ask me now.**

Do not repent later, saying:

**"We could not ask these questions when our Teacher was alive; we could not clarify this doubt at that time.' Therefore, if you have any question, ask me now. If someone does not want to ask a question because of his deference for me, get a friend to ask it on your behalf."**

He said so three times. But the monks kept silent.

*(Mahā Parinibbāna Sutta- Anguttara Nikāya-Chatukka Nipāta)*

Just consider the nature of this Chief, this Leader - this Teacher. He requested the monks from his death bed before He breathed His last, not once, but three times, to ask Him anything they wanted to know, or to clarify any doubt they had about His life, about His behaviour, about His ideas, about His brotherhood, or about things they did not know. **This demonstrates the purity of His life, and His earnestness to teach things that they did not know, even at the moment of His breathing His last.**

This also indicates His commitment to service to others even when He was breathing His last. **Is there any other**

**teacher, any other leader, any religious person, any mother or father, or any elder who made such a request at such a sad moment, in the whole of human history?** Isn't this a great example to those who serve, and to those who are under obligation to serve?

> **"O monks, give up evil. Evil can be given up. I would not ask you to give up evil if evil cannot be given up. I say this because evil can be given up. I will never say this if something bad or some suffering is likely to happen when evil is given up. I say this only because giving up evil is conducive to good and to happiness."**

*(Anguttara Nikāya- Dukkha Nipāta)*

Consider whether this does not contain the tone of an entreaty made by a mother or father appealing to their children, "My son, my daughter, do not do any evil thing. You can refrain from doing evil. That is why I ask you not to do wrong things. Only good will result if you avoid evil action." Have gods said such things? Not at all so.

> **"O monks, if others also know the value of giving just as much as I know, no one will eat anything without giving at least a morsel to others. They will never be miserly. If there is anyone to receive it, they will give part of the last portion of their meal they were eating."**

*(Itivuttaka Pāli - Ekaka Nipāta)*

**These are the words of a person of great generosity, who had given away much.**

Once, the Buddha was afflicted with a rheumatic illness. **Ven. Upavāna** was ministering to the Buddha. The Buddha said to that monk,

> **"Upavāṇa, bring me some warm water."**

*(Sanyutta Nikāya-Brahmana Sanyutta)*

**In this, too, we can see a human quality.**

Once, the Buddha went to the shade of a tree, accompanied by **Ven. Mahā Kassapa.** The Buddha indicated that He likes to sit under that tree. **Ven. Mahā Kassapa** took his silk robe and folded it four-fold, and placed it on the ground for the Buddha to sit on. The Buddha sat on it and said,

> "**Mahā Kassapa**, your robe is very smooth.'

**Ven. Mahā Kassapa** said,

> "Sir, please accept this robe in compassion for me."

The Buddha said,

> "**Kassapa**, do you like to wear my robe, worn out due to long use and made of cemetery cloth?"

**Ven. Mahā Kassapa** said,

> "Yes Sir, I like it. I will give my robe to the Buddha and put on the worn-out robe of the Buddha, made of cemetery cloth."

*(Sanyutta Nikāya - Kassapa Sanyutta)*

Here, the Buddha indicating that **Ven. Mahā Kassapa**'s silk robe was smooth, He persuaded **Ven. Kassapa** to give the Buddha his silk robe, taking the Buddha's worn out robe in exchange.

**This exchange shows signs of an equality and an intimate friendship that existed between the Buddha and Ven. Mahā Kassapa.**

Once, a Brahmin by the name of **Pañcavagga Dāyaka**, was taking his meal with his back turned to the courtyard of his house. The Brahmin's wife was serving him. Seeing that the two of them were ripe for spiritual achievements, the Buddha visited that house on his alms round. Seeing the Buddha, the Brahmin's wife thought, "If my

*"O Brahmin, a blue lotus, red lotus or white lotus is born in the water. It grows in the water. But , it remains uncontaminated and untouched by water. I, too, am like that. I was born among men of this world. I grew up among men in this world. But, I have risen above the world and ordinary men and women. I am not attached to the world. Therefore, O Brahmin, I am a superior human being who has destroyed all the weaknesses of ordinary human beings."*

*see page 2*

husband the Brahmin were to see the Buddha, he will offer the food he is eating to the Buddha. Then I will have to cook all over again. Thinking that way, the wife served her husband, obstructing the Brahmin's view of the Buddha.

The Buddha, too, stood there without budging. The Brahmin's wife gave a sign to the Buddha with her head, asking Him to go away. The Buddha, too, shook his head to indicate that He was not going. The Brahmin's wife burst into loud laughter seeing a great ascetic of a royal family shaking His head that way. Enquiring why she laughed suddenly the Brahmin turned round. Seeing the Buddha waiting for alms the Brahmin offered his half-eaten meal to the Buddha. The Buddha did not reject it because it was a left-over meal.

The Buddha said,

> **"O Brahmin, for us any part of the meal is all right, whether it is the first part, the second part, or the last part. We are like those ghost spirits (*paradattupajīvī) who depend on any type of meal they receive."**

The Brahmin was surprised and shocked that such a noble sage from a royal family should accept his offering without refusing it as it was a left-over meal. The Brahmin became exceedingly pleased with the Buddha.

*(Dhammapadaṭṭha kathā. Pañca Vagga Dāyaka Brāhmana Vatthu)*

The Buddha's dedication to serve others and to do good to others even if He had to do it, taking left-over meals, is demonstrated by this story.

One morning, the Buddha, wearing His robe with decorum, with His alms bowl in hand, went to the house of the Brahmin named **Udaya**, on His alms round. The Brahmin offered a full bowl of rice to the Buddha. Next day, too, the Buddha visited the same house. That day, too, the Brahmin gave a full bowl of rice. On the third day, too, the Buddha visited the same house. The Brahmin offered a full bowl of rice to the Buddha. He told the Buddha, "You come to my house again and again. You must be greedy for food."

The Buddha said,

> **"Cultivators sow again and again. They plough the field again and again. They give grains to the country again and again. Beggars beg again and again. Generous people give again and again. By giving they go to heaven again and again. Those who milk cows milk them again and again. The calf runs to its mother cow again and again. Beings faint again and again. Beings get shocked again and again. Life gets conceived in wombs again and again. Beings die again and again. Beings are taken to the cemetery again and again. The wise person attains the Deathless and is not born again and again."**

*(Saṃyutta Nikāya Brāhmana Samyutta)*

Here, the Buddha visited the house of Brahmin **Udaya** on three consecutive occasions on His alms round, not because of His greed for food, as the Brahmin thought at first, but because of Buddha's compassion towards the Brahmin who the Buddha knew had the capacity to realize truth.

The Buddha took as the theme 'again and again' for His dialogue with the Brahmin. He converted the Brahmin that way. **This, too, is a human quality of great**

*This is a kind of ghostly beings that can receive meals and other requisites given by humans-**paradattupajīvī** (**paradatta**-given by others, **Upajivi**-living)

**compassion.**

**"O Bhikkhus, gains, honours, glory, praise are all harsh. These pierce the outer skin of human beings. Then they pierce the inner skin. Then they pierce the muscles. After piercing the muscles they pierce the veins. Then they pierce the bones. Then they go and lodge in the marrow of the bones."**

***(Saṁyutta Nikāya - Lāba Sakkāra Saṁyutta)***

The person who stated that gains, honours, praises, power-hunger, hunger for wealth, greed for position, prestige, fame are all harsh, dreadful, destructive and harmful, is not a god. This was said by a superior human being who discarded them all in disgust, after understanding their true results through experience.

The Buddha addressed **Ven. Kassapa** this way:

"O **Kassapa**, you are very old now. The robe made of cemetery cloth and worn by me until it became thread-bare, is too heavy for you now. Therefore, put on an ordinary robe offered by devotees. Give up your alms-rounds. Accept invitations from homes for meals. Now, you must live close to me."

**Ven. Kassapa** replied this way:

"O Sir, I have been dwelling in the forest for quite a long while. I have extolled the virtues of forest-dwelling for a long while. For a long while I have depended for my food on the alms-round. I have invariably worn robes made out of cemetery cloth. I extol its virtues. For a long while I have been wearing the three-fold robes. I extol its virtues. I lead an unburdened life. I lead a life of leisure. I lead a solitary life away from crowds. I extol the virtues of that kind of life. I lead a diligent life. Therefore, Sir I like to continue my way of life."

The Buddha praised him,

"Your decision is very good, **Kassapa**. For the good of the many, for the well-being of the many, **Kassapa**, continue to wear the coarse robe made out of cemetery cloth, continue to obtain food from the alms-round, continue to dwell in the forest."

***(Saṁyutta Nikāya - Kassapa Saṁyutta).***

**This, too, emphasizes a compassionate human quality.**

"As you are old, do not wear coarse, heavy, thread-bare robes. Do not continue to go on alms-round. Do not continue to dwell in the forest. Stay close to me."

**What a friendly, compassionate, humane and kind affection is embodied in these few words! From hundreds of facts of this type it is evident that the Buddha is the greatest of human beings.** He has been deified not by Himself but by some of His devotees - by those who consider god to be greater than man.

**The Buddha is not a creator.** He was not born creating a world. He never accepted tasks that He could not perform. He never took over such responsibilities. The Buddha saw the world as established upon suffering. One day, someone asked the Buddha where the world was situated(**Kasmiṃ Loko Patiṭṭhito**).

The Buddha replied,

"The world is situated on suffering."
(**dukkhe loko patiṭṭhito**)

The Buddha saw the three characteristics of **anicca** (impermanence), **dukkha** (suffering), and **anatta** (soul-lessness) in all

*"O Ānanda, now I am decrepit, advanced in years, grown old. I am now eighty years old. Just as an old creaking chariot is kept going by binding pieces together, my body, too, is kept going now, bound together by my saintly powers."* *see page 2*

created things. The Buddha spoke about these quite often. But He never spoke about a creator - this is just because it is so futile a subject to ţalk about. The Buddha did not like to waste His precious time on such useless topics. He kept silent when such questions were asked. He did not reply such questions.

**The Buddha is not a saviour.** The Buddha who said that there was no permanent soul, did not save a soul that was not there. The Buddha indicated the path to the 'release from suffering'. The Buddha addressed a direct question to those who sought the help of others.
He asked them,

> "One is one's own saviour. How can another help him?"

**This Buddha Word is an effective answer to those who are bereft of self-respect, who expect external help, who do not appreciate the value of one's human wisdom, and one's labour, who have no power of inner virtue, who worship unseen forces, who pray, and to those who have servile minds. The Buddha did not 'save' anyone. But, He indicated quite clearly the path to free one's self from the sufferings of saṃsāra (the cycle of birth)**. Therefore, He is not a saviour.

From the above facts, it is evident that the Buddha is neither a god nor a saviour, but the most supreme human being who has appeared in human kind so far. He became the Buddha entirely because He was a human being. Becoming a Buddha is possible only for a human being. No god could achieve that state.

By becoming Buddha, He gave the highest possible place a human being could give, to human wisdom and to humanity. The Buddha is the only human being - the only religious Teacher - who demonstrated that the wise and virtuous human being is nobler, more powerful and greater than even god.

A deity who came to see the Buddha worshipped Him and stood on one side. **(aññatarā devatā bhagavantaṃ abhivādetvā ekamantaṃ aṭṭhāsi**).

Brahmins, coming to see the Buddha, knelt down on their right knee and asked Him questions with their two hands folded on their head in adoration. **(Atha kho Brahmā Sahampati ekaṃsaṃ uttarā sanghaṃ karitvā dakkhina jānu manḍalaṃ puthuviyaṃ nihantvāyena bhagavā tena anjaliṃ panāmetvā bhagavantaṃ etadavo ca).**

In a country and at a time when **Mahā Brahma**, gods and saviours were worshipped, the Buddha, who was a human being, received adoration from gods and Brahmas, while other human beings were looking on. They attended upon the Buddha. What other human being in that era could achieve such a miracle?

**The Buddha stated that even gods honour and respect men of high virtue and exalted moral quality.** Man attributed to god all those powers that cannot be either seen or understood. But the Buddha stated that one should help one's own self without expecting god's help (**Atta dīpā viharatha, atta saranā na añña saranā**).

Is there any other statement that is more analytical than this about self-reliance, self-confidence, self-respect, self-pride and the proper grammar of living? The Buddha stated that there was nothing in this world that cannot be accomplished by human wisdom, human effort and human potential, and that it is a shame for one's humanity to transfer all those powers to others, and to remain inactive without utilizing one's wisdom and effort.

**So saying, the Buddha encouraged His Moral Battalion like a General with such orders as 'Initiate good action', set out to perform such action! (Ārabhatha! nikkhamatha! yuñjatha! Buddhasasane).** (Start, set out, fight the battle of Buddha's Dispensation). The Buddha sent them forward.

**The greatest pleasure, satisfaction, consolation and pride we have as Buddhists is that the Teacher we follow is a supreme being with a history.**

## A Radiant Sun

*In this world of storm and strife, hatred and violence, the message of the Buddha shines like a radiant sun. Perhaps at no time was that message more needed than in the world of the atomic and hydrogen bombs. Two thousand five hundred years have only added to the vitality and truth of that message. Let us remember that immortal message and try to fashion our thoughts and actions in the light of that teaching. We may face with equanimity even the terrors of the atomic bomb age and help a little in promoting right thinking and right action.*

***Sri Nehru - Former Prime Minister of India***

*He requested Ven. Ānanda three times this way: "Ānanda, I am very thirsty. Fetch some water for me quickly."*

*see page 4*

CHAPTER 2

## THE SUPREME BUDDHA- THE GREATEST OF TEACHERS

The Supreme Buddha assumes a foremost place among teachers, professors and savants who have an expert mastery over educational science, educational technique and educational psychology.

Buddhists characterize the Buddha as **'Tiloguru'** - the Teacher of Three Worlds. A teacher who has won the genuine affection, genuine respect and the genuine devotion from his countless pupils as much as the Buddha, has never appeared in the line of teachers in the whole of human kind.

At first He had only five pupils. At the time of His Great Demise the number of His disciples who were scattered over hundreds of miles in various cities and provinces of India, exceeded hundreds of thousands. In the whole history of mankind the only lecturer, the only speaker, the only preceptor, the only teacher who converted a vast multitude towards him, through his discourses, through his talks, through his advice, and through his teachings, was the Supreme Buddha.

Hearing His Discourses, the devotees of other religious teachers began to take refuge in Him in their hundreds and thousands. Those religious teachers who lost their followers started saying that the Buddha was a magician and that He knew how to hypnotize.

Hearing this, the **Licchavi King Bhaddiya** asked the Buddha,

> "Is it true that you know the magic of hypnotizing people, of attracting and holding them to you?"

The Buddha replied,

> "O **Bhaddiya**, please do not accept anything simply because you heard it, or because it came down through generations, or because it was so recorded in history, or because it is stated so in the text, or because it squares with the logic and the theory. You must accept something only when you yourself see it as the truth, when you yourself understand it as the truth, and when you yourself realize it as the truth." "**Sutaṁ metaṃ bhante māyāvī samano Gotamo āvattanī māyaṃ jānāti. So añña tithayānaṃ sāvake āvattetī ti etha tumhe Bhaddiya mā paramparāya mā itikirāya attanāca jāneyyātha.**"

***(Anguttara Nikāya - Catukka Nipāta - Bhaddiya Sutta)***

So saying, the Buddha stated that what He does is only showing what is virtuous and what is evil, and that He has never asked anyone to become His disciple. This indicates clearly that seeing their disciples seeking the Buddha in their thousands, the other religious teachers were jealous of Him. The principal Teaching mode utilized at the time was the format in which the disciple listened while the Teacher lectured. The Pali for disciple is '**sāvaka**', which signifies 'listener'. Those who listened to the Buddha were described as '**Buddha Sāvakas**'. As the Buddha is all-compassionate, He never threatened the disciples. Nor did He reprimand them or intimidate them. He never chased them out. Nor did He give them corporal punishment.

In the course of His Teaching, He never used a single word that the disciples would not understand. The Buddha, who was adept in educational science and psychology, obtained a penetrating view of their character and their thoughts, and taught in a manner that befitted them. Those who came to see Him and to question Him, assuming that they were more learned and more knowledgeable than the Buddha, became His obedient disciples at the end.

This great Teacher possessed the power to see the minds of others and to recall past births (**paracitta vijānana pubbe nivāsānussati**). In consequence, He could figure out, immediately on seeing a person, that he had such and such character traits, his thoughts and ideas were such and such, and that he has had such and such a past. This was not all. The Buddha could see several of His past births, too.

The worst punishment that the Buddha imposed on a very stubborn student was '**Brahma Daṇḍa**'. The expression '**Brahma Daṇḍa**' implies the 'noble punishment'. In the course of this punishment the friends and associates of the punished person boycott him and refrain from talking to him.

**Ven. Channa** was given this punishment. **Channa** was born the same day as **Prince Siddhārtha**. He was the person who became **Prince Siddhārtha**'s closest associate from childhood on. Being inordinately proud of this, even after becoming a monk, he did not show due deference to such great arahants as **Ven. Sāriputta** and **Ven. Moggallāna**. He showed no deference to anyone other than the Buddha. In order to dispel his inordinate pride, the Buddha imposed '**Brahma Daṇḍa**' on him.

A special characteristic in the Buddha's Teaching style was His method of driving home a point using similes, metaphors, examples and instances. If calculated, the number of similes and metaphors He has used exceeds thousands. He has derived all these similes and metaphors from daily life and from His environment.

Here are some instances:

"as a cart-wheel following the bull's hoofs (**cakkaṃ va vahato padaṃ**);
like a shadow that constantly accompanies a body (**chāyāva anapāyinī**);
like a serpent sloughing off its old skin (**urago chinnamiva tavaṃ purānaṃ**);
like the moon emerging from a cloud (**abbhāmuttova chandimā**);
just as the wind topples the weak tree (**vāto rukkhaṃ va dubbalaṃ**);
just as the spoon does not know the taste of curries (**dabbī sūpa rasaṃ yathā**);
fattens like a bull (**balivaddo va jīrati**);
just as milk does not curdle immediately on being milked (**sajju khīraṃ va muccati**);
experts in water-management direct the water to any place they want (**udakaṃ hi nayanti nettikā**);
just as the cowherd directs the cattle to the pasture with his goad (**yathā**

***Vakkali, who was fascinated by the Buddha's incomparable physical beauty, became a bhikkhu (monk) only to keep on looking at Him. Once, the Buddha asked Ven. Vakkali, "Vakkali, what profit do you get from this impure body?"*** ***see page 4***

**danḍena gopalo gāvo pāceti gocaraṃ**);
weeds are a threat to the field (**tina dosāni khettāni**).

The Buddha's Teachings are full of such similes and metaphors.

The Buddha narrated thousands of stories and anecdotes to make the disciples appreciate a point. All the stories in the five hundred and fifty **Jātaka Tales** (Birth Stories) were narrated to the disciples on various occasions in relation to various incidents.

The Buddha performed His educational service by questioning, by responding to questions from students, by delivering Discourses on some specific topics, by discussions and introducing techniques that would enable the disciples to understand matters for themselves.

In all the monasteries He dwelt in, there were auditoriums. The pulpit in the centre of such auditoriums was always reserved for the Buddha. When the disciples were discussing some issue, the Buddha would visit the place and would occupy the pulpit reserved for Him. Then He would participate in the discussion that had been going on. He would ask the monks,

> "What were you discussing before I came in here?" (**Kāyanuttha Bhikkhave etarahi kathāya sannisinnāti**.")

One monk out of the whole totally silent congregation will stand up and say,

> "O Sir, we did not indulge in those thirty-two forms of talks, like talking about kings, thieves etc. (**rāja kathā, cora kathā**). We were discussing such and such an incident, relating to such and such a monk."

At that point the Buddha will reveal an aspect of the incident that no one knew until then. Those monks who listen to Him begin to admire the Buddha more and more.

The Buddha, unlike most other teachers, did not use only His monastery or His auditorium for teaching. **The Buddha taught His disciples mostly in the open air. The Buddha's class-rooms were public parks, cemeteries, rock-slabs, sandy stretches, shade of trees, fields, pasture-land, poor hovels, the public roads and the forest.** These were places that had an uncluttered environment. The Buddha quoted examples and instances from what was found then and there, right before their eyes.

The Buddha would teach in such a pragmatic way that when a disciple brings a vessel filled with water to wash his feet, He would use that itself as the topic to teach the disciple, leading to his attainment of **Arahantship** (Sainthood).

The Buddha instructed **Ven. Culla Panthaka** to rub a piece of pure white cloth with both his hands, looking at the sun, repeating '**Rajo haranaṃ - rajo haranaṃ.** ' (Removing blemishes). That young monk, who was dejected that he could not memorize just one stanza though he tried hard for four months, became an Arahant as a result of the Buddha's psychologically structured instruction.

When the Buddha visits a field where cultivators are at work He teaches making use of the plough, the ploughing, the farmer, the grains and the cattle as metaphors. When He visits a river where people bathe to cleanse themselves of sin, the Buddha teaches them putting forward valid reasons that sins cannot be got rid of by washing them away in a holy river. (**Kiṃ Sundarikā**

**karissati? Kiṃ Payāgā**?)

When He goes to a forest He compares what He has taught and what He has not taught to leaves that are fallen, dried leaves that still remain in the trees, respectively. When He goes to a cemetery He instructs the disciples, taking a dead body as the example.

The Buddha heard that **Sirimā**, the beautiful courtesan, had died suddenly. The Buddha instructed **King Kosala** not to cremate the body of that courtesan who had conquered the whole city with her bewitching beauty. He instructed the king to keep her body at the cemetery for four days, protecting it so that animals could not get near it. The Buddha requested the king to assemble the people of that city there on the fourth day. The king acted as instructed.

On the appointed day, the cemetery was totally crowded with the people who had assembled there on the king's orders. The Buddha arrived at the cemetery with His disciples at the appointed time. The Buddha requested the king to auction **Sirima**'s body which had been valued at thousands of gold coins per hour, when she was alive.

**King Kosala** started the auction, indicating an initial value of a thousand gold coins. He asked the people to make bids. There were no bidders. He lowered the price to five - hundred gold coins. And, at the end, he brought it down to one gold coin. Still, there were no bidders. Then the king asked the people to take it free. No one was willing to take away that body which, at that point, was bloated and was oozing at all orifices.

The Buddha gave those teeming crowds assembled there a Discourse on the impermanence of beauty, the illusion of beauty, and that it was folly to be overwhelmed by beauty. This way, the Buddha taught the people a practical lesson about the futility of being deceived by beauty.

On some occasions the Buddha refrained from teaching certain persons, from advising certain persons. He devised interesting methods. He enabled those people to understand things for themselves.

The only son of young **Kisā Gotamī** was dead. Born in an excessively affluent family she was not aware that a dead person could not be brought back to life. She got many physicians to treat her child, but to no avail. No one was able to bring back her dead son to life. After everything failed, she went to the Buddha with her son's dead body. She placed her son's dead body at the Buddha's feet, and asked Him to bring her son back to life.

The supremely compassionate Buddha, who was also a supreme psychologist, did not reject her request outright. The Buddha realized that there was no use giving her a religious Discourse when she was so deranged in mind due to her son's death. Therefore, He said,

> "All right, I will bring him back to life."

The mind of the young mother who had been sorely distraught as all the physicians had refused to treat him, was relieved, at least to some extent, when the Buddha accepted to treat him. "If you can get the medicine I prescribe, I will bring back your son to life," the Buddha said next. "What medicine, Sir?" "A pinch of mustard." "Oh, that is simple. I will bring it quickly."

So saying, she got ready to go.

> "But wait a bit. That pinch of mustard must be from a house where death had never occurred." "All right,

***"O Bhikkhus, if any monk present here has any doubt whatsoever either about me, or the Dhamma, or the Sangha, or the Path, or the rules, ask me now. Do not repent later."***

***see page 4***

Sir, I will bring the mustard."

**Kisā Gotamī** took her son's dead body and left **Jetavana** Monastery. She entered the main street of the city of **Sāvatthi**. She went into the first house she saw.

"The Buddha said that He will bring back my dead son to life if I can fetch a pinch of mustard. Could you please give me some mustard?"

The housewife runs into the house and brings a pinch of mustard. **Kisā Gotamī** takes the mustard and asks,

"Has anyone died in this house?" "Yes, our grandfather died, our father died, a brother died." "If so, I don't need this mustard. I need mustard from a house where no one had died. I will ask next door."

**Kisā Gotamī** went to the next house. There, too, she received mustard. But, since there too death had occurred, she went to another house. This way, she visited about a hundred houses in the city. Everywhere she received a similar answer. Truth began to dawn in her mind, little by little. She realized that death had happened not only to her son, but to a multitude. On the one hand reality dawned upon her. On the other hand the stench from the dead body was unbearable. Realizing the true nature of death she discarded the dead body in the cemetery, and went back to the Buddha. Worshipping the Buddha she asked Him to ordain her. The Buddha asked her,

"Did you bring a handful of mustard?"

"O Sir, I have now realized the true nature of death. Please ordain me and make me achieve the deathless."

The Buddha sent her to the nuns so she could be ordained a nun. Shortly after she was ordained a nun, she attained Sainthood.

This story shows how the Buddha taught a lesson without delivering a Discourse. **Kisā Gotamī** was a mother who was distracted to the point of madness due to the death of her son. It was not proper to preach the Doctrine to her at that time. Therefore, the Buddha did not deliver a sermon to her. He devised a method that would enable her to realize the nature of death, by herself.

Some teachers do not quite like the idea of students asking them questions to clarify issues they cannot understand. During Buddha's time there were six religious teachers - **Pūrana Kassapa** and others - who were senior to the Buddha. They were the teachers of exclusive ascetic groups. They appeared as religious leaders. They were famous and received considerable material support. They were philosophic and were respected by many. **Ascetic Sabhiya** went to meet each of these religious leaders and questioned them. But, they wouldn't answer. They get angry. They find fault with him. They say unpleasant things. They show their displeasure by their body language.

**Sabhiya** the ascetic then thought this way: "These teachers are mature, aged, have lived long, old, advanced in years, stable in their religious life. They are accepted by the world as saints. They have been in religious life for long." (**Jinnā, vuddhā, mahallakā, addhagatā, vayo anuppattā, therā, rattaññu cira pabbajitā.**). But, when they are asked a question, to get a clarification, they get angry, become irate, shout, find fault. If they are like this it is better to give up my ascetic life and become a layman.

Whatever it is I will meet Gotama and try to put my questions to Him. Gotama is very young. He is young and is junior in asceticism (**Samano hi Gotamo daharo ce va jātiyā, navo ca pabbajjāya.**). But, one must not look down upon him because he is young. He has great psychic power. He is of awe - inspiring prowess (**Samano kho daharoti na paribhavatabbo, daharopi vesa samano Gotamo mahiddhike hoti, mahānubhāvo**). Because of this I will go and question Him."

He went to the Buddha and after the initial pleasantries, he told the Buddha,

> "I have several doubts in my mind. I want to question you about these. Will you answer them, Sir?"
>
> "**Sabhiya**, you came over a long distance of 700 yojanas to ask questions. Ask all the questions you want. I will answer your questions one by one, systematically, according to the law, according to the significance," said the Buddha (**Dūrato va āgatosi Sabhiya - pañhe pucchituṃ ākaṃkhamāno tesantakaro bhavāmi te pañhe te puṭṭho - anupubbhaṃ, anudhammaṃ vyākaromī te**).

**Sabhiya** was extremely surprised.

> "It is quite surprising, indeed. It is impossible to get permission from other teachers to ask questions, not to say anything about asking questions. But, this ascetic Gotama allowed it very pleasantly." (**Acchariyaṃ vatabho, abbhūtaṃ vatabho yāvatāhaṃ aññesu samana Brāhmanesu okāsa kamma mattampi nālatthaṃ kiṃ me idhaṃ samanena Gotamena okasa kammaṃ kataṃ.**) He, overwhelmed with joy, began to ask questions.
>
> *(Sutta Nipāta - Sabhiya Sutta)*

One can appreciate the greatness of the Buddha as a Teacher from this story. When Buddha was asked questions, He responded to them fearlessly. He never displayed a displeasure at being questioned. He was happy when questions were asked. The Buddha could visualize, through His wisdom, the heart, the inner workings of all those who came to ask Him questions. Seeing the hearts and minds of the questioners, the Buddha will answer their questions in terms of their specific needs, and in terms of their thoughts. By His efficient answers to their questions the Buddha removes the pride in the minds of the questioners.

When the Buddha has created a humility in the minds of the questioners, He can get the questioners themselves to say:

> "O Samana Gotama, your resolution of questions is really great. You explained the Doctrine in a variety of ways, as if you are turning up a vessel that had been turned down, as if you are revealing something that had been concealed, and as if directions are being shown to a bewildered person who has lost his way. We take refuge in you, in the Dhamma, and in the Sangha. Please consider me from today as a devotee who has taken refuge in the Triple Gem, until the end of my days."[3]

***"O monks, if others also know the value of giving just as much as I know, no one will eat anything without giving at least a morsel to others. They will never be miserly. If there is anyone to receive it, they will give part of the last portion of their meal they were eating."***

*see page 5*

Even such Brahmins as **Saccaka, Ambaṭṭha, Sonadanda, Kūtadanta, Potthapāda, Pāyāsi, Sabhiya, Sela** who were adept in the Three Vedas, and such demons as **Ālavaka,** could not defeat the Buddha by asking Him questions. One novice monk behaved badly in the presence of the Buddha. The Buddha, who knew his past thoroughly, did not become displeased with him. He continued to show him compassion.

"A householder from an affluent family in the city of **Sāvatthi** became a monk after his wife died. He got down into the temple all the furniture, clothes, grains and other effects that were in his house. He got his servants to cook him rich meals. He spent his days eating and drinking at a level of high luxury. He would not wear at night the robe he put on during the day, he would not put on during the day, the robe he wore in the night. He lived in the midst of many possessions. He was known as the 'possessor of many things'.

One day, he kept his robes, bed-sheets etc., in the sun, and was waiting until they dried. At that time, some monks from provincial areas were visiting the monastery. Seeing robes and clothes drying in the sun as at a washerman's point, the monks asked, "Whose effects are these?" The monk 'possessor of many things' said, "They are all mine."

The monks said, "The Buddha has permitted only three-fold robes and an alms bowl, hasn't He? Being a monk in the Buddha's Order who advocates few possessions, why have you hoarded such a vast array of possessions?" The monks took him to the Buddha and complained against his behaviour.

The Buddha said to him,

> "I extol the virtues of a life with few possessions. Why do you hoard these things, without donating whatever things you get?"

The monk became angry. He discarded his robe right in the midst of the four-fold congregation, and asked,

> "Do you want me to be like this?"

The assembly of monks was stunned and bewildered by the unseemly and stubborn behaviour of the monk.

The Buddha extended His incomparable compassion to that monk and said,

> "O Monk, this is an occasion when we have to show you the greatest compassion. Although you display a lack of shame and fear today, you kept on seeking the meaning of 'shame and fear' for twelve long years when you were born in a previous birth as a 'water demon' ***(Devadhamma Jātaka-Birth tale Devadhamma)***. When you were so concerned with 'shame and fear' during that birth, why do you behave so shamelessly in the midst of this assembly, while being ordained in such a noble Order as this?"

The monk regained his senses and quickly picked up the discarded robe and put it on again

***(Saddharmaratnāvalī - The Story of the Bahubhāṇḍika Thero)***

**In such instances, the Buddha displayed the incomparable compassion of a great teacher.**

In ancient India, among those erudite teachers in all branches of knowledge such as the Vedas, medicine, astrology, drama, music etc., there was the strong tradition of teachers keeping some secrets for themselves. In short, they never taught their wisdom fully to their pupils. For self-protection, they kept a very exclusive part of their expertise to themselves.

Buddha, born in such an age, taught everything He knew, and all the things the people wanted, without any selfishness. The Buddha said,

> "**Ānanda**, in the Buddha's Teachings there is no part that is kept as 'teacher's secret'." (**Natthi Ānanda Tathāgatassa dhammesu ācariya muṭṭha**.).

This was said by the Buddha Himself to Ven. Ananda. The Buddha's urge to teach others what He knew was so strong in Him that even when He was in His death bed at the age of eighty, He asked the monks three times,

> "O Monks, if you have to know anything from me, ask me now itself. Do not repent later saying we were not able to know these matters when the Buddha was still alive. Therefore, ask me now itself, whatever you want to know. If a given monk cannot ask me directly, get a friend to ask me. I will gladly answer any question you have to ask."
>
> ***(Mahā Parinibbāna Sutta)***

All other religious teachers, saviours, creators, leaders etc., never even hinted at the appearance of another like themselves. They never wished such an appearance. But, the Buddha was happy if everybody in the world was a Buddha like Himself. He taught the technique to achieve that state. His sincere wish was that the greatness he won - the supreme Enlightenment He attained - should be reached by all.

> "If one endeavoured, if one strove,
> if one fulfilled the perfections,
> everybody could be a Buddha,"

He said.

The Buddha never threatened anyone, saying, "Do it this way. If you do not do it this way, I will punish you this way." The Buddha pointed out what was good and what was bad, and their relative results, with a compassionate kind heart, saying, "This is good, this is bad; if you do good, such good results will ensue; if you do bad, such evil results will follow." There was not even a trace of selfishness or self-gain in this great, compassionate Teacher.

This great Teacher never expected adoration, gain, profit or worship from His pupils. He kept on rejecting gain, profit, glory, praise as harmful, and as a danger to the achievement of Sainthood which is the highest spiritual victory.

This unique Teacher never categorized anyone as 'bad'. Never got rid of anyone. Never chased out anyone. He went in search of those who were castigated by society as bad. He met them, talked to them with compassion, and transformed them into good men.

**Angulimāla**, who became a symbol of devotion to teachers, was a fierce murderer for all the people in India. When they merely heard his name the king and his men trembled in fear. All efforts to destroy him were in vain. None of these was able to see

*"Mahā Kassapa, your robe is very smooth. Ven. Mahā Kassapa said, "Sir, please accept this robe in compassion for me." The Buddha said, "Kassapa, do you like to wear my robe, worn out due to long use and made of cemetery cloth?" Ven. Mahā Kassapa said, "Yes Sir, I like it."*

*see page 5*

that, concealed within this ferocious murderer, there dwelt an Arahant. In other words he had the potentiality for becoming an Arahant. Only the Teacher of Three Worlds was able to see this.

Seeing this he went to meet **Angulimāla**, while the people gathered on either side of the road, made a worshipful entreaty, saying,

> "O Sir, please do not walk that way. **Angulimāla** is lurking there. He kills whomsoever he sees, and cuts their fingers. If you went that way, he will kill you too, and cut your fingers."

This fearless Teacher disregarded all those pleas. Like a kind father going in search of a disobedient son, He went to **Angulimāla**, subdued him, tamed him, and made him attain the highest rung, or the highest peak of non-violence, which is the Arahanthood. He achieved this not through the power of some magic, but through the power of great compassion.

When **Ambapāli** the renowned courtesan visited the monastery and invited Him for a meal at her residence, He did not reject that invitation, saying, "You are a well-known courtesan. If I visit your residence and take a meal, there will be all kinds of gossip in the country." Instead, He accepted the invitation gladly. The **Licchavi** kings, too, invited the Buddha for meals, the very same day. But, as the Buddha had accepted the previous invitation from **Ambapāli**, He could not accept the invitation from the **Licchavi** kings.

The Buddha visited **Ambapali**'s residence with His disciples. The Buddha had His meals there, and preached the Doctrine to her. He transformed her into a great female devotee who had totally given up the courtesan's profession.

All teachers are likely to have great qualities as well as minor shortcomings. Pupils have a unique ability to measure the quality of a teacher. But, the only teacher a single shortcoming of whom no pupil could ever detect, was the Buddha. Not one pupil out of thousands of His pupils could properly understand His superior quality. He possessed all the qualities essential for a teacher.

He was a great Teacher full of thousands of such virtues as loving-kindness, compassion, patience, purity of character, being exemplary, possessing true knowledge of all subjects taught, highest level of wisdom, capacity to explain so that the pupils will understand thoroughly, having nothing that will arouse the slightest suspicion of pupils, not doing wrong even secretly, sympathy for others, and being devoid of such weaknesses as jealousy and hatred.

Kings came to this great Teacher, giving up their royal splendour, guild-masters sought Him, giving up their affluence, Ministers came to Him, giving up their Ministries, husbands came giving up their wives, wives came, giving up their husbands, parents came, giving up their children, children came, giving up their parents, householders came to Him, giving up their households. They all came and became His pupils.

When the Buddha visited the market town of **Āpana** in **Anguttarāpa**, a line of 1, 250 pupils marched in single file behind Him. Seeing the line of monks headed by the Buddha, walking serenely with restraint, the whole of the market town was quite impressed. All the people left their homes and stood on either side of the road. An affluent Brahmin called **Keniya**, pleased at the sight of this Bhikkhu pageant, invited them to his house for next day's mid-day meal. The Buddha did not accept the invitation, saying,

> "We are a very large group. It will be extremely difficult to prepare the mid-day meal the next day for such a large group."

The Buddha accepted it after he extended the invitation three times. **Keniya** assembled all the people in the village and put various people in charge of various tasks. Thus, he offered meals the next day to 1,250 monks headed by the Buddha. The Buddha was fully aware of the logistical problems that will have to be faced by the donors when they had to prepare meals to such a large group as 1,250 persons.

*(Sutta Nipāta - Sela Sutta)*

The Buddha did not want to accept invitations that will entail difficulties to others. It is clear by His non-acceptance of the invitation three times. This great Teacher highly esteemed the deference to teachers.

Immediately on attaining Enlightenment His first concern was to see whether He had a teacher who should be honoured, and to obtain advice from. When He searched, He found that He did not even have another person like Him, not to say anything about a person who could be recognized as His teacher. (**Na me ācariyā atthi sadisā mena navijja ti.**).

> **"I do not have a teacher. Not even a person who is similar to me."**

**Therefore, the Buddha kept Dhamma (the Doctrine) as His teacher.**

**The Buddha is an example to all the teachers in the world. Teachers, when they educate their pupils, must consider quite carefully how the Buddha disciplined His pupils, how He taught them, how He subdued His pupils, how He directed His pupils along the right path, how He made the lives of His pupils successful, and how He fulfilled the aims of His pupils.**

## Buddha is like a physician

*The Buddha is like a physician. Just as a doctor must know the diagnosis of the different kinds of illness, their causes, the antidotes and remedies, and must be able to apply them, so also the Buddha has taught the Four Holy Truths which indicate the range of suffering, its origin, its cessation, and the way which leads to its cessation.*

***Dr. Edward Conze, "Buddhism"***

*On the third day, too, the Buddha visited the same house. The Brahmin offered a full bowl of rice to the Buddha. He told the Buddha, "You come to my house again and again. You must be greedy for food."*

*see page 7*

CHAPTER 3

## THE BUDDHA IS THE GREATEST EXPONENT OF NON-VIOLENCE

The Buddha, when He converted a non-Buddhist, got the convert to promise five things. These five promises are called '**Panca Sīla**' (The Five Precepts).

The first promise of these five is that 'I promise not to kill any living being.' This indicates that the primary quality a Buddhist should possess is non-violence. The Buddha denounced all forms of violence. The Buddha asked loving-kindness to be extended not only to men, but even to all animals.

**Sabbe tasanti daṇḍassa**
**Sabbe bhāyanti maccuno**
**Attānaṃ upamaṃ katvā**
**Na-haneyya naghātaye**.

All are frightened of punishment. All dread death. Therefore, since one is frightened of punishment and death, taking one's own self as the example, refrain from killing others.
You must not destroy.

**Sabbe tasanti daṇḍassa**
**Sabbesaṃ jīvitaṃ piyaṃ**
**Attānaṃ upamaṃ katvā**
**Na-haneyya naghātaye.**

All are frightened of punishment. All love life. Therefore, since one is frightened of punishment and death, taking one's own self as the example, refrain from killing others. You must not destroy. Only the Buddha and **Mahāvīra** showed kindness to animals. Other religious leaders did not. Those other religious leaders encouraged the killing and eating of animals. In consequence, those other religious teachers will not receive the respect of animals.

**Mahāvīra** went beyond the extremes of non-violence. His main Doctrine is non-violence. He thought even water had life. He considers the sailing of ships and canoes suppressing water, as a sin. Since minor insects get killed when we breathe in and breathe out, he suggested that we should cover our nose and mouth with a piece of cloth. He does not even approve of '**tikotipārisuddha māṃsa**' (flesh that is harmless in three ways) which has been allowed by the Buddha.

As a result of this, no follower of Jainism takes meat or fish. Due to this extreme non-violence, Jainism became a difficult religion to practise. Jainism never spread outside India. Since insects get killed even in the cultivation process, the Jains do not indulge in any other industries or crafts, than trade.

The Buddha's Teaching is the middle-path. Therefore, He gave up extremes. In consequence, His system can be followed by any citizen anywhere since it is not an extreme position. The Buddha considered the life of any being - whether friendly or unfriendly, big or small, known or unknown, seen or unseen - as being dear to that particular being. In extending loving-kindness, He included all beings of all levels.

**Apādakehi mama mettaṃ**
**Mettaṃ dvipādakehi me**
**Chatuppādehi me mettaṃ**
**Mettaṃ bahuppādehi me.**

I extend my loving-kindness to such beings as serpents that have no feet. I extend my loving-kindness to beings with two feet. I extend my loving-kindness to such beings as centipedes that have many feet.

**Sabbe sattā sabbe pānā**
**Sabbe bhūtā ca kevalā**
**Sabbe bhadrāni passantu**
**Mā kañci pāpa māgamā.**

May all beings, may all those possessing life, may all sentient beings see only good. May no evil come to them.

This way, the Buddha taught the people to extend loving-kindness to all. There is not even a stray reference in His Teachings that is likely to cause any pain or harm or loss to anyone. There is not even a reference that is likely to create such a harm, even remotely.

In **Kakacūpama Sutta** the Buddha states:

"O Monks, if ferocious bandits were to cut up a person into pieces with a two-handled saw, and if the person who is being cut up were to have an anger towards those bandits, then that person has not followed my Teaching. O Monks, even under such circumstances you must think this way: 'Our mind never changes. We will not speak harsh words to them. We will pity them and extend loving-kindness to them. We will extend limitless compassion to the whole world that comes within the purview of our loving-kindness. We will extend limitless non-hating compassion to them. O Monks, you must get used to thinking that way, even about an enemy."

***(Kakacūpama Sutta - Majjhima Nikāya)***

The Buddha says, "If a person were to have anger, without extending loving-kindness, even towards the enemy who cuts up one's body into pieces, that person has not followed the Word of the Buddha. He is not a person who believes in the Buddha's advice."

A Buddhist gets no room from the Buddha's Teachings to hurt, to torture, or to be unkind to anyone for any reason whatever. Therefore, the Buddha is the true exponent of non-violence. Among Buddhists who follow the Buddha genuinely, there is no occasion whatsoever for hurting, torture, killing, fighting, arguing, resentment, abuse or blood-shed. If these things occur in some groups, the implication is that they are not true Buddhists. **The Buddha, who is the symbol of loving-kindness, is also the symbol of non-violence.** A great emperor like **Asoka** who, after achieving conquests through wars, stopped waging war completely. Such righteous kings as **Sirisangabo** came into being. Such world-famous non-violent leaders as **Mahatmā Gāndhi** and **Jawaharlāl Nehru** appeared.

The Buddha's noble tradition of non-violence still continues uninterrupted. The concept of non-violence recceives accceptance all over the world today.

*One day, someone asked the Buddha where the world was situated. The Buddha replied, "The world is situated on suffering." The Buddha saw the three characteristics of anicca (impermanence), dukkha (suffering), and anatta (soul-lessness) in all created thin*

*see page 8*

## CHAPTER 4

# THE BUDDHA IS THE PERSON WHO SUFFERED MOST

The Buddha endured endless suffering, both when He was Ascetic **Siddhārtha**, and even in a large number of births before that. The Aspirant Buddha endured all the possible sufferings, following the advice of those ascetics who believed that self-mortification was the only path to Liberation. He tried out all forms of austerities that involved the torturing of the body.

"O **Sāriputta**, I lived without wearing clothes, naked, like a naked ascetic, giving up civilized ways; I had food served on my palm and licked it. If I was invited to a home for meals, I rejected such invitations. I followed the rites of not accepting food prepared for me; food taken out of an ordinary pot; food taken out of a cooking-pot; food served over the threshold; food served over a log; food served over a rice-pounder; food served by one of two persons taking meals; food given by an expectant mother; food given by a woman suckling a baby; food served without giving it to a dog that looks on, and food served at a fly-infested place. I did not accept flesh, fish or intoxicating drinks.

"**Sāriputta**, I went for meals only to one house. I lived on just one lump of food. I went to just two houses for meals. I lived on just two lumps of food. I went to seven houses for meals. I lived only on seven lumps of food. I lived on a small plate of rice, on two plates and on seven plates. I took meals once a day, once in two days, once in seven days, and once in a fortnight.

"I took only raw greens for my meals. I practised austerities eating only millet, raw rice, skins and offal, rice-bran, wild rice, grass, wild roots, windfall fruits. I wore coarse hemp, clothes of mixed varieties of thread, shrouds from corpses, bark-strips, leopard skins, grass strands, clothes of human hair, blankets of horse-hair, and clothes of owl-feathers.

"Instead of shaving my hair and beard, I plucked out my facial hair with seeds of palms. I practised the austerity of not sitting in any seat. I practised the rites of lying supine, sitting on my heels, walking on thorns, and sleeping on thorn-beds.

"**Sāriputta**, so severe were my austerities that I refrained from bathing for years. As a result of this the sweat caked on my body and it split in places. My body was like an ancient pillar that had split with age. But, it never occurred to me either to rub off this layer of caked sweat, or to get another to rub it off. One can imagine how severe my austerities were.

"**Sāriputta**, I hated sin so much that I walked about carefully, lest tiny insects should die. I showed kindness, thinking that even in a drop of water there was insect life. **Sāriputta**, in the forest I sought total solitude. If I saw a cow-herd, a grass-cutter or a forest frequenter, I would leave that part of the forest and go to another part. Just as a wild animal would run from one forest-grove to another at the sight of men, I totally refrained from seeing humans, thinking may I not see humans, and may humans not see me.

"**Sāriputta**, I who was an ascetic in the quest for purity, spent the whole night in the forest during winter when the snow fell heavily, shivering in the cold. **Sāriputta**, I lay down to sleep in a cemetery, with bones and skeletons as pillows. Children of cow-herds would come there and spit and urinate on me. They showered me with dust and stuck twigs in my ears. But, I never had an evil thought about them.

**"Sāriputta**, just like some ascetics I also thought that purity comes from food. On one occasion, I subsisted on a single jujube fruit. You may perhaps think that at that time, jujube fruits were large. But, in reality the jujube fruits were of the same size as they are today. There is no difference, then and now. When I subsisted on a single jujube fruit, my body became exceedingly emaciated. My body became like withered creepers. My buttocks became like the hoofs of animals. My spine was like a string of beads. My ribs were like the rafters in a dilapidated house. The pupils of my eyes in their deep sockets gleamed like the reflections of stars in a deep well. The skin of my skull was shrivelled like the skin of a raw bitter gourd that had been dried in the sun.

"**Sāriputta**, I was so emaciated due to the little food I took that when I touched my belly, it was my back-bone that I stroked. When I touched my back-bone, it was my belly that I felt. Due to the scant food I took my back-bone and my belly wall were cleaved together. When I tried to answer calls of nature, I would fall flat on my face. If I stroked my body my body-hair, decayed at their roots, would fall off.

"**Sāriputta**, I too followed these ascetics and recluses who believed that, with austere food habits, one would be able to achieve purity. I too subsisted upon a green-gram or a grain of rice. **Sāriputta**, you may think that a grain of rice at that time was larger than it is today. But, it is not so. At that time too it was of the same size as now.

But, **Sāriputta**, even with these austerities, I was not able to obtain the noble insights and intellect that would raise me from the level of ordinary human intelligence to the higher level of wisdom of an exalted person."

***(Majjhima Nikāya - Mahā Siha Nāda Sutta)***

Buddha gave this account of the tremendous suffering He endured not to any ordinary

*He asked them, "One is one's own saviour. How can another help him?" The Buddha did not 'save' anyone. But, He indicated quite clearly the path to free one's self from the sufferings of samsāra (the cycle of birth). Therefore, He is not a saviour.* *see page10*

person, but to **Ven. Sāriputta**, His Chief Disciple. This description will show clearly how much the Buddha had suffered. No individual in the whole of human history has suffered as much as the Buddha has. He endured all this suffering not for self-gain, but because of His compassion for men - to seek out the Truth - to realize **Nibbāna** (Liberation).

He suffered the worst possible privations a human being could. He revealed this suffering, with all the humility, to His Chief Disciple. Most people are given to the habit of being reluctant to talk about their past suffering once they achieve success from small beginnings, after having suffered and having been poor. Most people tend to think it demeaning or an insult. But, the Buddha did not realize supreme Enlightenment by living a life of luxury in vast palaces. He stated that He realized Enlightenment by renouncing all that luxury and through the experiments and experiences of suffering, privation and austerity. The life of the Buddha is excellent proof to establish the fact that, to achieve great ideals, and reach greatness, it is essential to endure suffering. Those who rendered a great service while enjoying luxury, are rather rare. Those who realized high ideals while enjoying luxury are also rare.

If one wants to render a high service, one must undergo suffering. One must give up luxuries. Must come down to the level of ordinary folk. Must witness the suffering endured by the masses. One must taste that kind of life. The sufferings of others cannot be eradicated unless one endured that kind of suffering. If one were to serve mankind genuinely, one must possess experiences acquired through suffering, like the Buddha.

## First Missionary

*Buddhism is the first missionary religion in the history of humanity with a universal message of salvation for all mankind. The Buddha after his Enlightenment sent out sixty-one disciples in different directions asking them to preach the doctrine for the weal and welfare of mankind.*

***Dr. K. N. Jayatilleke, "Buddhism and Peace"***

CHAPTER 5

## THE BUDDHA IS THE RELIGIOUS LEADER WHO MADE THE GREATEST SACRIFICES FOR MANKIND

Supreme Enlightenment is a status that should be achieved by making endless sacrifices over an unthinkably long period of time, spanning aeons.

Among the ten perfections that should be fulfilled to become a Buddha, generosity takes the first place. A Bodhisatta (an Aspirant Buddha) should sacrifice wealth, time, effort, possessions, wife and children, eyes, heads, flesh of one's own body, blood, and the total body, not just once or twice but tens of thousands of times. Therefore, there is no other human being more generous than the Bodhisatta. There is nothing that one can say as not been sacrificed by a Buddha. The only great person who has known the value of generosity is the Buddha. The Buddha said,

> **"O Monks, if others know as much as I do, about the value of giving and distributing, no one will eat without giving at least a handful of rice. They will not remain miserly. If there is someone to take, they will give even the last portion of rice on one's plate."**
>
> *(Itivuttaka Pali)*

There is no one who is clever enough to state the number of sacrifices made by the Bodhisatta aspiring to Buddhahood. There is no one who is quite capable of quantifying the sacrifices made by the Bodhisatta (The Aspirant Buddha) to achieve Buddhahood. In short, there is hardly any sacrifice that He did not make. In **Sivi Rāja** Birth Tale, King **Sivi** spoke thus:

> "If a beggar were to ask me for any organ or any part of my body, I will consider it even nobler than being crowned. If a beggar were to ask me for my heart, I will cut open my chest with a sword, I will take out my heart, as if plucking a lotus, and will present it while blood oozes drop by drop. If someone asked for my flesh, I will cut my body with a sharp weapon, and give it to him. If someone asked me for blood, I will crush the whole of my body and will donate buckets full of blood. If one were to ask me for my eyes, I will take them out like the kernel of a nut and give them to the beggar. There is nothing I have not given out of these that could be donated." So saying, he gave both his eyes to the blind Brahmin.
>
> (*Sivirāja Birth Tale*).

When the Bodhisatta (The Aspirant Buddha) was born as **King Vessantara,** the tears that issued from the eyes of his two princely children, began to fall on the Bodhisatta's feet which were like fully blossomed red lotuses. The tears from the eyes of the Bodhisatta (The Aspirant Buddha) fell on the children's backs which were like red slabs. Then The Bodhisatta got the children to stand up and said, comforting them,

"Children, I want to cross over

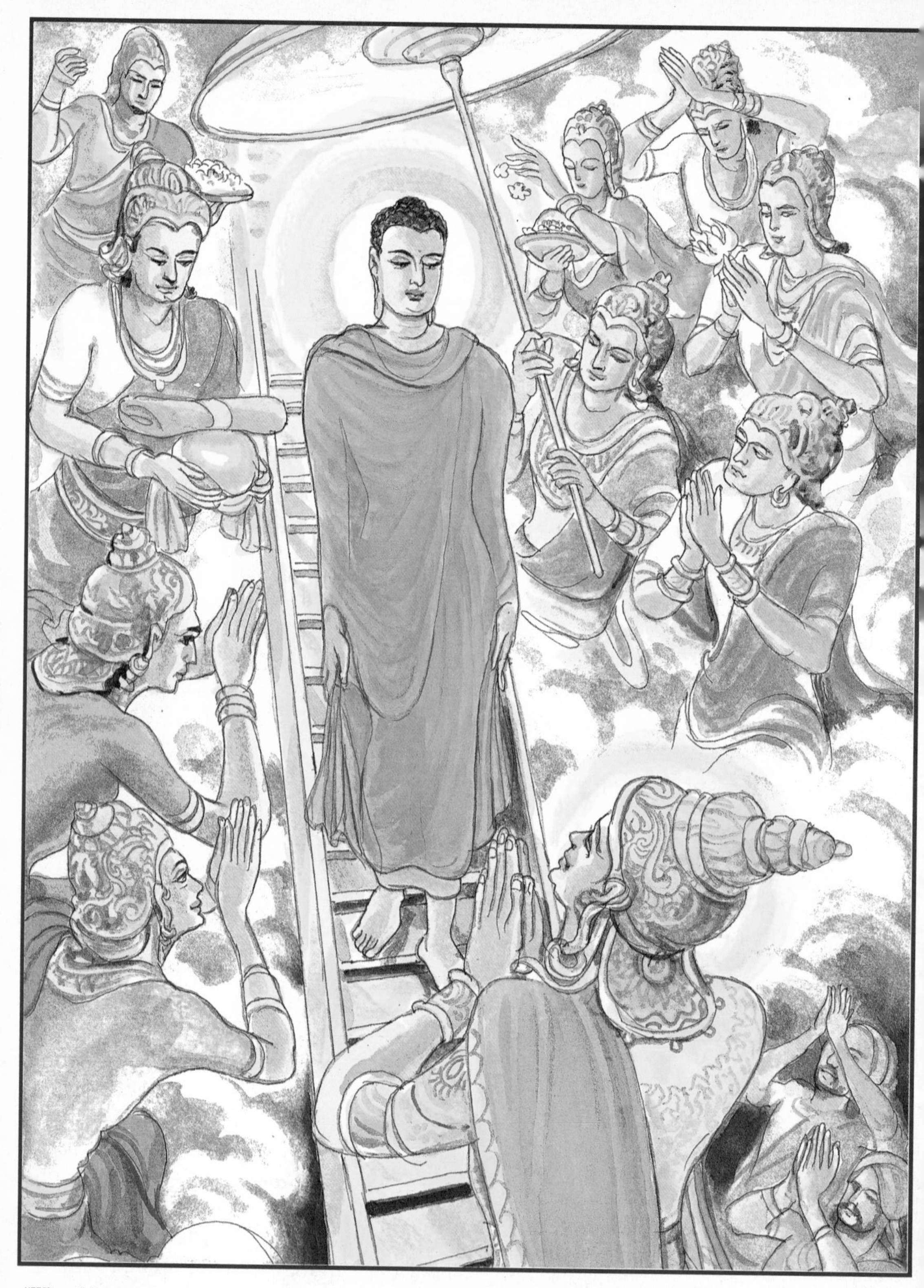

*"When, Mahā Brahma, gods and saviours were worshipped, the Buddha, who was a human being, received adoration from gods and Brahmas, while other human beings were looking on. They attended upon the Buddha.*

*see page 10*

to the other side of this ocean of becoming (**samsāra**) which is difficult to cross. I will cross over, and then I will get you and all the beings, including the gods, to cross over. Children, are you not aware of my charitable intentions? Children, please allow me to fulfil my perfection of generosity."

Comforting them that way, He took the hands of the children and said,

"Brahmin, come here. I give my children not because I do not love them. To me, attainment of supreme Enlightenment is worth ten-thousand times more. I will give my children away and with the merits of that action, I will attain supreme Enlightenment in the future and do good to the whole world."

So saying, He poured water from His water-vessel on the Brahmin's hands, and gave away the children. The children went away weeping and wailing,

"Don't you see the blood oozing from our backs? Did you bring us up applying red powder, bathing us in perfumed water, placing us upon jasmine flowers only to make us suffer this way?"

When they wept and wailed like that The Aspirant Buddha was immensely saddened. His heart melted. As the nose was incapable of coping with the force of inhaling and exhaling, extremely hot breath went in and out of His mouth. Tears began to rain from His eyes. A tremendous sorrow that nearly split his heart kept on rising. But He subdued the sharpness of the pain by continuing to contemplate Supreme Enlightenment

***(Vessantara Birth Tale)***

One can become aware of the sense of sacrifice of the Aspirant Buddha from the above two Birth Tales of **Sivi Rāja** and **Vessantara**. Prince **Siddhārtha**, who enjoyed the highest luxuries a human being could enjoy, gave up His wife and his only son, and went into the forest, took a rag that wrapped a dead body fully infested with worms, washed it, dried it in the sun, put it on, and became an ascetic. There is no other human being with the exception of Prince **Siddhārtha**, who made such an overwhelaing sacrifice, in the whole of human history. He made this unparalleled sacrifice, this incomparable renunciation, not for anything else, but for Supreme Enlightenment - for the welfare of others - for the service to the world, in quest of truth.

Considered this way, the primary quality of an Aspirant Buddha is generosity. No greatness can be achieved without a sacrifice. No service can be rendered without generosity. Service, done without any sacrifice, is not the right kind of service. It is not a genuine service.

Ascetic **Sumedha** was a very affluent guild leader before he became an ascetic. He found that his ancestors had hoarded wealth in their treasury over a period of seven generations, but these ancestors never took that wealth along when they passed away. What did he do deciding to take that wealth with him? He summoned the people by beat of drum, and asked them to take away the whole wealth as they wished. He had all the doors of his palace opened, took a seat in the courtyard, and enjoyed the sight of people taking away the wealth.

Giving has a tremendous power. There is hardly any achievement that is not possible through generosity. There is no greatness on earth that cannot be obtained through generosity. No one can realize Supreme

Enlightenment without the highest possible sacrifice. On the one hand, generosity helps others. On the other, "the blemish number one" in the human mind, which is craving, gets reduced.

The greatest obstacle to the realization of **Nibbāna** is craving. The Buddha said that the people entrenched in craving tremble just like a hare that had run fast. The Buddha extolled the virtues of generosity in various places, in a variety of ways. The Buddha said, "The world exists and is maintained by craving. All are under the sway of this one force - craving."

> **Tanhāya nīyatī loko**
> **Tanhāya parikassati**
> **Tanhāya ekadhammassa**
> **Sabbeva vasaman vagu**

Those who possess wealth should not think of hoarding, adding more and more to one's wealth. Instead, they must give to those who do not have. They must exert for the well-being of others. They must think of others. They must work for others.

This way, anyone can become generous. Those who are not generous are unfortunately dominated by craving. There is hardly anyone who suffers mentally, as the miserly and the stingy. Even though he may be a millionaire, if he is miserly, he is an unfortunate person. Wealth is utilized as the measure of good fortune, because of the ignorance of Buddhism. When He saw a bundle of gold coins the Buddha showed it to **Ven. Ananda**, saying,

> "**Ananda**, there is a serpent over there." The wealthier one is, greater the craving. Greater the craving, **Nibbāna** is more and more distant.

Those who are fully aware of the generosity of the Buddha will utilize one's wealth for one's own self, and will reap its best results by using it for the well-being of others. When we contemplate the Enlightened One we can never forget His supreme generosity.

## Buddha is for whole mankind

*The Buddha is not a property of Buddhists only. He is the property of whole mankind. His teaching is common to everybody. Every religion, which came into existence after the Buddha, has borrowed many good ideas from the Buddha*

***A Non- Buddhist Scholar***

***The Licchavi King Bhaddiya asked theBuddha,"Is it true that you know the magic of hypnotizing people, of attracting and holding them to you?" The Buddha replied, "O Bhaddiya, please do not accept anything simply because you heard it,......"*** ***see page 13***

## CHAPTER 6

### THE BUDDHA IS THE BRAVEST AMONG HUMAN BEINGS

In the whole of human history no person braver than the Buddha has been born, to-date. The feeling called 'fear' had been totally eliminated from His being, forever. The only cause for 'fear' is craving. (**Tanhāya jāyatī bhayaṃ**).

Craving brings fear into being. The expression '**bhaya**' is a word for sense-desires. Why is it considered a word for sense-desires? The person who is agitated by sense-desires gets attached to phenomena. He will not free himself from the fears that occur in this world. In consequence, the word 'fear' (**bhaya**) is yet another synonym for sense-desire.

People experience fear due to several reasons. Beings are likely to feel a sense of fear because of their love of life, or because they do not want to die, or else, because of their attachment to their spouses and children, their attachment to their houses and lands and other property. The Buddha does not have any such possessions to which he wanted to feel attached. As a result He had a surprising fearlessness. No trepidation or trembling could happen in him in any way. Once, the Buddha said:

> **"That people, when they are shaken by fear, go to rocks, forests, groves for protection and refuge."**

The Buddha stated that fear is a mean quality and a blemish that is found in human beings, and that a human being should never be frightened of another human being, or even of a demon, for that matter.

Shame and fear should be there only when it comes to committing evil actions. One must be frightened and ashamed only when one does wrong things. One must not be frightened by people. **The Buddha, who is the supreme symbol of fearlessness, never frightened others.** Cowards became brave and fearless when they saw the Buddha. If those monks living in the forest experienced fear, they were asked to think of the Buddha. They were advised to think of the Buddha and be fearless. The Buddha stated:

> **"O Monks, I will advise you this way. When you go to the forest, or to the foot of a tree, or to an abandoned house, if you experience a fear, a trepidation, or if you experience your hair standing on end with horror, then just think of me."**

*(Dhajagga Sutta)*

'**Ālavaka** the demon who threatened to take Him by his feet and throw Him into outer-space, **Angulimāla** the murderer who ran towards Him to kill Him, the intoxicated elephant **Nālagiri** which was deployed along the main road to trample and break Him, **Suciroma** the demon who tried to pierce Him with his body-hair, **Saccaka** who tried to make Him perspire through his debating skill, the chief of **Asuras**, who was proud of his physical stature, four-thousand eight-hundred yojanas in height, **Baka** who had the illusion that there was none greater than him, ascetic **Uruvela Kassapa** who boasted that there were no Buddhas like him in the world, and **Devadatta** who hurled a stone at Him, were all subdued by the Buddha, stated the author of the classic **Butsarana**, upholding the Buddha's fearlessness.

When **Ālavaka** saw the Buddha in his abode, he ordered the Buddha to leave his house. The Buddha left, saying, "All right, friend." **Ālavaka** called Him in again. The Buddha was ordered this way three times. On the fourth occasion the Buddha said fearlessly, "No, I am not leaving. Do whatever you can." Then **Ālavaka** said, "Monk, I will ask you a question. If you do not answer me I will make you deranged. I will split your heart. Or else, I will throw you to outer-space, taking you by your two feet."

On hearing this the Buddha fearlessly responded,

> "**Ālavaka**, I have not seen anyone either in the world of space of gods, **māras** and **Brahmas**, or in the world of terrestrial beings, anyone capable either of making me deranged, or else splitting my heart, or throwing me to outer-space, taking me by my feet. But, whatever that may be, if you feel so, you can ask me any question you like."

A Brahmin called **Sela** went to see the Buddha with a retinue of three-hundred young Brahmins. When nearing the place where the Buddha was, Sela addressed the young men this way:

> "Friends, do not make much noise. Tread softly and come along. Friends, Buddhas are like lions, they live alone. It is difficult to get near them. When I talk to ascetic Gotama, do not interrupt. You come in only after I have spoken to Him."

This clearly establishes that even Brahmins, learned in the Three Vedas, had an awe towards the Buddha.
The Buddha, speaking about Himself, once said,

> "After hypnotizing all my enemies, bringing them all under my sway, I live in joy without fear."Others said of him, "Sir, you are a lion king who has shed all fears."

Such ferocious demons as **Ālavaka, Suciroma, Khararoma** and **Āravāla,** such **nāga** chieftains like **Cūlodara, Mahodara, Agnisikha, Dhūmasikha , Mucalinda,** such debators as **Saccaka,** such young men like **Ambaṭṭha,** such proud Brahmins like **Pokkharasāti, Sona Daṇḍa, Kūṭa Danta and Kasībhāradvāja, and** such king elephants like **Nālāgiri,** knelt before the Buddha.

All those who follow such a fearless religious leader must themselves become fearless. They must be people who could not know what fear is. Being cowardly is a shame on humanity. It is demeaning to Buddhists. It is degrading for one human being to be frightened of another. One must not be afraid of either parents, teachers, elders, demons, gods, even of the Buddha. We must respect those noble beings.

We must be obedient to them. We must care for them. But, we must not be frightened of them. People are frightened when they do wrong.

Fear is a blemish that occurs when we do wrong, or due to ignorance, or due to

*The worst punishment that the Buddha imposed on a very stubborn student was 'Brahma Danda'. Ven. Channa was given this punishment. Channa was born the same day as Prince Siddhārtha. He was the character who became Prince Siddhārtha's closest associate from childhood on. He was inordinately proud of this, even after becoming a monk. In order to dispel his inordinate pride, the Buddha imposed 'Brahma Danda' on him.*

*see page 14*

craving. It is a weakness. This blemish is not found in Arahants or in Buddhas. One must be frightened of, or ashamed of, not people but of doing wrong.

Therefore, if you want to be true Buddhists, follow the Buddha and cultivate within you fearlessness which was a very significant quality of the Buddha.

## Man who achieved a great victory

*One of the first scholars to begin the work of translating the Pali Literature into English, was the son of a well-known clergyman. His object in undertaking the work was to prove the superiority of Christianity over Buddhism. He failed in this task but he achieved a greater victory than he expected. He became a Buddhist. We must never forget the happy chance which prompted him to undertake this work and thereby make the precious Dhamma available to thousands in the West. The name of this great scholar was Dr. Rhys Davids.*

***Ven. A. Mahinda, "Blue Print of Happiness"***

CHAPTER 7

## THE BUDDHA IS A RELIGIOUS TEACHER WITH AN AUTHENTIC HISTORY

Most religious leaders, creators, saviours and gods are not historical persons. There is no acceptable historical evidence to prove that they actually lived. But, there is a vast variety of evidence to uphold the fact that the Buddha was a truly historical personage, and that He actually lived.

The whole world has now accepted the fact that He is a historical figure. His line (the **Sākyas**), His clan (**Gotama**), His name (**Siddhārtha**) are all recorded in ancient Indian Literature. They are mentioned in **Hīnayāna** and **Mahāyāna** books. His birth-place, the place where He delivered His first sermon, the site at which He realized **Nibbāna**, can still be seen. Emperor Asoka visited many of these sites mostly on foot. He had rock edicts set up at these sites. Cities, villages, rocks, rivers mentioned in His sermons and Discourses, exist even today.Those persons He met, **King Bimbisāra**, **King Kosala**, **King Ajātasatta**, and the **Licchavi Kings**, are also historical personalities.

Emperor **Asoka** who visited **Lumbini**, the site at which **Prince Siddhārtha** was born, set up a stone pillar there to mark that sacred spot. The legend on the Pillar reads this way:

> '**Devānaṃ piyena Piyadasinā Lājinā visati vasāhī sitena atana āgāca mahīyite hida Budhe jāte Sākya munīti silā vigada hivā kālā pita, silā thabheva usa pāpite hida bhagavaṃ jāteti Lunmini gāme ukhalike kate ata bhāgīyeva.**' (**King Devānaṃpriya Priyadarshi** visited this place personally in the twentieth year of his enthronement, and had offerings made here as this was the site where **Sākya Muni** Buddha was born. A stone wall was also set up. He established a stone pillar. The village of Lumbini was freed from taxation. One-eighth of the income was also given to the village.)"

***(Lumbini Rock Inscription)***

In several inscriptions set up by Emperor Asoka the Buddha's name is mentioned. In a variety of contexts the places where the Buddha resided are referred to. '**Sāvatthiyaṃ Viharati Jetavane**'(in the **Jeta Grove** in **Sāvatthi**); '**Sakkesu Viharati Kapilavatthusmin**'(at **Kapilavatthu**); '**VesāliyaṃViharati Mahāvane**' (at **Vesāli** in the Great Forest); **Rājagaha**);'**Kosambiyaṃ ViharatiGhositārāme**' (in **Ghositārāma** at **Kosambi**); '**Rājagahe Viharati Mora Nivāpe**' (at **Mora Nivāpe** in **Rājagaha**); '**Sāketa Viharati Kālakārāme**' (in **Kālakāṛāma** at **Sāketa**); **Rajagahe Viharati Gijjhakūṭe Pabbate**' (in the **Gijjhakūta** Rock at **Rājagaha**); '**Rājagahe Viharati Veluvane Kalandaka Nivāpe** (in **Veluvana**, **Kalandaka Nivāpa**, at **Rājagaha**); '**Antharā ca Ukkuṭṭhaṃ antharā ca**

*The Buddha, unlike most other teachers, did not use only His monastery or His auditorium for teaching. The Buddha taught His disciples mostly in the open air. The Buddha's class-rooms were public parks, cemeteries, rock-slabs, sandy stretches, shade of trees, fields, pasture-land, poor hovels, the public roads, and the forests.* *see page 16*

**Setavyaṃ**' (walking between the cities of **Ukkuṭṭha** and **Setavya**); '**Bhaggesu Viharati Suṃsumāragire**' (in **Bhagga** at **Suṃsumāragira**); '**Koliyesu Viharati - Sajjanelaṃ**' (in **Sajjanela** in the land of the **Koliyas**); '**Kusinārāyaṃ Viharati Mallānaṃ Sālavana**' (in the Sala Grove of the Mallas in Kusinārā); '**Sāvatthiyaṃ Viharati Pubbārāme**' (in **Pubbārāma** at **Sāvatthi**); '**Bhagavānālike Viharati Nīculavane**' (in **Nīculavana** at **Bhagavā Nālike**); '**Bārānasiya Viharati Gijjhakāvasathe** (in **Gijjhakāvasatha** in **Bāranasi**); '**Kimbilayuṃ Viharati Isipatane Migadāye**' (in **Kimbila** in **Isipatane**); '**Ālaviyaṃ Viharati Aggalāve Cetiye**' (in **Aggalāva** Monastery at **Ālaviya**); '**Campāyaṃ Viharati Pokkharani Tīre**' (at **Campā** near the Pond); **Magadhesu Viharati Manimālake**' (in **Manimālaka** in **Magadhe**).

All these places are found in North India even today. Some of the rivers the Buddha mentioned, like **Gangā, Yamunā, Aciravatī** and **Godhāvarī,** still continue in their courses. Some of the mountains He referred to, **Himālaya** and **Gijjhakūta,** for instance, still stand. Brahmins, who like those who asked Buddha various questions, are there in India today, too. Those sacrifices and rituals which the Buddha pointed out as futile are practised today, too. The caste cleavages that existed at that time flourish today, too. Those regions in which He travelled exist there still. The Buddha referred to four places that should move devoted householders. They should see these four places. These four places are the place the Buddha was born, the place where He realized Buddhahood, the place where **Dhammacakka Pavattana Sutta** was preached, and the place where the Buddha passed away. These four places are **Lumbini, Buddha Gayā, Isipatana** and **Kusināra (Cattārimāni Ānanda Saddhassa Kulaputassa dassanīyāni samvejanīyāniṭhānāni.Katamāni cattāri: idha tathāgato jātoti;idha tatāgatho anutharaṃ sammāsambodhiṃ abhi sambuddhoti;idha tathāgatena anuttaraṃDhammacakkaṃ Pavattitanti; idha tathāgato anupādisesāya Nibbāna dhātuya parinibbuto ti)**

(*Mahā Parinibbāna Sutta*)

Thousands of devotees go to see these four sacred sites referred to by the Buddha Himself. Seeing these places they really are moved. The places the Buddha told Ananda were pleasant spots,can still be seen. **(Ramanīyā Ānanda Vesālī, ramanīyaṃ Udena Cetiyaṃ, ramanīyaṃ Gotamaka Cetiyaṃ, ramaniyaṃ Sattamba Cetiyaṃ, ramaniyaṃ Bahuputta Cetiyaṃ, ramanīyaṃ Ānanda Sārānanda Cetiyaṃ; ramanīyaṃ Cāpāla Cetiyaṃ).**

(*Mahā Parinibbāna Sutta*)

The places the Buddha referred to as especially pleasant are - **Vesāli, Udena Cetiya, Gotamaka Cetiya, Sattamba Cetiya, Cāpāla Cetiya.**

When the Buddha was nearing His last days Ananda spoke to Him thus:

> "Sir, this is but the suburb of a minor city. Please do not pass away in such a small town. In India there are such great cities as **Campā, Rājagaha, Sāvatthi, Sāketa, Kosambi** and **Bāranasī.** Please pass away in one of those great cities.
>
> (*Mahā Parinibbāna Sutta*)

As has been indicated by the Buddha the sixteen Great Kingdoms of India, during Buddha's time were - **Anga, Magadha,**

*Lumbini*

*Buddha Gaya*

*Kusinara*

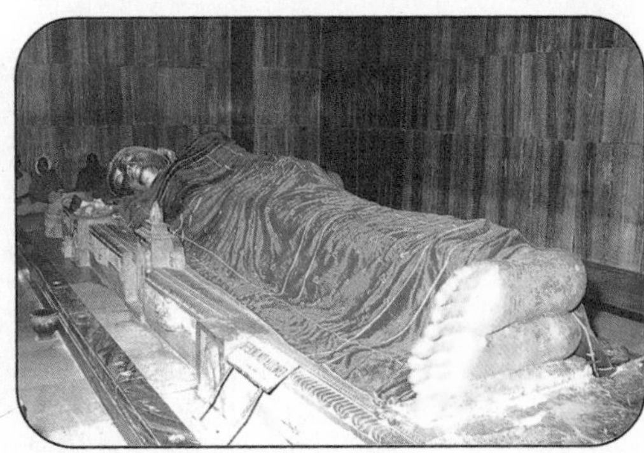

*Parinibbana, Kusinara*

*Saranath, Dhammika Cetiya*

*Vajrasana, Buddha Gaya*

*Relics Casket from Kapilavastu (Delhi Museum)*

*Kapilavastu (Stupa with Buddha-relics)*

*Buddha Gaya*

*Buddha Gaya*

*Buddha Gaya - Ambulatory*

*Vesali*

*Ajanta Cave Sculptures*

*Buddha's foot-print Buddha Gaya*

*Ancient Kapilavastu*

**Kāsi, Kosala, Vajji, Malla, Ceti, Vanga, Kuru, Pañcāla, Maccha, Sūrasena, Assaka, Avanti, Gandhāra** and **Kāmboja.**

The black soil that was burnt at the cremation of the Buddha's body can be seen even today. The Bodhi Tree under which the Buddha realized Enlightenment exists today, too. A sapling of this Bodhi Tree has grown in **Anurādhapura**, Sri Lanka. Two caskets containing the relics of Ven. **Sāriputta** and Ven. **Moggallāna**, the two Chief Disciples of the Buddha, were brought back to India from the Victoria and Albert Museum in England, and were deposited at **Sāñchī Stūpa**. The two words '**Sariputasa**' and '**Mugalanasa**' are carved on the caskets. A tooth relic is deposited at the Temple of the Tooth Relic in **Kandy, Sri Lanka.**

The Buddha's Word in **Tripitaka** is preserved in Buddhist countries. The line of Bhikkhus initiated by the Buddha still flourishes and there are tens of thousands of Buddhist Bhikkhus in Buddhist countries. Buddhist **King Kanishka** of the 1st Century A.D. minted a coin with the image of the Buddha on it. The two pilgrim monks from China, **Fa-Hien** and **Huien-Tsiang,** visited all the important Buddhist sites in the 5th and 7th Centuries A.D. In those countries in Asia, where Buddhism flourished, Buddha's images are found not in thousands, but in hundreds of thousands. **This way, the Buddha is a Great Man with a history, who made history. The Buddha occupies the foremost place among those great people who adorned human history, and world history.**

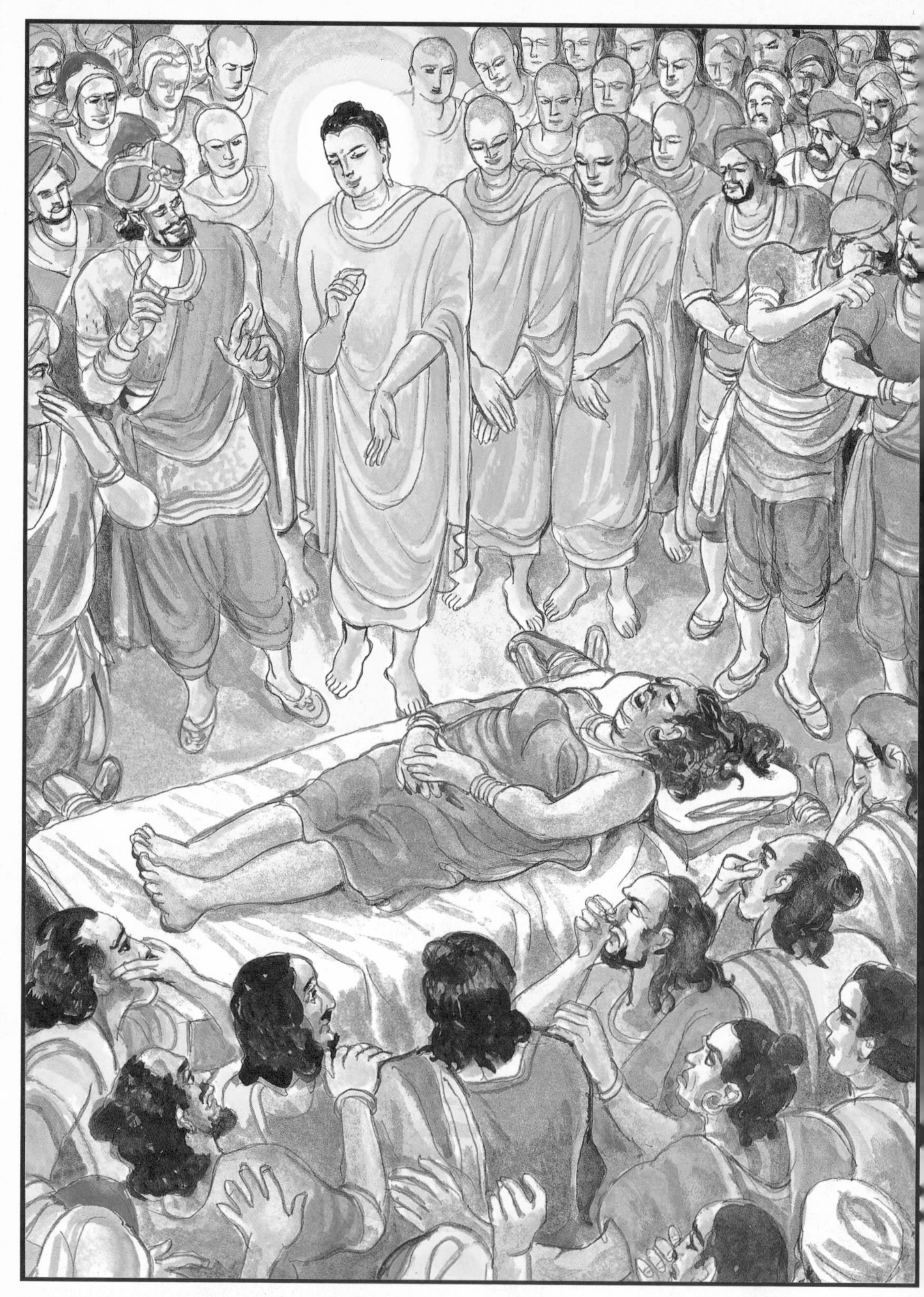

*On the appointed day, the cemetery was totally crowded with the people who had assembled there on the king's orders. The Buddh[a] arrived at the cemetery with His disciples at the appointed time. The Buddha requested the king to auction Sirima's body which ha[d] been valued at thousands of gold coins per hour, when she was alive.*

*see page 1*

CHPATER 8

## BUDDHA WAS THE MOST BLAMED SOCIAL WORKER

There is no one who was not found fault with when engaged in service to the country, to the nation, to religion, to society, and to the world. In all countries, in all nations, in all societies, there are groups opposed to social service. There are those who misinterpret service. Also, there are some who suffer loss because they wanted to serve people. It is natural that they should oppose social service.

In all countries one comes upon traditional ways that are harmful to the country entrenched beliefs, strong cults and obsolete thoughts that are problematic. A progressive social worker fights against such harmful forces. Others try in a variety of ways to get rid of such social workers. We have heard of such social workers eliminated in many countries.

The Buddha initiated a tremendous revolution of social mores and notions in ancient India. He started it non-violently, with loving-kindness and compassion, and with restraint and patience. In consequence, His life was saved.

When He began to stand out among other religious teachers, when He became more and more popular, the numbers who venerated Him began to increase. At the same time the number of people who opposed Him also increased. But, the Buddha travelled about in villages and in market cities, both alone and with His retinue. He was never given police protection. The Buddha's great qualities protected Him.

Of the royal dynasties in ancient India, **Sākya** line was considered most proud. When a prince born in such a proud royal line became a beggar, going along streets for his alms round, giving up all his royal privileges and luxuries, the event dealt a stunning blow to the capitalist system of the day, to the dictatorships of the time, to caste prestige, to those who lived lives of ultra-luxury, and to Regal Majesty. Kings and members of royal families resented Prince **Siddhārtha**'s renunciation. Some people did not like the idea of a person at the highest peak of luxury giving up all that, descending to the level of ordinary people, and becoming a have-not.

Those other religious leaders who were earlier known as popular personalities, and their followers, too, were opposed to the Buddha. Many Brahmins resented the Buddha's opposition to caste concepts of those Brahmins who, deceiving naive folks, enjoyed luxuries. **Devadatta** and his devotee **Ajāsattha**, too, opposed the Buddha.

The Buddha had to render service to mankind while so many powerful persons were ranged against Him. They toppled stones to kill Him. Sent archers to assassinate Him. Deployed an intoxicated elephant to destroy Him. They levelled the worst possible changes against Him through the female ascetic **Sundarī** and **Ciñci Mānavikā**. They levelled a charge of murder against Him. This way, He endured abuses and charges from numerous opponents. One Brahmin abused the Buddha directly, calling Him **Vasala** (outcast) and **Mundaka** (shaven head). But, the Buddha remained unshaken by all this. He showed them the same kind of compassion He displayed to His son **Rāhula**, and that, too, without any change.

The Buddha was not even vestigially disillusioned by abuses, insults and resentments. He never thought of leaving the country. He did not think of reducing the service He rendered. He never contemplated revenge. He was not at all afraid. He was not shaken. He showed everyone the same level of loving-kindness. Because of the power of His loving-kindness He was able to subdue all His opponents. They were restrained. With every opposition His greatness increased in proportion. Had it not been for **Devadatta** His greatness would not have been so greatly pronounced. **Devadatta** came into being because of his urge for revenge. The Buddha came into prominence because He extended loving-kindness without resorting to revenge. **Devadatta** is the worst possible example of revenge. The best example for refraining from revenge is the Buddha.

The Buddha is the greatest possible ideal for those social workers, rulers and leaders who lose their temper when abused, and those who do not like to be abused. Those who cannot endure abuse should not enter into the field of social service. People must enter into the field of social service with the expectation of being abused. Those who do nothing can remain unabused. But, they are not as great as those who do social service and get abused and insulted. Being abused when serving people is an index to the value of the service rendered.

If one were to become discouraged or disillusioned because of abuse, he is not a true social worker. When you serve people and when you get abused and insulted, think of the Buddha. Please try to follow His path. As Buddhists, whenever we get abused one must remember how the Buddha was abused and how He endured all that with patience.

## A wise father

*Buddha is one who sees his children playing in the consuming fire of worldliness and employs different expedients to bring them out of this burning house and lead them to the safe asylum of Nirvana.*

*Prof. Lakshimi Narasu, "The Essence of Buddhism"*

*Then the Buddha accepted to treat him. "If you can get the medicine I prescribe, I will bring back your son to life," the Buddha said next. "What medicine, Sir?" "A pinch of mustard." "Oh, that is simple. I will bring it quickly." So saying, she got ready to go. "But wait a bit. That pinch of mustard must be from a house where death had never occurred." "All right, Sir, I will bring the mustard."*

*see page 17- 18*

CHAPTER 9

## THE BUDDHA WAS THE LEADER TO DISPLAY THE HIGHEST PRINCIPLES

Legal experts and politicians in various countries have formulated and promulgated many and various laws, constitutions, regulations and ordinances. But these have not been conducive to the well-being of all the people in the world. They are not universally valid. There are some shortcomings in these laws and principles.

But, the Buddha, through a very long effort and after years of suffering, discovered the principle of the Middle Path, by research, by experimenting, and by implementing. No one has ever been able to discover such an admirable principle which will continue to be valid as long as the world exists, which will be applicable as long as human society progresses.

When He was a prince, ascetic **Siddhārtha** enjoyed limitless luxury. When He was an ascetic He endured limitless suffering. He realized fully and comprehensively the futility of both these extremes, and said in joy,

> "Eye arose on phenomena never known before. Wisdom arose. Knowledge arose. Insight arose."
> **(Cakkuṃ udapādi, paññā udapādi, vijjā udapādi, āloko udapādi)**

The Buddha took immediate steps to place that unique knowledge, that unparalleled light before the generality of the people in the world. In short, He was able to realize supreme Enlightenment while being established in that principle It was possible to realize Enlightenment through the principle of the Middle Path. What is the progress or well-being that cannot be achieved through the principle of the Middle Path? The principle of Middle Path is the law that ensures the protection of the world. Even the planets move in the orbit of the Middle Path. If the planets go beyond their orbits they will get destroyed. Even our Earth rests on the principle of the Middle Path.

In everything, in every action, straying beyond limits will spell destruction. Our daily rice sustains our life. But, if we took several plates of rice or a whole pot of rice all at once, that will bring about destruction. Drinking water sustains our life. But, if we drank several bucketfuls of water, it will be extremely harmful. Those who take intoxicating drinks excessively die early. Those who break rest excessively will become deranged. Even if medicine is taken in excess it will prove harmful.

There is a limit to the work that people should do. There is a limit within which a person should live. To exceed those limits is harmful. There is a limit to a woman's behaviour. If she trangresses that limit it is destructive. There is a limit to a monk's behaviour. If he goes beyond that it is harmful. There are limits even officials, kings, ministers, people's representatives and prime ministers should observe.

If they go beyond those limits it will bring about destruction. There are limits to countries, to nations, to communities. If these limits are transcended their destruction will come about.

Extremism is harmful - destructive. Buddha experimented with it and rejected it as low, common, belonging to ordinary folk, ignoble, conducive to misery. There are countries with extreme political power. Sri Lanka is foremost among countries that have shaped their political systems over a long period of time, along the principle of Middle Path. They built tanks throughout the country, improved cultivation and fed the people well. **Vihārās**, monasteries and places of worship were set up. Religious feelings were inculcated in the minds of men. Thoughts of peaceful co-existence were promoted among the people. All this was achieved with the inspiration of the Middle Path principle of Buddhism.

The Buddha advocated a balanced existence as a means of worldly welfare. What was meant by the expression 'balanced existence' was a way of life in which the expenditure was in keeping with the income. The Buddha's principle of Middle Path was so highly esteemed by Emperor **Asoka** that, in his Rock Edict No. 3, he has proclaimed:

> "It is good to strike a balance between income and expenditure.'

He had this written down for the benefit of the people. In consequence, the Buddhists should follow the Middle Path, and no other policy.

The only system, the only principle that any individual, that any society, that any country, any nation or any community can sustain, is the principle of the Middle Path.

Those countries which develop fast and those people who rise rapidly, have all collapsed quickly. We have witnessed this kind of thing. Therefore, we have to lead our lives strictly according to the principle of the Middle Path.

When an individual walks along the Noble Eight-Fold Path of Right Views, Right Thoughts, Right Words, Right Activity, Right Livelihood, Right Effort, Right Mindfulness and Right Concentration, his policy will automatically be that of the Middle Path. All Buddhist lives should be led in terms of this noble policy.

## Mind Training

*We hear much nowadays of thought-power, but Buddhism is the most complete and effective system of mind-training yet placed before the world.*

***Dudley Wright***

***He went to the Buddha and after the initial pleasantries, he told the Buddha, "I have several doubts in my mind. I want to questi you about these. Will you answer them, Sir?""Sabhiya, you came over a long distance of 700 yojanas to ask questions. Ask all th questions you want. I will answer your questions one by one, systematically, according to the law, according to the significance, said the Buddha.***

***see page2***

CHAPTER 10

## BUDDHA IS THE YOUNG RELIGIOUS LEADER WHO SET UP A YOUTH ORGANIZATION CALLED THE SANGHA ORDER

Ascetic **Siddhārtha**, when He realized Enlightenment, was a youth of thirty-five. His first group of disciples of sixty persons, including **Yasa** the householder, was a youthful crowd.

The second group of missionaries, consisting of the thirty **Bhaddavaggiya** princes, was also made up of young people. Next, He ordained five hundred including the ascetic **Uruvela Kassapa**, three hundred including **Nadī kassapa**, and two-hundred including **Gayā kassapa**. These one-thousand ascetics were all youths.

After this, **Koliya** and **Upatissa** were ordained along with their retinue of two-hundred and fifty persons. These two were made the Buddha's Chief Disciples. This, too, was a group of youths. Later on, those ordained at **Kapilavatthu**, the **Sākya Princes Nanda**, **Rāhula**, **Baddiya**, **Anuruddha**, **Ānanda**, **Bhagu Kimbila**, **Devadatta** and **Upāli** the butler, were all young people who were not mature in body, in years, in appearance, in strength and in wisdom. These young monks, numbering about one-thousand and five-hundred, were a group of young missionaries who were young and healthy, were capable of walking hundreds of miles, and had the capacity to resist both heat and cold.
Hindu life in India is divided into four stages described as **Brahmacāri, Gruhastha Vānaprastha and Sannyāsi.** People remain **Brahmacāri** until marriage. They get married at the proper age and perform their household duties. When they are above fifty or sixty they go to a hermitage or a forest-abode. That is the end of traditional Hindu life.

The Buddha did not recognize this system and built an entirely new religious institution. While He was young Himself, a majority of His followers also were young. With the passage of time the members of this young group of monks became elderly. But, we have to accept the fact that, at the beginning the majority were young, and that even in later years, a majority of the people who joined newly were young. In consequence, there is no harm in characterizing this as an organization of young monks.

All the contemporary religious leaders of the Buddha in India were older than the Buddha. (**Jinnā, vuddhā, mahallakā, addhagatā anuppattā**). They were grown old and decrepit.

Respecting the elderly and the aged was a noble tradition that existed among the Aryans for quite a long time. But, the Buddha never displayed any deference to any elderly person who came to see Him. This was because no one was superior to Him in wisdom, in moral achievement, and in the discipline of the mind. One day, an elderly, mature Brahmin, by the name of **Veranja**, came to see the Buddha. He asked the Buddha,

"Sir Gotama, I have heard that you do not show deference to elderly Brahmins who come to see you, by worshipping them, by getting up from your seat, and by giving them a seat. Is it true? If it is true, is it not a major fault?"

The Buddha answered,

**"I do not see anyone, either among gods or men, who should be honoured by me by worshipping and by other gestures. A person does not deserve to be honoured merely because his hair is grey. If someone possesses truth, righteousness, non-violence, restraint, wisdom and absence of blemishes, such people should receive veneration as elders."**

One day, King **Kosala** went to see the Buddha. He asked the Buddha,

"Sir, do you state that you have attained Enlightenment, which is the highest state?"

The Buddha replied,

"Great King, if in truth it has to be said about someone, that he has attained Enlightenment, which is the highest state, it is about me it has to be said. Great King, I have realized Enlightenment which is the highest state."

Hearing this, **king Kosala** said,

"Sir, other religious leaders who have a vast following of ascetics, who are the leaders of groups of ascetics, who have a wide-spread fame and who are venerated by many, do not say that they have realized Enlightenment. But you are young in years. Young in asceticism. Still, you say you have realized Enlightenment. How can I accept this?"

**"O Great King, there are four types of people in this world who should not be denigrated because they are young. These four are the royal prince, the serpent, the fire and the monk.** You must not denigrate them because they are young. If you anger the royal prince he will avenge it when he becomes king. The serpent, though young, can destroy a human life by stinging. The fire, though small, can burn your finger. It can expand and destroy a whole region. The monk, though young he may be, if he is high in moral attainment, he is very strong and powerful."

***(Samyutta Nikaka - Kosala Samyutta).***

In the Buddhist order, there were only a few persons who became monks when they were elderly. Those who become monks in old age are described as '**Buddhapabbajita**' (those who were ordained when old). It was an old monk by the name of **Subhadra** who said thus to the monks, weeping at the Demise of the Buddha,

"Don't weep. Feel happy. We can do whatever we want now as we do not have a leader."

Ven. **Thūlatissa**, who received veneration from senior theras, was another of those who became a monk in old age. A monk is well suited to the life of a Bhikkhu when his Bhikkhu life evolves from childhood on. The Buddha did not intend to make His order a Home for the Aged. Therefore,

*The Buddha said to him, "I extol the virtues of a life with few possessions. Why do you hoard these things, without donating whatever things you get?" The monk became angry. He discarded his robe right in the midst of the four-fold congregation, and asked, "Do you want me to be like this?"*

*see page 22*

He ordained many young people. This Great Order He planned out with vast vision, has continued over 2,500 years because He gave priority to youth, wisdom and discipline. No organization that does not give the due place to wise, young persons, can become strong or permanent. By the prohibition to ordain blind people, deaf people, cripples and the sick, it is evident that the Buddha wanted the Order of Monks to consist of only strong monks. This also indicates that the Order should consist of able, wise people who can perform services.

## Knowledge is the key to higher path

*Without sensuous pleasure would life be endurable? Without belief in immortality can man be moral? Without worship of a God can man advance towards righteousness? Yes, replies the Buddha, these ends can be attained by knowledge; knowledge alone is the key to the higher path, the one worth pursuing in life; knowledge is that which brings calmness and peace to life, which renders man indifferent to the storms of the phenomenal world.*

*Prof. Karl Pearson*

CHAPTER 11

## IS BUDDHISM A RELIGION THAT SHOULD BE RESTRICTED TO BOOKS AND RITES AND RITUALS ONLY?

To judge from how Buddhism is practised by its adherent in some countries before long, Buddhism, will get transformed into a religious system that is totally different from what the Buddha intended.

The five precepts, which are cardinal virtues of a Buddhist, have now become five phrases recited at the beginning of a ceremony or a meeting. The five precepts which should be implemented hundred per cent have now become a series of Pali words that are hundred per cent non-implemented.

Today, the five precepts are found only in the monk who administers five precepts to the devotees. Out of thousands of people who recite the five precepts in all these places, only about one or two will observe them. The only human community that pledges to abstain from five sins, that people do or that may happen accidentally is the Buddhist community. If these pledges are scrupulously kept the greatness of that human community could be maintained.

Buddhism is a religion that one must practise while living it. Buddhism means the best way a human being should live. Buddhism is the religion that teaches the right way to conduct life. It is of no use that Buddhist subject- matter should be found in books, or that one should keep on thinking about it. The virtues and principles found in Buddhism should be adapted to one's daily life, and must be experimented with. If that does not happen one cannot say that real Buddhism, true Buddhism, exists.

Rites and rituals and **stūpas** and shrines are not the essence of Buddhism. These, too, are necessary for the survival of a religion, just as the bark is necessary for the tree to exist. When religious structures and religious rites and rituals get eroded, the religion dies off. Therefore, they, too, are necessary. But, they are not the true essence of a religion. Religions are not there for the use of animals but exclusively for the use of man. If man does not follow religion, or else if man does not make use of the religion, if he does not lead his life in accordance with religion, that religion will get restricted to books and to external rites and rituals.

Religion in some countries, is getting transformed into that kind of status. In reality, the Buddha did not think of a group of people who would sculpt, carve, build or draw his image in terracotta, clay, wax or stone, and would keep on worshipping them. It is all right to worship them. There is no harm in that. But, that is not exactly what the Buddha expected of the Buddhists. **The only thing He expected was that they would tread the Noble Path He indicated. But, without following that Path, if they kept on worshipping Him from morning till night, not just one day, but a hundred years, one cannot realize Nibbāna. If one must realize**

*Angulimāla, who became a symbol of devotion to teachers, was a fierce murderer for all the people in India. When they merely heard his name, the king and his men trembled in fear. All efforts to destroy him were in vain. None of these was able to see that, concealed within this ferocious murderer, there dwelt an Arahant.* *see page 23*

**Nibbāna one must invariably tread the Path He indicated. One can become a true Buddhist only if one followed the Noble Eight-fold Path He advocated.**

Buddhism is not a religion that adores a given person. It is a religion that upholds virtues. We consider the Buddha to be our religious Teacher because of His great and noble virtues. We worship not His body but His virtues. This way, our religious Leader is the body of noble virtues. When there are no virtues there is no Buddhism. There are thousands of such virtues as generosity, charity, loving-kindness, compassion, sympathy, humility, equanimity, being of service to others, and patience. Where there are no such virtues, there is no Buddhism. We must explore our own selves and must try to see not casually but honestly and seriously, how many of those virtues are found within ourselves. We must give thought to this.

Most of those who describe themselves as Buddhists are filled with thousand of such vices as thievery, deceit, dishonesty, falsehood, grasping, jealousy. Many are engrossed in a tremendous struggle impelled by hunger for wealth, for power, for glory, and for office. They have forgotten what is seemly and human, not to say anything about Buddhism. Those who think of religion regularly are rare. It is restricted to funeral service, alms giving, protective chants, and to the observing of five precepts. Buddhism is one particular place. Buddhists are elsewhere. When you consider these matters we find that it is high time that we had a discussion to devise ways and means to introduce Buddhism into the daily lives of people in a practical and pragmatic way. If society distances religious practices and the religious way of life there must be a reason for it. We must try and find out what that cause is.

Religion has to be adapted to the needs of human life, and also to the needs of the present time. But, it should be so adapted that no harm is done to the primary principles and main aims of the religion.

If people cannot be corrected by sermons, and if people do not follow the Doctrine they have heard, that format has to be given up and a new method that is more suitable, should be explored. Such a new system should be implemented.

The Buddha did not preach the Doctrine to **Kisā Gotami**, who was sorely distraught because of her love for her child. He devised a method that would enable **Kisā Gotami** herself to understand the nature of death. Therefore, there are many ways in which those who cannot be disciplined by sermons could be corrected.

The most outstanding feature of the Buddha's way of teaching, was his capacity to understand the needs of each individual person. In consequence, The Buddha's way of teaching had a freshness of approach, in terms of the audience. His supreme method should inspire today's Buddhists.

## CHAPTER 12

### THE SUPREME BUDDHA - GREATEST OF GUIDES

Buddhas are indicators of the Path (**Akkātāro Tathāgatā**) said the Buddha, Enlightenment One Himself. The Buddhas are described also as '**Maggaññu**' (Knower of the Path), '**Maggavidū**' (He who has realized the Path), and '**Maggakovido**' (One who is wise about the Path).

All these signify 'the person who knows the true Path - the Noble Path'. This true Path is the Path to obtain relief from suffering, that is, the Path to **Nibbāna**. The Path realized by the Buddha's wisdom. It is the Path that men should tread. No one who followed the Path has ever gone wrong. The only concern of the Buddha was to direct beings who went stray into the right Path. This true Path is **Ariya Aṭṭhangika Magga** (the Noble Eight-fold Path).

The principle of the person who treads this Path is the Middle Path - the Middle Path that does not go to extremes (**Majjhima Paṭipadā**). This Path consists of these: **Sammā Diṭṭhi** (Right Understanding), **Sammā Saṃkappa** (Right Thought), **Sammā Vācā** (Right Speech), **Sammā Ājīva** (Right Livelihood ),**Sammā Kammanta** (Right Bodily Action ), **Sammā Vāyāma** (Right Effort), **Sammā Sati** (Right Mindfulness), and **Sammā Samādhi** (Right Concentration).

The Buddha discovered this noblest of Paths, consisting of eight stages. If an individual were to follow at least one of those eight, he will become great among human beings. If he follows two, he will become a greater man. If he follows all these eight, he will become greater than gods and brahmas.

Buddha indicated these to us in this manner: "This is good. This is bad. These are virtuous actions. These are evil actions. These are the things that should be done. These are the things that should not be done. These are the things that should be acquired. These are the things that should not be acquired. These are the things that should be followed. These are the things that should be given up. If you do good, such and such good results will follows. If you do bad, such and such bad results will ensue. I do not say these things without reason. I say these through experience - through doing. Therefore, do the right things. Give up what is bad."

The Buddha indicated to us the good path, the right path, the true path, like a kind father, kind mother and a kind instructor. How can we make the best possible use of the noble indicator of the Path? Is it by continuing to worship Him, or by making offerings to Him? Is it by constructing large statues of the Buddha? Or is it by travelling along the right Path He indicated with His finger? We are indebted to Him for showing us the path

*"O Monks, I compare the Doctrine to a raft. It is necessary for crossing a river or a stream. It is not for carrying on your shoulders. O Monks, the Doctrine I expounded is only to help a person to cross the ocean of 'samsāra' (becoming) - and not for carrying on one's shoulders or on one's head."*

*see page 69*

to **Nibbāna** (the Eternal Bliss). We must honour Him and make offerings to Him. This will make us accrue merit. But, those material offerings alone are not sufficient for us to realize **Nibbāna**. **Nibbāna** is with us. We must acquire it ourselves - we ourselves must discover it - realize it. It is not something we can acquire through the help of others.

The Buddha never intended to assemble a vast array of disciples and to live like a great leader surrounded by that retinue of disciples. He intended to assemble a group of persons who will tread that true path - the Path of purity

He discovered after enduring the worst sufferings a human being could undergo. He wanted a group of people who would follow Him - who would emulate Him - who would think like Him - who would work like Him. He wanted a group of people who would talk like Him, who would live like Him. In short, He did not need a group of people who passively listen to Him, who would write down what He said and memorize it, or else who would keep on worshipping His Words. He needed a group of people who would do what was said - who would experiment and who would implement what was said. **Nibbāna cannot be realized merely by honouring the Buddha's name or His image.**

Let us take an example. A person who arrives at the railway station asks someone there directions to the Independence Building. That person tells him the road he should take. If the man who asked directions remained there, worshipping, honouring and thinking the person who gave him directions without going, he will not be able to go to the Independence Building. He will then never know the Independence Building. He must thank him, and go along the path he indicated. He could reach the Independence Building only if he trod the path that was indicated.

The Noble Eight-fold Path indicated to us by the Buddha is a thousand times nobler than the path to the Independence Building shown by the man at the railway station. We must worship at least three times a day that noble Being who indicated to us that Noble Path - that path to the Eternal Bliss of **Nibbāna** - must make offerings to Him - must honour Him.

But, in order to realize **Nibbāna** such material forms as worshipping, making offerings, honouring, etc., are not sufficient. There is no other path to **Nibbāna** than the one He indicated. We must invariably tread that Path.

Here is a good example to prove this. When the Buddha was in His death bed, the worldling Bhikkhu (those who had not reached the paths or fruits of spiritual attainment) started crying and lamenting. Those monks who were bereft of blemishes contemplated the nature of formations. At this stage a monk by the name of **Dhammārāma** determined this way:

> "Before our Buddha breathes His last, I will somehow follow His advice and will obtain some result."

Making up his mind that way, he went to a secluded spot, did solitary meditation and obtained the purity of mind. Those other monks who were crying and lamenting saw monk **Dhammārāma** who, without any thought of their all-compassionate Teacher breathing His last, was all alone in a secluded spot. Those other monks took him by the hand and pulled him alone to the Buddha saying,

> "When our immortal Leader, the Buddha, is about to leave us for ever, this monk only has no sorrow or sense of loss. This is a fellow without a heart."

The Buddha in His death bed saw a reluctant monk being dragged by others towards Him. He asked those monks, "Why do you drag along this monk?" The other monks replied,

> "O Sir, you are about to pass away. There is no use living without you. By looking at whose face can we gain solace? Who would advise us with such a compassion-filled heart? Therefore, our sorrow is limitless. But, only this monk has neither sorrow nor sense of loss. He was seated at a secluded spot, looking down silently. That is why we pulled him along to you."

The Buddha asked that monk, "Are they saying the truth?"

> "Yes Sir, I did not want to cry and lament in a futile manner like them. Without crying and weeping I followed a golden advice you have given us, and was determined to make use of it before you close your eyes for ever. My effort and my determination were extremely successful. I have overcome the immature state of crying and weeping like these monks," the monk replied.

Realizing that he had become an Arahant the Buddha, while in His death bed, put His palms together and said, "**Sādhu, Sādhu, Sādhu**." He addressed the weeping monks this way:

> **"Monks, you who weep and cry for me do not have a genuine affection for me. This monk who, following one Word of mine, achieved high spiritual results is the person who has the true and proper affection for me. Honouring my Word does not only mean writing it in gold sheets or silver sheets or on stone to protect and preserve it, and worshipping it and honouring it. One must live according to my Words. My Words and advice must be implemented. You must conduct your life in accordance with my Words. Those who worship me offering me only fragrant flowers, do not worship me properly. Only those who follow my advice and my Words worship me and honour me properly."**
>
> ***(Dhammapadaṭṭha Kathā)***

From the above story we can quite clearly see who the Buddha really is and what His aim was. He did not want to build a retinue of thousands of disciples who were hypnotized either by His radiant body, or by His appearance, His pleasant voice, His nobility, or His incomparable personality, and to get them to honour Him, respect Him, and to hero-worship Him. He did not want to give them advice, to order them about, to keep them under control, to suppress them, to make them obedient, and to uphold His own leadership.

What the Buddha wanted to set up was a fearless, courageous, virtuous and disciplined society that adhered to the Doctrine, that tried out the Doctrine, that

*The Order of Monks was founded on high principles. They discarded selfishness fully. They were the symbol of common interests. They were free of all such bonds as bondage to lay-life. They had given up all such desires as craving for material things and craving for sensualities. They, like birds who had only the burden of their wings, could go anywhere they listed.* *see page 69*

considered righteousness their way of life and their life-style, that would give their life to uphold principles, that gives the proper place to straight forward attitudes, that would respect law and order, that would honour truth, that would go forward, and that will not go back. The noblest segment in that society is the Order of Monks.

This Order was founded on high principles. They discarded selfishness fully. They were the symbol of common interests. They were free of all such bonds as bondage to lay-life. They had given up all such desires as craving for material things and craving for sensualities.

They, like birds who had only the burden of their wings (**sapattabhāro pakkhi sakunā vīya**), could go anywhere they listed. Those who followed the Buddha were a group of people who symbolized high culture.

The Buddha did not approve of exaggerated honour and respect, not only to Himself but also to His Doctrine.

> "O Monks, I compare the Doctrine to a raft. It is necessary for crossing a river or a stream. It is not for carrying on your shoulders. If one were to think, 'This raft was exceedingly useful to me. I was able to cross because of it. Therefore, I must take it along either on my head or on my shoulders," it is not a wise thought. In the same way, O Monks, the Doctrine I expounded is only to help a person to cross the ocean of '**saṃsāra**' (becoming) - and not for carrying on one's shoulders or on one's head."

*(Majjhima Nikāya - Alagaddūpa Sutta).*

The Teachings of the Buddha are not merely for the purpose of writing down in books and keeping them in library shelves for veneration. Nor are they to be kept concealed. These should be made available to all for reading and spreading the Word of the Buddha, everywhere.The Buddha said,

> **"O Monks, the Doctrine preached by the Tathāgata shines more and more when it is open. It does not shine when it is concealed."**

*(Anguthara Nikāya - Nika Nipāta)*

All these establish the fact that the Buddha wanted to be a true guide to the world, and to show the world the Right Path. He was keen that the men and women of the world trod the Right Path. He was not at all keen to get honour and respect from the world. He was never concerned either about the praise or the blame He received from the world. The true significance of the expression "**Buddhaṃ Saranaṃ Gacchāmi**" is that "I follow the Buddha" - that I tread the Path trodden by the Buddha.

The Buddha passed away in the Great Demise over 2,500 years ago. How can we request assistance from a person who is not alive today? What is the use of such a request? The only assistance, the only help, and the only use one can get from Him who is not there today, is treading the Path He trod, and following His advice.

Realizing the truth that He realized with such tremendous difficulty, whatever else one did without following Him that way, would not at all mean that we took refuge in the Buddha in the proper manner.

The true significance of the expression

"**Dhammaṃ Saranaṃ Gacchāmi**" is that "I follow the Doctrine". The Doctrine (Dhamma) is not a person. It is not a thing. The only use one can make of it is to follow it.

The true meaning of "**Ṣanghaṃ Saranaṃ Gacchāmi**" is that "I will receive advice and guidance from the Sangha. I follow the Sangha. I will cultivate within me the virtues of the Sangha." It is in that way that one can take refuge in the Sangha.

With the passage of time Buddhists drift further and further away from the Buddha. Many people do not have a true awareness of Him. By following the Buddha with wrong awareness and with uncritical devotion, one cannot obtain the true results.

The primary obligation of a Buddhist is to become aware who truly the Buddha is. No one without a true awareness of the Buddha will be able to become a true Buddhist. Therefore, all efforts should be made to tread the Noble Eight-fold Path which is the purest of paths - the Path of Purification shown to us by the Buddha who is the greatest guide to the spiritual Path to-date in the whole of humanity.

## Negative Answer of The Buddha

*If we ask, for instance, whether the position of the electron remains the same, we must say 'no'; if we ask whether the electron's position changes with the time, we must say 'no'; if we ask whether it is in motion, we must say 'no'. The Buddha has given such answers when interrogated as to the conditions of a man's self after his death; but they are not familiar answers for the tradition of seventeenth and eighteenth century science.*

***J. Robert Oppenheimer***

*The Middle Path that does not go to extremes (Majjhima Patipadā). This Path consists of these: Sammā Diṭṭhi (Right Understanding), Sammā Saṃkappa (Right Thought), Sammā Vācā (Right Speech), Sammā Ājīva (Right Livelihood), Sammā Kammanta (Right Bodily Action ), Sammā Vāyāma (Right Effort), Sammā Sati (Right Mindfulness), and Sammā Samādhi (Right Concentration).* *see page 64*

CHAPTER 13

## BUDDHA IS THE FIRST RELIGIOUS LEADER WHO BROUGHT ABOUT A THOUGHT AND SOCIAL REVOLUTION

From the earliest times Man had got into the habit of emulating parents, teachers, elders, priests, kings and leaders. Majority of men and women thought the way those leaders thought. They acted in terms of the orders of those leaders. They got attuned to the idea that doing things contrary to the wishes of the leaders was a breach of tradition, breaking the laws, a disobedience, and a sin.

As a result of this state of thinking man's capacity to think became curbed in a variety of ways - it became restricted. In ancient India the thought processes of the ordinary masses were strongly controlled by Brahmins who had a place of high prominence in the Indian society of that day. Everyone from the king downwards received advice from the Brahmins. If a Brahmin makes a statement everybody had to accept that as the truth.

The Buddha appeared at a time when the society was filled with such strong traditional views and customs. In consequence, He had to bring about a powerful revolution in thought and in society. He brought this about not in the revolutionary mode of such later revolutions as the French Revolution in Europe, and the Russian Revolution. He did not bring about His revolution through blood-shed, through torture and mayhem, through murder, through compelling speeches, or by stirring the minds of men and women into anger. He brought about His revolution entirely through His limitless compassion, through a policy of non-violence and peaceful compassion. The results of those are deeply etched and embedded in the minds of millions in a large number of countries in the East.

Such non-violent leaders as **Emperor Asoka** who, after an initial period of waging fierce war, gave up wars and violence for ever, came into being as a result of the all-powerful, all-compassionate thought revolution of the Buddha. The Buddha pointed out very compassionately, but fearlessly, the fallacies, superstitions, wrong beliefs, cruel forms of sacrificial offerings, customs and traditions that tended towards social deterioration, and questionable forms of rites and rituals.

Prince **Siddhārtha**, who was born in a royal family full of princely affluence and splendour, displayed a tendency towards revolutionary thinking from His early days on. When ascetic **Kāladevala**, who was a favourite of King **Suddhodana**, came to see infant Prince **Siddhārtha**, the king was keen to get the infant Prince to worship ascetic **Kāladevala**. But, what the infant Prince Siddhartha did was placing His feet on the turban of ascetic **Kāladevala**. As a young person when He saw a sick person for the first time, He asked Minister **Channa** a whole series of such questions as,

"Who was that person who had an unusual look? What made him look so? Are there more people like that? Can I, too, become sick?"

Later, when He saw an old person, a dead body, and an ascetic, He asked a similar series of questions.

These four omens stirred in Prince **Siddhārtha**'s mind a whole series of questions: What is 'life'? What is the purpose of 'life'? What is the end of 'life'? For what reason is 'life' continued? In other words, these sights brought about a thought revolution in Him. When He continued to think about sickness, ageing and death, the Prince became disillusioned with the royal splendour He enjoyed. He saw the whole palace as a huge fire full of roaring flames. "If all those who are born will invariably and inevitably die, what is this farce that people enact?' the Prince thought.

He saw that all human beings were caught up in a mass of suffering. He decided to find out the cause of this suffering, and the path to the eradication of suffering.

He was disillusioned with the whole world. Prince **Siddhārtha** grappled violently with His mind. The royal dancing girls danced, sang and played music for several hours in the night. But, they could not detect even a trace of a smile on the Prince's face. Tired, the dancing girls lay down and slept in various places. The sight of dancing girls sleeping in various ways and guises made Him leave the householder's life sooner. Prince **Siddhārtha** is the only young man, nay the only human being in the whole of human history, who renounced His country, His kingdom, His royal splendour, His wife and child, disgusted by the sight of a bevy of beauties, dedicated exclusively to give him pleasure, sleeping at night on the floor in one place. He saw the place where beautiful dancing girls were sleeping, as a cemetery.

A father knows no greater pleasure than the hearing of the news that his wife has borne him a son. But, when a messenger informed Prince **Siddhārtha** that **Yasodharā** (His wife) gave birth to a son, at once He said,

"That is a bond - a grip." (**Rāhulo jāto bandhanaṃ jāto.**).

The only father in human history to make such a statement is Prince **Siddhārtha**.

Making a secret renunciation, giving up His wife, His child, His royal palace, His kingdom and His royal splendour, He entered the forest. He took a rag in which a dead body was wrapped, shook of the myriad's of worms that infested it, washed it, dried it in the sun, and wore it. He sank to the very bottom of the simple life. He is the only royal prince in human history to have done all that. This is a tremendous revolution in lives of limitless luxury.

For six years Prince **Siddhārtha** frequented the abodes of sages and ascetics to learn their religious systems. He was not all satisfied with their systems. Realizing that they did not possess what He was looking for He started to grapple with the blemishes in His own mind. He was victorious in that war.

After He attained Enlightenment, He once visited his father's palace. He had His meals there. The next day, He started His alms round along the same street where

*The Buddha indicated to us the good path, the right path, the true path, like a kind father, kind mother and a kind instructor. How can we make the best possible use of the noble indicator of the Path? We ourselves must discover it - realize it. It is not something we can acquire through the help of others.*

*see page 64*

the royal palace stood. An heir to the throne, who had run away from his royal palace, became an ascetic, returned to the same city, though seeing his royal palace, went along the main street with the begging bowl from house to house, seeking alms. This is an event that would shock a country, a kingdom and a whole nation. This is a tremendous revolution of a royal line, of regal majesty, of kingly power, of royal splendour, and regal pomp and glory. This was a denigration of the capitalist world. A death-blow to royal pride.

The king, His father, became totally distraught by this sight and ran after Him, his royal clothes in disarray. He told the Buddha,

> "Do not denigrate our royal Dynasty."

The Buddha replied,

> "O King, you are of the royal line. But, I am of the Buddha line. Begging is a custom of the Buddhas."

This statement is a great saying that must issue only from the mouth of a Buddha, from a person who brought about a revolution in thinking.

> **"Do not believe in anything simply because you have heard it. Do not believe in traditions because they have been handed down for many generations. Do not believe in anything because it is spoken of and rumoured by many. Do not believe in anything simply because it is found written in your religious books. Do not believe in anything merely on the authority of your teachers and elders. But, after observation and analysis, when you find that anything agrees with reason and is conducive to the good and benefit of one and all, then, accept it and live up to it."**
>
> ***(Kālāma Sutta - Anguttara Nikāya)***

This is a fell blow dealt by a religious leader on blind faith and irrational conventionality. It is the theme of a thought-revolution. The only religious leader, the only thinker, the only man who made such a progressive scientific pronouncement 2,500 years ago, is the Supreme Buddha.

At a time not only those in India, but people all the world over, believed in a soul, the Buddha appeared and announced boldly that there was no soul (**anatta**). He reduced soul-champions to silence. The statement that "there is no soul" was a direct blow of revolutionary thought on the belief of all those other religious leaders who held that there was a soul.

At a time when the caste system had been accepted as an indispensable institution by the whole society, and by the whole country, the Buddha put forward a view totally opposed to contemporary social division, saying,

> **"No one becomes an outcast by birth; no one becomes a Brahmin by birth; one becomes an outcast or a Brahmin only by deed."**

The only person who remained unassaulted, unattached and unassassinated after speaking out against caste division in India at that time was the Buddha.

Those Brahmins who had been long classified and honoured by society were not recognized by the Buddha as 'true Brahmins'.

> **Na jaṭāḥī na gottena**
> **Na jaccāhoti brāhmano**
> **Yamhi saccaṃ ca dhammo ca**

**So suci soca brāhmano**

"Neither by the turban on the head, nor by clan, or by birth, does one become a Brahmin. If, within a person one can find truth and righteousness, he is a Brahmin."

**Yassa kāyena vācāya**
**Manasā natthi dukkataṃ**
**Saṃvutaṃ tihi ṭhānehi**
**Tamahaṃ brūmi brāhmanaṃ**

"If one does no wrong through body, word and mind, if one is restrained in three doors of perception, I describe such a person as a 'Brahmin'."

**Kiṃ te jaṭāhi dummedha**
**Kiṃ te ajina sātiyā**
**Abbhantaraṃ te gahanaṃ**
**Bāhiraṃ parimajjayī**

"Of what use is your turban and matter hair, foolish person? What is the use of your leopard-skin garment? Inside, you are filled with impurities, but you keep yourself bright and clean on the outside."

One day, the Buddha visited the residence of **Brahmin Aggikabhāradvāja.** He had kindled a fire and was performing a fire-ritual. The Brahmin became angry at the sight of the Buddha approaching. He started abusing the Buddha, calling Him,

"Shaven head - outcast."

The Buddha remained unperturbed by the abuse, retaining His pleasantness. He asked the Brahmin,

"O Brahmin, do you know who an outcast is? Or what makes an outcast?"

The Brahmin said,

"I do now know. If you know could you explain them to me?"

Then the Buddha said,

**"A person does not become an outcast or a Brahmin by birth. He becomes an outcast or a Brahmin only in terms of his deeds. Those who get angry quickly, those who harbour hatred, those who are evil and ungrateful, those who cover up their faults, those who kill animals, those who have no love of beings, terrorists and bandits who destroy villages and market towns, who borrow and do not return what is borrowed, those who do not look after the aged parents even when they can care for them, those who denigrate the Buddha and religious persons, those who exalt themselves but demean others, those who get angry constantly, those who are extremely stingy, those who are bereft of shame and fear, those who utter falsehoods, and those who are seen with the wives of others, however high their caste, their clan, their family or their community, they are outcasts."**

This was a deadly blow on wrong-doers in general, and on Brahmins in particular. The Buddha applied the term '**vasala**' (outcast) not to those who were born in such families, but to those who did wrong and unvirtuous deeds.

Seeing those in His contemporary Indian society who sought the protection of trees, rocks, forests and shrines, the Buddha characterized them as cowards. To end suffering there is no use seeking their protection, the Buddha said. He said this directly to those who resorted to that kind of practice:

**Bahuṃ ve saranaṃ yanti**
**Pabbatāni vanāni ca**

*The Buddha asked that monk, "Are they saying the truth?" "Yes Sir, I did not want to cry and lament in a futile manner like them. Without crying and weeping I followed the golden advice you have given us. I have overcome the immature state of crying and weeping like these monks," the monk replied. Realizing that he had become an Arahant, the Buddha, while in His death bed, put His palms together and said, "Sādhu, Sādhu, Sādhu,"*

*see page 67*

**Ārāma rukkha cetiyāni**
**Manussā bhaya tajjitā**
**Netaṃ kho saranaṃ khemaṃ**
**Netaṃ saranamuttamaṃ**
**Netaṃ saranamāgamma**
**Sabba dukkhā pamuccati**

***(Dhammapada)***

"Many who are frightened seek the protection of rocks, forests, trees, groves. Seeking their refuge no one can achieve Liberation. Seeking their refuge no one can overcome suffering."

In the days of the Buddha there were those who worshipped the sun, the moon, fire water and snakes. There were other forms of cults, too. The Buddha demonstrated the futility of such cults. He made the people think rationally about the futility of those. He broke the bends of long standing superstitions in order to make ignorant people think rationally and scientifically about these issues.

On one occasion the Buddha saw young **Sigāla** who kept on worshipping the six directions. The Buddha pointed out that worshipping such directions as North, South etc., was a futile act. The Buddha pointed out that parents constituted the East, teachers the South, sons and daughters the West, friends the North, servants the region below, and the religious persons constituted the region above.

Contemporary Buddhists may not exactly worship directions like **Sigāla** the householder but, still, the practice of respecting directions, which the Buddha characterized as superstitious, is there among them.

These phenomena the society conventionally considered to be auspicious were not thought of as fully auspicious phenomena by the Buddha. When the Buddha was asked what the most auspicious phenomena were (what the greatest blessings were), what He declared were not those held as great blessings by the contemporary society - but, a whole series of new phenomena.

Among these are: **Avoiding evil company, keeping the company of good people; honouring those worthy of honouring; residing in a congenial environment, having acquired merit in the past birth; restraint in mind; being well-informed; being adept in arts and crafts; being disciplined; being pleasant in speech; caring for one's parents; indulging in uncluttered livelihood; being generous; looking after spouse and children; acquiring ten forms of merit; helping friends and relations; respecting those who deserve respect; being pleasant and courteous in behaviour, being content; being grateful, patient, obedient; being virtuous; being of good behaviour; and being unshaken when fortune fluctuates.**

Some, out of the statements made by the Buddha on various occasions, are as follows:

"One is not a learned man just because he talks much. (**Na tena paṇḍito hoti yāvatā bahu bhasati**)"
"One does not become a mature elder merely because one's hair is grey. (**Na tena thero hoti ye nassa palitaṃ siro.**)"
"An unvirtuous person will not become a religious person merely because he is shaven-headed. (**Na muṇḍakena samano abbato alikaṃ bhana**)"

"Those who do not become sages merely because they keep silent. (**Na monena muni hotī.**)"

"Can the waters of **Sundarikā**, **Bāhukā** and **Payāga** wash off the sins of people? If water can wash off sins, fishes frogs etc.,who live permanently in the water, must be totally devoid of sins. (**Kiṃ Sundarikā karissanti kiṃ Payāgā, kiṃ Bāhukā nadī**?)"

There is no other human being who placed his life in jeopardy not once but tens of thousands of times, for the cause of liberty. Such expressions as '**mukti**', '**vimukti**', '**moksa**', '**vimoksa**' and '**Nibbāna**' all imply liberation from bonds, from the grip of craving - that is obtaining release from the cycle of rebirths.

The Buddha pointed out that all such phenomena as parents, kingship, spouse and children, being ministers, peoples' representative, wealth, power, glory and egotism tend to negate one's liberty. They are all shackles that bind people, the Buddha said. When we give up our craving for all these, along with our egotism, both our mind and our body get liberated.

The Buddha introduced to the people a form of thinking that enabled them to contemplate the true nature of things **(yatā bhūta ñāna)**, and to see the cause and effect of all things. The Buddha never did any harm or evil to anyone **(yoniso - manasikāra).**

Sir Edwin Arnold described the Buddha as 'Light of Asia'. The Buddha Himself, immediately on realizing Enlightenment, declared "**Vijjā udapādi**" (Knowledge arose) and **"Āloko udapādi"** (Light arose). It is a great consolation to us that the Buddha, who brought about a revolution in thought and a social revolution by giving the people freedom of thought and freedom of expression, is our religious leader. The greatest respect we can confer upon Him is getting attuned to thinking liberally and wisely.

## Wisdom id the sword and ignorance is the enemy

*Not a single page of Buddhist history has ever been lurid with the light of inquisitorial fires, or darkened with the smoke of heretic or heathen cities ablaze, or red with blood of the guiltless victims of religious hatred. Buddhism wields only one sword, the sword of Wisdom, and recognizes only one enemy - Ignorance. This is the testimony of history, and is not to be gainsaid.*

***Prof. Bapat "2500 years of Buddhism"***

*"One is not a learned man just because he talks much., One does not become a mature elder merely because one's hair is grey, An unvirtuous person will not become a religious person merely because he is shaven-headed, Those who do not become sages merely because they keep silent, Can the waters of Sundarikā, Bāhukā and Payāga wash off the sins of people? If water can wash off sins, fishes frogs, etc., who live permanently in the water, must be totally devoid of sins."*

*see page 78*

## CHAPTER 14

## THE BUDDHA IS THE GREAT HERO WHO REALIZED THE TRUTH

There have been heroes of many kinds in the world. Some became heroes by winning wars, by conquering lands, and by building empires. Some became heroes by inventing new things. Some became heroes by discovering new things. Some became heroes by travelling to planets and returning to earth. Still, others became heroes protecting their country from foreign attacks.

**But the Buddha became a hero by sacrificing His life for an ideal of those others. The Buddha became a hero by realizing the absolute truth with the foremost intention of freeing the beings from suffering.**

During thousands of births He sacrificed eyes, heads, flesh, blood, wives, children and His own life in quest of truth. Even in His last birth, He suffered all possible mortifications, tried out all possible experiments, and finally discovered the absolute truth, real truth - the Four-fold Noble Truth. In consequence, there is a great difference between the heroism of the Buddha and the heroism of the others. In the heroism of other heroes there is an implicit selfishness. But, in the heroism of the Buddha there is implicit a universality and a supra-mundane quality.

Because of this He has been described by such other names as **Buddhavīra** (Buddha the Hero), **Mahāvīra** (the Great Hero), **Sākya Sinha** (the Lion of the Sākyas), **Loka Nātha** (the Support of the World), **Dasabala** (the Person of Ten-fold Power), **Loka Vidu** (the Knower of the world), **Sabbaññu** (the All-Knowing One), and **Jina** (the Conqueror). He was described as **Mahāvira** (the Great Hero) even before He was born, not by human beings but by gods of Tusita Heaven.

In this context the Buddha was addressed as Hero by **Mahā Brahma Sahampati.**

> "O Great Hero, it is high time you were born in a mother's womb." (**Kāloyaṃte Mahāvira, uppajja mātukucchiyaṃ**) "O Hero, who won the battle against **Māra** (Death),
> Caravan Leader, O Noble One who has no debt called sense desire, stand up." (**Uṭṭhehi vīra, vijita sangāma, satthavāha anana**)
>
> ***(Majjhima Nikāya - Ariyapariyesana Sutta)***

Before the Buddha discovered the Four Noble Truths He went to various ascetics as a seeker after truth. He followed various methods under them. He realized that the truth they knew was not the absolute truth. He then gave up self-mortification and followed the Middle Path. He resolved that

> "I will get up only after I realized the Truth."

At last, He realized the Truth. Immediately on His realization of Truth a strange knowledge, a strange wisdom, a strange awareness, and a strange light occurred within Him. (**Pubbe ananussutesu dhammesu cakkhuṃ udapādi, ñānaṃ udapādi, paññā udapādi, vijja udapādi, āloko udapādi.**)

That change, that Enlightenment, that wisdom which occurred to Him that day, at the foot of the Bodhi Tree, cannot be described by any other person than the Buddha Himself. His joy was boundless.

"I conquered. I won. I discovered.
I discovered "

He exulted. He did not stop there. He set out, determined to place before the world this absolute Truth, this strange status, this unique knowledge and this unparalleled awareness. He expounded it to the Five-fold Bhikkhus. He preached these views to them while they were still fresh - still 'hot'. He expounded to them the results of extreme luxury and extreme self-mortification, and the advantages of the Middle Path and the Noble Eight-fold Path.

The Buddha's new discovery became popular not only among the various ascetics of the day, but also among the ordinary folk. The Buddha began to travel in villages, market towns, cities and suburbs surround, like the moon by the stars, by the newly ordained monks.

From this great Ascetic and His disciples who numbered about five-hundred, there emanated an Ascetic grace, a tranquil, restrained and appealing demeanour, subdued postures of coming and going, sitting and standing, and a pleasant, wise and methodical organization. All those who saw this scene were charmed. People began to follow them giving up their homes, properties, and even their wives and children. The news that the scion of the **Sākyas** - Gotama the Ascetic - with a retinue of monks was travelling to such and such a village, or such and such a city, began to spread fast. Those who heard the news were quite keen to see Him, to give Him alms, to listen to His Discourses, to question Him and to have discussions with Him. His fame began to extend to various parts of India.

"A strange ascetic of the **Sākya** Clan has discovered a strange phenomena (Four-fold Truth)." The Brahmin Chief **Pokkharasāti** came to know the Buddha's glory. **"Assosi kho pokkharasāti Brāhmano samano khalū bho Gotamo sakya putto, sakyakulā pabbajito Kosalesu cārikaṃ caramāno mahatā Bhikkhu Sanghena saddhiṃ panca mattehi Bhikkhu satehi"** "The Brahmin **Pokkharasāti** heard that the Ascetic Gotama, son of the **Sākyas**, who has gone forth from the **Sākyan** Clan, is now travelling through the Kosala Kingdom with a retinue of a large number of monks numbering more than five-hundred."

***(Dīgha Nikāya - Ambaṭṭhagha Sutta)***

It would have been a very impressive sight to see the Buddha walking along serenely through villages, market towns and cities with about 500 Arahants following Him in single file, in order of seniority, with their eyes downcast. This will evoke a mental picture even today in the mind of anyone who has seen about a hundred monks walking in line in single file.

There is no other hero than the Buddha who sacrificed His life to truth - to absolute Truth. He is described by such names as **Buddha** (the Enlightened One), **Sam Buddha** (Fully Enlightened One), **Sammā Sambuddha** (Fully and Supremely Enlightened One), because He

***Many who are frightened seek the protection of rocks, forests, trees, groves. Seeking their refuge no one can achieve Liberation. Seeking their refuge no one can overcome suffering. In the days of the Buddha there were those who worshipped the sun, the moon, fire, water and snakes. There were other forms of cults, too. The Buddha demonstrated the futility of such cults. He made the people think rationally about the futility of those.***

***see page 78***

realized the absolute Truth, the Noble Truth. Buddhism is the religion that follows the Truth and the Noble Person who discovered it.

If there is something devoid of truth, it is not Buddhism. When we honour the Buddha we do so not to His physical form, but for the Buddha prowess which He acquired after excruciating suffering. Buddhism is the religion that worships, that honours, that esteems wisdom. Buddhism is the religion that exalts wisdom. If anything is written about the Buddha, that is devoid of truth, it just cannot be Buddhism. It just could not be the Word of the Buddha. The greatest duty of the Buddhist is to follow the Buddha who is the Hero of Truth, and establish one's self in Truth, always. His duty is to honour Truth. Where there is no truth there is no Buddhism - not even a Buddhistic trace. The main characteristic of Buddhism is being truthful. Even one's life has to be sacrificed to protect Truth. We must be determined to sacrifice it.

There is no greater heroism than being a Buddha. No one other than a great hero can ever become a Buddha. There are ten perfections (**Pāramitā**) he should fulfill. These ten are: **Dāna Pāramitā** (Giving - Liberality); **Sīla Pāramitā** (Morality); **Nekkhamma Pāramitā** (Renunciation); **Paññā Pāramitā** (Wisdom); **Viriya Pāramitā** (Energy); **Khanti Pāramitā** (Patience - forbearance); **Sacca Pāramitā** (Truthfulness); **Adhiṭṭhāna Pāramitā** (Resolution); **Metta Pāramitā** (Loving-kindness); and **Upekkhā Pāramitā** (Equanimity).

While fulfilling these ten, the person who aspires to Buddhahood must be ready to sacrifice his life for each of these. Buddhahood has to be achieved by fulfilling each of these at the highest possible level. No one who does not possess these ten essential qualifications can become a Buddha. One of these is the Perfection of Energy (**Viriya Pāramitā**). '**Viriya**' is the quality of a **vīra** (hero).

A human mind first thought of becoming a Buddha, when a son was grappling with the sea, carrying his mother on his back. Every action of the Bodhisatta (the aspirant Buddha) prior to becoming Buddha was a heroic act. Extending thoughts of loving-kindness to those who cut off his limbs; giving to those who asked all the things they wanted, finally even his life; spending six years in self-mortification without eating and drinking properly; not losing one's virtues, even though one may lose one's life; not harming a person or hurting a person, or not making a person suffer loss, even if one were to lose one's life; not uttering lies, even though one may lose one's life - the Buddha has done such acts not once, but tens of thousands of time, before He became Buddha.

He did all these things not with a selfish motive - not with the intention of enjoying luxuries. He did all this to find out the nature of suffering, the cause of suffering, the cessation of suffering, and the path to the cessation of suffering.

He did all this to discover these truths and to place them before the world, with the intention of liberating the human kind from suffering. The Buddha endured vast suffering to discover these. He made a tremendous effort.

We cannot underestimate that tremendous

effort. We must constantly reflect upon this. Honouring the Truth, and affirming the Truth are a way of respecting the Buddha. If you disregard Truth, it amounts to disregarding the Buddha.

As a result of the passage of a long period of time there could be found, even in Buddhism and in the Doctrine, certain untruths that could have crept in due to blind devotion. If such things have crept in, we must set them aside without any hesitation. We must not accept these. Just like the husk around the coconut, there could be much exaggeration and hyperbole around the Truth.But, such exaggerated descriptions are not an obstacle to the discovery of Truth. In the true Word of the Buddha, one finds hundred per cent truth. Such Teachings as the Four Noble Truths, Noble Eight-fold Path and **Paticca Samuppāda** (Dependent Origination) are real Buddha Words. We can see the Buddha's wisdom and image through them.

All those who follow Him should become seekers of the real truth in everything and everyone. They must be respecters of Truth, who always speak the Truth.

## Salvation without God

*For the first time in the history of the world, Buddha proclaimed a salvation, which each man could gain for himself and by himself in this world during this life, without the least help from a personal God or Gods. He strongly inculcated the doctrine of self-reliance, of purity, of courtesy, of enlightenment, of peace and of universal love. He strongly urged the necessity of knowledge, for without wisdom psychic insight could not be got in this life.*

***Prof. Eliot, "Buddhism and Hinduism"***

*He asked the Brahmin, "O Brahmin, do you know who an outcast is? Or what makes an outcast?" The Brahmin said, "I do now know. If you know could you explain them to me?" Then the Buddha said, "No one becomes an outcast by birth; no one becomes a Brahmin by birth; one becomes an outcast or a Brahmin only by deed."*

*see page 75*

## CHAPTER 15

## THE BUDDHA IS AN ELOQUENT EXPONENT OF THE DHAMMA

Among men there are only a few orators. Even of these orators, there are only a handful who can get the ear of all to his oration. Even from among them there are only a meagre number who can compel listeners through their hypnotic words.

Of all these orators, if there was a speaker who was capable of addressing the people with an awareness of the minds of all listeners, it was only the Supreme Buddha. During the Buddha's day the art of writing had not progressed as it has today. Every idea had to be orally presented. The Supreme Buddha expressed His noble ideas and views eloquently in the presence of four-fold audiences consisting of thousands, throughout His mission of forty-five years.

When He spoke His audiences of, say, hundreds or tens of thousands or of hundred thousands, listened to Him in perfect silence with rapt attention.

There were no buzzes, whispers, groans or private conversations when He spoke. Everybody thought that the Buddha addressed him personally. "He speaks specifically to me," they all felt.

There were no reporters, as in our day, to write down the immortal Words that escaped His lips. The Buddha's Words were so pleasing, so precious that it was as if some strange being were pouring forth pearls, gems, diamonds, rubies and other forms of invaluable gems along with His Words issuing from the mouth.

Just as those who esteem the value of such gems and jewels would fill vessels with them to be made due use of, His disciples constantly gathered round Him to fill their mind-vessels with them to be recorded later in their memories delibeately. They took in these words more valuable than pearls and gems, as they emanated from His sacred lips, cooled by the touch of His compassionate and cool heart.

These disciples committed these Words into memory, recited them day and night lest they slipped their mind, brought them down through a mnemonic tradition, protecting those Words as great legacy.

Later on, they enshrined them, inscribing on gold plate or silver plate. They preserved them inscribing them on rocks or writing them down on the leaf. The Words from no other orator's lips have been preserved in this manner.A tremendous power people possessed those days was the power of memory. Disciples blessed with this exceptional power of memory preserved the Tipitakas containing the Buddha's Words, for centuries. These memory experts were described as **Dīgha Bhanakas** (those who memorized the **Dīgha Nikāya**), **Majjhima Bhānakas** (those who memorized the **Majjhima Nikāya**), **Saṃyutta Bhānakas** (those who memorized the **Saṃyutta Nikāya**), and so on. Those who had memorized the whole of the **Tipitaka** were described as **Tipiṭaka Dhārī** (bearers of the **Tipiṭaka** in memory).

The voice that arose from inside the Buddha who was totally blemishless, was exceedingly sweet. Words were kind. They were so fascinating that one could have gone on listening to Him not only for hours, but for days, for that matter. His Words were meaningful - were of practical use.

There was no exaggeration or hyperbole in His Words. There were no empty verbal flourishes - no repetitions. There were no falsehoods in His Words. There were no empty statements. These Words were filled with a supra-mundane taste. Every Word was conducive to good - both here and in the next world.

The Buddha knew a multiplicity of things. He preached only a little of it. This was demonstrated by Him in a Simsapa Forest. He picked up a handful of those leaves that had fallen on the ground, and said, **"Ananda, what I have preached is about the few leaves in my hand. The quantity I have not preached and I have to preach is about the amount of leaves in this great forest."** This gives us an idea.

For forty-five years He went on preaching without any consideration of night or day, or of rain or shine, or of distances involved, or without a regard for the rich or the poor. He never discriminated thinking this a powerful person or this is a weak person. He expounded His Doctrine for the good of all. Of the vast quantum of the Doctrine what is left for us today is only a modicum. What is left is only what Ven. Ananda remembered. Ven. Ananda, wrote down in his mind-book with the pen of his memory all events and incidents connected with the Buddha's life and all the statements that issued forth from the Buddha's lips. In almost all the books and almost all the Suttas (Discourses) we have the prefatory statement 'Evam me sutam' (Thus have I heard). What a truthful and what a cultured statement is it? He gave credit to the Buddha for the Buddha Word and He remained at the level of a person who only heard. This demonstrates his humility and his respect for the Word of the Buddha.

In all the statements made by the Buddha you have a beginning, a middle and an end. There is a wholesome meaning. There is a wholesome thought. There is not a single word that cannot be understood. There is not a single meaningless word. In consequence there was no one who did not understand Him when he listened to Him. There was no one who was not pleased.

Many people who were pleased listening to Him, spoke thus Sir Gotama, your preaching of the Doctrine is excellent. Sir, it was like turning up a vessel that had been turned down. It was like revealing a concealed treasure. It was like giving proper directions to a person who had lost his way. You preached the Doctrine as if you were holding up a well-lit, well-oiled torch in the dark, saying "May those who have eyes see the figures!' You have indicated many things in your Sermon. I

*"Do not believe in anything simply because you have heard it. Do not believe in traditions because they have been handed down for many generations. Do not believe in anything because it is spoken of and rumoured by many. Do not believe in anything simply because it is found written in your religious books. Do not believe in anything merely on the authority of your teachers and elders. But, after observation and analysis, when you find that anything agrees with reason and is conducive to the good and benefit of one and all, then, accept it and live up to it."*

*see page 75*

take refuge in the Buddha, in the Dhamma, and in the Sangha. Sir, please consider me a devotee who has taken refuge until the end of my days." This is a praise that had been showered upon the Buddha by those who were exceedingly pleased with His expositions. Some of those who listened to Him expressed the wish to be ordained under the Buddha. Some became monks the same day. Some eradicated all human weaknesses and attained Arahanthood.

The Buddha preached the Doctrine only after exploring whether there was the potential for some people to take refuge, some people to become ordained, and preached according to their needs. When the Teacher preached according to the needs of a person He first gave an introductory statement. The introductory talk consists of a discussion regarding generosity, morality, reaching pleasant states (Heaven), the ill-effects of sense-desires, their lowliness, their dirtiness, and the virtues of renunciation.

The Buddha initiates the discussion with a description of the advantages of generosity, charity, lack of miserliness and the good results of service to others. Next, the Buddha indicates the value of being virtuous without resolving to evil, and the value of the moral life. He describes how those who give and lead virtuous lives go to pleasant states (Heaven), and that Heaven is a place of sensual pleasures. He describes the futility of sensuality. He describes that the householder's life is full of troubles and miseries. He next indicates the high pleasures of the life in solitude. When the Buddha presents His methodical presentation, that has an appeal to the decidedly disillusioned with lay-life and desire to be monks. Those people who cannot become monks due to various obstacles become devotees of the Buddha, taking refuge in the Triple Gem and observing the Five Precepts.

A Brahmin who was exceedingly happy after listening to the Buddha behaves this way. Then Brahmin Brahmāyu got up from his seat. Adjusted his shawl properly. He worshipped the Buddha, placing his face on the feet of the Buddha. He kisses the Buddha's feet with his lips. He strokes the Buddha's feet with his hands. He spoke thus to the Buddha: "Sir, I am Brahmin Brahmaya." Thus, he introduces himself by his name.

When He delivers a Sermon the Buddha presents what He has to say in a timely, topical style. He tells only the truth.. He speaks only sense. He does not utter even a single meaningless word. He delivers His Sermons only in terms of the Nine-fold Supra-mundane factors of His Dispensation. He delivers His Sermons only in terms of the discipline what should be acquired - what should be avoided

It is said that of those who speak, the Buddha is the greatest (Buddho vadatam varo.) The Buddha is described as the greatest among those who speak (Vadatam pavaro). Therefore, through the spoken Word, through the Words that escaped the lips, the man who has done the greatest service in this world is the Buddha.

**In other words the Buddha is the greatest and the most compelling religious orator of mankind.**

## CHAPTER 16

# THE BUDDHA IS THE MOST PROGRESSIVE OF ALL THE RELIGIOUS LEADER

The Buddha flourished more than 2,500 years ago. But the Doctrine He preached is not for only one age or for one period of time. It is not restricted. It fits all time. As societies become more and more progressive, Buddhism becomes eminently suitable for that kind of progressive society.

Buddhism marches with time. The ideas and teachings of some become outdated and obsolete with the passage of time. But the Buddha has never expounded an idea that would become obsolete. Truth is always true. A word that is not true never escaped the Buddha's lips.

Buddha did not advocate that everybody should renounce. He never asked everybody to become monks. Nor did he ask everybody to become male and female lay devotees. What he did was revealing Truth - explaining to others the Truth He discovered. What He did was showing the Path to Liberation - to **Nibbāna**.

The Buddha encouraged His disciples to "Get started, go out and get engaged actively in the Buddha's Teachings." He impelled them that way. He encouraged them. He looked down upon slothfulness. He described diligence as the path to immortality.

The Buddha, even in His death-bed, advised the monks this way:

> "**Vaya dhammā sankhārā - appamādena sampādetha** (All component things disintegrate - work out your Liberation with diligence.)."

The Buddha frequently advised the monks to keep on striving without getting disillusioned. He said:

> "**Appamattā na mīyanti - ye pamattā yathā matā** (Those who do not strive are like the dead. Diligent ones never die.)."

The Buddha extolled the virtues of "**uṭṭhānavato**" (irrepressible effort), and "**dalhaviriyo**" (hard striving). He praised those who strove hard. Right Effort is one of the Ten Perfections necessary for a person to be a Buddha.

The Buddha looked down on lazy, effortless, sleepy and reluctant monks. He praised those monks who were progressive, fearless and courageous. Considered this way, the Buddha is a very progressive religious Teacher. The Buddha praised those who made progress.

In **Parābhava Sutta** (The Discourse on Decline) the Buddha indicated those who were prone to decline. He also described the causes of decline. The Buddha was a genuine, dedicated social worker who spent the greater part of his twenty-four-

*The Buddha though seeing his royal palace, went along the main street with the begging bowl from house to house, seeking alms. The king, His father, became totally distraught by this sight and ran after Him, his royal clothes in disarray. He told the Buddha, "Do not denigrate our royal Dynasty." The Buddha replied, "O King, you are of the royal line. But, I am of the Buddha line. Begging is a custom of the Buddhas."*

*see page73*

hour long day working. He worked solely for the service of others.

**Āraddha viriyo paramattha pattiyā**
**Alīnacitto akusītavutti**
**Dalhanikkamo thāmakhalupapanno**
**Eko care khagga visānakappo**

*(Sutta Nipāta - Khaggavisāna Sutta)*

The effort goes non-stop until they reach the place where there is no sorrowing **Nibbāna** (**Gacchati anivattantaṃ yattha gantvā na socati**). **Viriyena dukkhaṃ acceti** (Through effort suffering is overcome.) **Uṭṭhānā vindate dhanaṃ** (The person who is full of effort acquires wealth.) **Sangāme me mataṃ seyya yañce jīve parājite** (It is better to die in battle than living defeated.) **Uṭṭhahata nisīdatha ko attho supinena vo** (Get up, sit up, what on earth is the use of sleeping?)"

*(Sutta Nipāta - Uṭṭhāna Sutta)*

"O Monks, this way I have preached the Doctrine well. I have made it quite clear. I have revealed it. I have proclaimed it. I have purified it. When there is a Doctrine made quite clear by me, revealed by me, proclaimed by me, and purified by me, the householder who has obtained ordination through devotion must make a determined effort resolving this way; 'I will not cease my effort until I achieve the goal which has to be attained through human strength, human vigour and human prowess, whether the skin, veins and bones of my body remain or whether my flesh and blood dry up.

Monks, the lethargic, slothful person engages in wrong, harmful actions. He lives miserably. Monks, the person who makes a sustained effort will free himself from wrong, harmful actions. He lives happily."

He achieves the fulfilment of his great purpose. It is not possible to achieve the high state of an **Arahant** (Perfected One) by an individual whose confidence, effort, mindfulness and concentration are quite limited. The Highest Fruit of being an Arahant can be achieved only by a person who possesses a high level of confidence, effort etc.

"Monks, this holy life - this great way of living - is like a pleasant and delicious drink. You have already met the great Teacher. Therefore, make an effort to reach a status you have not reached, to realize a form of knowledge you have not realized, and to see for yourself the Teaching you have not been able to see for yourself. This way, our monastic life will not be fruitless. It will not be empty. It will be fruitful. It will keep on growing. You must discipline yourself so that you can confidently assure yourself that: 'If we make use of the Four-fold Requisites someone offers us, their offerings to us will bring about great results.' Monks, those of you who expect self-profit or your own personal gain must immediately become diligent. Even those of you who serve others must also be diligent."

*(Saṃyutta Nikāya- Abhisamaya Saṃyutta - Dasabala Sutta)*

There are hundreds of such progressive statements in the Buddha Word. Buddhism is not a religion that makes beings pessimistic. It is not a religion that will make beings retrograde. It is not a religion that makes beings lethargic. It is not a religion that makes people shy. On the other hand, it is an extremely progressive religion. The Buddha preached a Doctrine that will make people happier and more joyous in this life than in the next.

The Buddha declared the way in which human life should be organized - how it should be adapted. He declared how people should live in society. The Buddha pointed out what is good and what is bad. He indicated what should be done and what should not be done. He indicated those with whom one should be associate, and those who should be shunned. In this manner, the Buddha provided all the advice and guidance necessary for the building of a cultured and progressive society. The Buddha demonstrated to society the path it should take. The Buddha did not have any reactionary views at all.

He attacked reactionary Brahmanic ideas quite vigorously. He gave women human rights. He always disregarded such divisions as nations, clans and castes. He extended the same kind of loving-kindness to all (**"Sabbe sattā bhavantu sukhitattā**" - May all beings be happy and well.). In His loving-kindness there were no grades. It was similar to all. **His Teaching agrees well the progressive world. There is no other progressive society than one that is organized in terms of His Teachings. A society like that cannot be organized by the teachings of any other person. In terms of all these, the most progressive of all religious teachers is the Buddha.**

## A Buddhist is not a slave to anybody

*A Buddhist is not a slave to a book or to any person. Nor does he sacrifice his freedom of thought by becoming a follower of the Buddha. He can exercise his own free will and develop his knowledge even to the extent of attaining Buddhahood himself, for all are potential Buddhas.*

**Ven. Narada Maha Thera, "What is Buddhism"**

***Making a secret renunciation, giving up His wife, His child, His royal palace, His kingdom and His royal splendour, He entered the forest. He took a rag in which a dead body was wrapped, shook of the myriad's of worms that infested it, washed it, dried it in the sun, and wore it. He sank to the very bottom of the simple life. He is the only royal prince in human history to have done all that. This is a tremendous revolution in lives of limitless luxury.***

***see page 73***

CHAPTER 17

## THE BUDDHA WAS A GREAT STORY TELLER AND A CREATOR OF VERBAL IMAGES

The Buddha never uttered a word that the listeners could not understand. He spoke in an idiom that everybody could appreciate.

When He addressed cultivators, He used similes and metaphors relating to the field, the field ridge, paddy, rice, empties, goad, plough, winnowing-fan, oxen, cowherds, carts, grain and water. On one occasion the Buddha was residing in the Brahmin village of **Ekanālā** in the province of **Dakkhina Giri** in **Magadha** country. One morning, the Buddha went to the site where the Brahmin named **Kasībhāradvāja** was ploughing the fields with about five-hundred ploughs. The Buddha went for alms to the place where the Brahmin and his people were taking their meals. The Brahmin spoke to the Buddha:

"O Ascetic Gotama, as for me I plough the field, sow seeds, get a yield of grains and eat. You too must plough, sow, get a yield, and eat."

Then the Buddha replied:

"I too plough. I sow and obtain a yield, and eat."

The Brahmin said:

"You say that you plough, sow, and eat the yield. But I have never seen your plough or goad or oxen."

The Buddha replied:

**"In my form of cultivation the seed paddy is devotion. Morality is the rain-water. My Insight Knowledge and my Knowldge of the Path are my plough. Sense of shame is the head of my plough. Mind is the plough-share. My concentration is the goad."**

**Saddhā bījaṃ tapo vuṭṭhi**
**Paññā me yuganaṃgalaṃ**
**Hiri īsā mano yottaṃ**
**Sati me phālapāvanaṃ.**

*Kasībhāradvāja Sutta*

He made it clear to the Brahmin that he, too, was a kind of cultivator. He preached the Doctrine to the Brahmin. After listening to the Buddha he became a monk. Later, he attained Arahanthood. Even when preaching to the monks, the Buddha made use of similes and metaphors from cultivation

**"Tīnimāni bhikkhave kassa kassa Gahapatissa pubbe karaniyāni. Katamāni tīni idha bhikkhave kassako gahapati patigacceva khettaṃ sukaṭṭhaṃ karotva Sumati kataṃ kālena bījāni patiṭṭhapeti. Kālena bījāni patiṭṭhapetva samayena udakaṃ abhinetipi apanetipi imāni kho bhikkhave tīni kassakassa gahapatissa pubbe karaniyāni."**

"O Monks, there are three preliminary tasks a cultivator must do. Firstly, he must smoothen the field. Secondly, he must sow the seeds in time. Thirdly, after sowing he must provide water in time; must drain out the water in time. These are the three preliminary tasks that the cultivator should perform."

When the Buddha preached to kings, He would quote instances, metaphors, stories and images about tyrannical rule, wars, battles, victories and conquests, anger, revenge, greed, etc. ("**Jayaṃ veraṃ pasavati** - Victory brings hatred").

When He explained the Doctrine to Brahmins He would point out the futility of pride, caste-prestige, and sacrificial offerings and rituals. He would establish that one does not become a Brahmin by birth, and that one becomes a true Brahmin only by deeds. This way, He attacked their false views. These similies are found in such Discourses as **Alagaddūpama vatthūpama, Cula Sihanāda, Mahā Sīhanāda, Madhupinḍika, Kakacūpama Vammika, Culla Hatthipadopama, Mahā Hatthipadopama, Mahā Ṡāropama, Cula Sāropama** and **Rathavinita.** There are thousands of such similes and metaphors in the **Tipiṭaka**.

Such four-footed animals as lions, elephants, horses, leopards, wolves, unicorns, dogs, oxen, deer, jackals occur in the Buddha's similes and metaphors. Of reptiles the cobra and the boa, of birds vultures, hawks, eagles, peacocks, swans, cranes, sand-pipers, cuckoos, parrots, and of insects bees, ants and white-ants, are referred to in the Buddha's similes and metaphors.

He refers to such forms of trees as mango, **sāla**, palm trees, banyan trees, fig trees, bamboo and sugar-cane. He makes reference to such fruits as mango and nelli, and to such varieties of seeds as paddy, mustard, sesame. Of flowers He refers to lotus varieties. Such precious metals as gold and silver are referred to. He talks also of pearls and gems, as well.

Among the rivers He refers to are **Gangā**, **Yamunā** and **Aciravatī**. He refers to the ocean, too. **Mahā Meru** and the **Himālayas** are the hills He refers to. The sun and the moon, stars, sky, clouds, ponds, rain, peaks, parks, pastures, sandy stretches, lakes, flood, fords, banks, waves, ships and rafts also occur in the Buddha's images.

When He preached to the monks He would very often talk about the advantages of virtuous Bhikkhu life and the ill-effects of unvirtuous life of a monk. He has narrated five-hundred-and-fifty tales about His past births. These are described as **Jātaka Tales** (Birth Stories). These tales have become part of world literature.

One of the Buddha's epithets is '**Loka Vidū**' which implies the individual who knows the world well. There is no one who knew the world and the lives of human beings as much as the Buddha did. Another epithet for the Buddha is '**Sabbaññu**'. This means the all-knowing One. He knew everything that a Buddha should know. He knew much. But He expressed to us only very little of what he knew.

Once, He was travelling through Simsapa forest with Ven. Ananda. He picked up a handful of those leaves from the ground and asked **Ven. Ānanda**:

"What is bigger, the quantity of leaves in my hand, or the leaves of the same kind in this great forest?"

"The quantity of the forest is about a thousand times bigger,"

Ven. Ananda replied.

*Prince Siddhārtha is the only young man, nay the only human being in the whole of human history,who renounced His country, His kingdom, His royal splendour, His wife and child, disgusted by the sight of a bevy of beauties, dedicated exclusively to give him pleasure, sleeping at night on the floor in one place. He saw the place where beautiful dancing girls were sleeping, as a cemetery.*

*see page 73*

**"All that I have preached to you so far is like the quantity of leaves in my hand. But the quantity I have not preached is as large as the leaves in this great forest."**

Once, a horse-trainer named **Kesī** came to see Him and stood on a side. The Buddha asked him:

"**Kesī**, you are an expert in the training of horses. What is the first thing you do to train an untamed horse?"

"O Sir, firstly, I train the horse softly. At times, I train horses harshly, too. At times, I train a horse both softly and harshly."

**"Kesī**, if you cannot train the horse in all three ways what would you do?" "O Sir, if I cannot train it in any one of those methods, I will kill it so that my tradition of training will not get a blemish."

Next, **Kesī** put a question to the Buddha.

"Sir, I am described as '**assadamma sārathi**' - expert in training horses. In the same way you are described as '**purisa damma sārathi**' - the expert in the training of men. I described to you now, how I tame horses. Could you please tell me how you train men?"

The Buddha said:

**"Kesī**, I too train them with soft, kind words. I train them in harsh ways, too. I train them softly by telling them: 'This is virtuous odily practice. This is the result of virtuous bodily practice. This is correct verbal behaviour. These are the results of correct verbal behaviour. This is right mental behaviour. This is the result of such good mental behaviour.' Deities are like this. Human beings are this. I train them mildly by explaining things in that way.

"I tame men harshly by telling them this: 'This is evil bodily behaviour. These are its ill-effects. This is evil verbal behaviour. These are its ill-effects. This is bad mental behaviour. These are the evil results of that kind of behaviour. This is the nature of the evil state (hell). This is the nature of the animal state. This is the nature of the ghost-spirits.' I train them, at times mixing these two methods - kind methods and harsh methods. It is this way.

"I tell them thus: 'This is evil bodily behaviour. These are its ill-effects. This is virtuous bodily behaviour. These are its good effects. This is good verbal behaviour. These are its good results. This is bad verbal behaviour. It has these bad effects. This is good mental behavour. These are its pleasant results. This is evil mental behaviour. These are its ill-effects. This is how I train them using both kind and harsh methods."

"O Sir, if you cannot train someone using all these three methods, what will you do?"

The Buddha said:

"I will kill him." **Kesī** asked Him: "Sir, isn't it unseemly for Buddhas to kill? They must not kill, isn't it, Sir?" "Yes, that is true, **Kesī**. If I cannot train him in all those three methods, I will refrain from instructing him - from advising him.

I will give him up as a person who should not be advised or instructed. Those other wise friends of his will also give him up as a person who cannot be corrected. **Setting aside a person, refraining from advising him both by myself and my disciples, is, in terms of the code of the Discipline of the Noble Buddhist Dispensation, like 'killing'. It is the most severe punishment.**"

**Kesī** was highly pleased and became a life-long disciple of the Buddha.

*(Anguttara Nikāya - Catukka Nipāta - Kesī Sutta).*

One day, the Buddha placed a few grains of sand on his thumb nail. He asked the monks:

"What quantity of sand is greater - the quantity on my thumb nail, or the quantity on earth?"

The monks said:

"The quantity on earth is greater."

The Buddha said:

"In the same way, Monks, those beings who will be born as human beings are as few as the grains of sand on my thumb. Those who are born as other beings than human beings are as great as the sand on earth."

(Samyutta Nikāya).

One day, a Brahmin came to see the Buddha and abused Him roundly. The Buddha listened to it all, quite calmly. The Buddha called him back to him and said:

"You abused me to your heart's content. I endured it all in silence. But, could you answer a question?"

The Brahmin said:

"All right, go ahead:Ask your question."

The Buddha asked him:

"O Brahmin, if a guest were to visit your house, what will you do?"

The Brahmin said:

"I will treat him well, with food and drink."

The Buddha asked him :

"If the guest does not partake of all the things you give him what will you do?"

The Brahmin said:

"I will enjoy all that with my wife."

The Buddha said:

**"Exactly in that manner, you abused me roundly just a little while ago. That 'treat' you gave me I did not accept. Therefore, you take it and enjoy it with your wife."**

One day, the Buddha visited **Ven. Rāhula** in his monastic cell. **Ven. Rāhula** received the Buddha with due honour, prepared a seat for Him, and brought water to wash the Buddha's feet. The Buddha took that water little by little in a small vessel, pouring water on His feet with it. He placed the small vessel upside down and asked **Ven. Rāhula**:

**"Is there any water in this little vessel now?"**

**Ven. Rāhula** replied:

**"As it is turned upside down there is no water in it at all."**

The Buddha addressed **Ven. Rāhula** and said:

"**Rāhula, just as no water remains in a vessel that is upturned, not even a vestige of virtue will remain in a person who utters lies."**

On one occasion the Buddha was lying down on some Simsapa leaves in the Simsapa forest in **Alavaka** country. Next morning, when royal prince **Hatthaka**

*He asked Minister Channa, "Who was that person who had an unusual look? What made him look so Are there more people like that? Can I, too, become sick?" Later, when He saw an old person, a dead body, and an ascetic, He asked a similar series of questions. These four omens stirred in Prince Siddhārtha's mind a whole series of questions: What is 'life'? What is the purpose of 'life'? What is the end of 'life'? For what reason is 'life' continued?*

*see page 73*

**Alavaka** was walking along, he saw the Buddha sleeping on the leaves. He worshipped the Buddha and asked Him whether He had a good night's rest. The Buddha said:

"Yes, Prince, I am one of the persons in this world who sleeps comfortably."

"O Sir, this is winter. This is the snow season. It is exceedingly cold at night. The ground is very rough. The ground is broken up by cart-wheel ridges. Even the leaves spread on the ground are quite thin. The tree is also withered and has no leaves. Even your yellow robe is cold. There is a strong cold wind blowing. With all this you say you are one of those in the world who sleeps well."

"O Prince, I will ask you a question about this matter. You can reply if you like. Just consider, a given householder or the son of a householder as a tall house which is secured against cold air from outside with well-made doors and windows. He has a bed spread with blankets of the softest wool. There are costly carpets on the floor. There are canopies above. Lamps with perfumed oil are lit at the foot and the head of his bed. He is attended upon by four young maidens of exquisite beauty. When all these conditions are there, O Prince, do you think that householder or that son of a householder will sleep well?"

The prince replied:

"Yes, Sir, I think he is one of those persons in the world who sleeps well." "Do you admit, O Prince, that householder or the son of the householder who sleeps like that with four beautiful maidens will experience his body and mind burning due to the fire of sensual desire - fire of lust, and that he sleeps miserably because of that fire?

"Yes, Sir, I admit it."

**"O Prince, I have fully and completely eradicated the fire that burns the body and mind due to lust, hatred and ignorance. I have eradicated that fire so that it will never occur again. That way, I am one of the persons in the world who sleeps well."**

*(Anguttara Nikkāya -Tika Nipāta - Devaduta Vagga)*

On one occasion, the Buddha sat with His upper body erect, deep in meditation, in a forest glade in **Kosala** kingdom. At that time, a Brahmin of the **Bhāradvāja** clan entered that forest looking for fourteen heads of his cattle that had gone stray. Seeing the Buddha, he described how fourteen heads of his cattle had gone stray. In addition, he recounted his domestic grievances. He told the Buddha:

"Sir, as you are devoid of all these you live happily."

At that, the Buddha spoke thus:

"O Brahmin, you have been wandering around for six days, looking for your fourteen heads of cattle gone stray. I do not have cattle. Therefore, I am happy. I have no sesame filed with one-leaf and two-leaf plants. Therefore, I am happy.

"O Brahmin, in your empty barn, the mice run about. I do not have any such problem. Therefore, I live happily.

"O Brahmin, your grass mat which is seven months old is infested with worms born in it. I have no such problem. Therefore, I am happy.

"O Brahmin, you have one son. You have seven widowed daughters with two sons. I do not have even one. Therefore, I live happily.

"O Brahmin, your cat-eyed Brahmin wife, whose body is full of honey-coloured moles, wakes you up when you are asleep, by kicking you. I have no such problem. Therefore, I am happy.

"O Brahmin, your creditors come early in the morning and ask you to pay back the loans. When you don't, they abuse you. I have no such problem. Therefore, I live happily without suffering, like you."

*(Samyutta Nikāya - Brāmana Sanyutta - Arahanta Vagga)*

Using the description given by the Brahmin himself, the Buddha shows how the Brahmin suffers, but now is happy.

One day, King **Kosala** came to see the Buddha immediately after he had taken about four measures of rice, as was his habit. The king sat on a side panting, huffing and puffing. Seeing how he was panting, knowing also how much rice he had taken, the Buddha told him:

**"The person who takes his meals, aware of a sense of proportion, will have no pains whatsoever. He can fully digest the food he takes. This protects his life-span, too."**
**Manujassa sadā satimato mattaṃ jānato laddhabhojane tanu tassa bhavanti vedanā sanikaṃ jīrati āyupālayanti."**

The king's attendant, a young man called **Sudassana**, stood behind the king. The king went back to the palace and told **Sudassana**:

"Go back to the Buddha, learn that stanza by memory and recite it every day, seated near me when I take my meals. I will give you a salary of hundred kahapanas."

**Sudassana** did as instructed. The quantity of rice taken came down gradually and, at last, it came down to a single **nālika**. With that, the king's prominent paunch, too, got reduced. The obese body became slimmer. He stroked his body with his hands, saying:

"Our Buddha shows me his affection for me both in matters relating to spiritual development and to worldly development. "**"Ubhayena vata maṃ so Bhagavā atthena anukampi diṭṭhadhammikena ceva atthena samparāyikena ca."**

*(Saṁyutta Nikāya - Kosala Saṁyutta - Donapāka sutta)*

Here, the Buddha pointed out the ill-effects of taking food, without a sense of proportion, in a manner that will not hurt his feelings.

Once, **King Kosala** went to **Jetavana** Monastery to see the Buddha. When they were in conversation a royal messenger came to the king and respectfully whispered something in the king's ar. He said that **Queen Mallikā** passed away. The moment the king heard it he prostrated himself, and was sorely distraught by deep sorrow. **Evaṃ vutte rājā Pasenadi Kosalo dukkhi dummano pattakkhandho adhomukho pajjhāyanto appanbhāgo nisīdi.**The Buddha, seeing King Kosala distraught at

***He did not bring about His revolution through blood-shed, through torture and mayhem, through murder, through compelling speeches, or by stirring the minds of men and women into anger. He brought his about not in the revolutionary mode of such later revolutions as the French Revolution in Europe, and the Russian Revolution. He brought about His revolution entirely through His limitless compassion, through a policy of non-violence and peaceful compassion.***

*see page 72*

the news of the death of his queen, consoled him thus:

**"O great King, there are five things in this world that even the greatest person cannot get. They are - remaining without growing old; remaining without falling ill; remaining without losing years; remaining without dying; and remaining without changing. Even if a man, or a god, or a Brāhmin, or a Māra, or any other great man, were to expect that these things will not happy to him, or were to wish, these things can in no way be achieved."**

The Buddha travelled the kingdom of **Kosala** with a retinue of Bhikkhus. In the course of His travels He visited a Brahmin village called **Icchānangala**. The Buddha resided in a forest there. Hearing that **Gotama**, the scion of the **Sākya** clan who had become a monk, has arrived in this village, Brahmins from the village came to see Him, bearing varieties of food and drink and offerings.They assembled at the gate to the forest, and began to shout at the top of their voice. At that time it was **Ven. Nāgita** who attended on Him. The Buddha spoke to **Ven. Nāgita:**

"**Nāgita**, who are those who are shouting as at a fish market?" (**"Ke paneto Nāgita uccā saddā, maha saddā kevaṭṭā maññe maccha vilopeti?"**)

Ven. Nagita said:

"O Sir, the Brahmin villagers of **Icchānangala** have brought along alms for the Buddha and His disciples, and are assembled there at the outside."

The Buddha said:

**"I don't need material goods, praise or glory. I do not want to have any link with these, and these material gains, praise and glory should also not have any link with me (Māhaṃ Nāgita yasena samāgamo; mā ca mayā yaso). I have joy in my renunciation. I have joy in my solitude. The joy of tranquility is qute sufficient for me."**

Ven. Nagita said:

"O Sir, wherever you reside, all the people in that area turn in your direction. They get attracted to you. ("**Yena, yena padesaṃ Bhante Bhagavā gamissati tanninnāva bhavissanti Brāhamana, gahapatika negamā ceva jānapadā ca.**") Therefore, O Sir, please accept these offerings. O Sir, after a heavy rain-fall all the water rushes to the lower ground. In the same way, if you visit some area, all the Brahmins, householders, villagers, citizens of market towns, all get attracted to your direction. They flood in. Why do they do it? It is entirely because of your virtue and unparalleled wisdom. ("**Taṁ kissa hetu tathā hi Bhante Bhagavato sīlapaññātaṃ.**") Therefore, O Sir, please accept their offering."

**"Nāgita, I have nothing to do with material gains, praise and glory. I never establish such links. Those things must not have anything to do with me. Nāgita, I treasure solitude, liberty, tranquillity. I must have that without any interruption. Eating, drinking, tasting are not important tasks. Their result is body-waste. (Asita pītakhāyita sāyitassa kho Nāgita**

**uccārapassyāvo, Eso tassa nissaando.**)

**(Anguttara Nikāya - Pañcaka Nipāta - Nāgita Sutta)**

One day, Prince **Abhayarāja** offered alms to the Buddha in his house. At the end, while carrying his two-year old infant son, Prince **Abhayarāja** asked Him a question: "Sir, you at times speak words that hurt others. '**Devadatta** will go to the evil state. No one can help him.' When you said such things, he got angry. When you speak such harsh words, there is no difference between yourself and ordinary worldlings."

The Buddha replied: "O Royal Prince, I speak the truth as it is, but, I never say harsh thing to anyone. Let us take an example. If this infant in your hand were to put a pebble or a morsel of dirt in his mouth, what will you do?" The prince said: "I will take out the pebble or the morsel of dirt." Then the Buddha asked him: "If it is not easy to take them out?"

The prince said: "I will hold the child's head with my left hand, put a finger of the right in the infant's mouth, bend it and probe the mouth, and will try to take out what he has put in his mouth."The Buddha then said: "When you do that, the child's throat might bleed. It may hurt the child. Isn't it?" The prince answered: "Yes, Sir." The Buddha again asked: "Did you do it because of your love of the child, or because you did not love the child?" The prince said: "Certainly because I love the child."The Buddha said: **"In the same way, when I speak out the truth as it really is, some people may feel hurt. Some may even get angry. But, I do not say these things to hurt them. I say this kind of thing because of the limitless compassion I have for them."**

In the **Tipitaka** this kind of story occurs not in hundreds but in thousands. It is quite clear that the Buddha used stories and similes extensively when He wanted to make Himself clear to the ordinary people.

Even today the ordinary folk, when they listen to a sermon, remember only a story that was told in the course of that sermon. The masses adore this style of the Buddha's Discourses, even in our own day, too.

## Appreciation of Buddhism

*Although one may originally be attracted by its remoteness, one can appreciate the real value of Buddhism only when one judges it by the result it produces in one's own life from day to day.*

***Dr. Edward Conze, A Western Buddhist Scholar***

*Immediately on His realization of Truth a strange knowledge, a strange wisdom, a strange awareness, and a strange light occurred within Him. His joy was boundless. "I conquered. I won. I discovered. I discovered," He exulted. He did not stop there. He set out, determined to place before the world this absolute Truth, this strange status, this unique knowledge and this unparalleled awareness. He expounded it the Five-fold Bhikkhus.*

*see page 82*

## CHAPTER 18

# THE BUDDHA IS THE GREATEST PSYCHIATRIST

Doctors are of two kinds - those who treat the body, and those who treat the mind. Illnesses, too, are two-fold - illnesses of the body and mental illnesses.The Buddha stated thus:

> "O Monks, illnesses are of two kinds; They are illnesses of the body and mental illnesses. There are those who live for one year, two years, three years, four years, five years, ten - twenty years, thirty, forty years, fifty years and, in some instances, even hundred years, without being afflicted by physical illnesses. But it is difficult to find those who are free of mental illnesses, even for one moment. The only exception are the Arahants (the Holy Ones).
>
> **Dissanti bhikkhave sattā kāyikena rogena ekaṃpi vassaṃ ārogyaṃ paṭijānamānā, dvepi vassasāni ārogyaṁ paṭijānamāna .... vassa sataṃpi ārogyaṃ paṭijānamānā - te bhikkhave sattā dullabhā lokasmiṃ ye cetasikena rogena muhuttaṃpi ārogoyaṃ patijānāti, aññatva khināsaveti.**
>
> **(Anguttara Nikaya - Chatukka nipata - Roga sutta)**

Of the two kinds of doctors referred to above, the Buddha is a psychiatrist - a doctor of the mind. There has never been a greater doctor than the Buddha, to cure mental illness. The Buddha, who eradicated all the mental illnesses in His mind, next cured hundreds of thousands of people who had the same kind of mental illness.

The Buddha has seen all worldlings as mad (**Ummattakā viyahi sabbe putujjanā dissanti**.). Many, though physically well, are mentally ill. The Buddha recognized quite clearly those blemishes in the human mind, diagnosed the cause of those quite effectively, and administered the fitting therapies. That explains why he told the Brahmin names **Sela**:

> **"O Brahmin, I am the Supremely Enlightened One. And I am the greatest surgeon." ("Sohaṃ Brāhmana Sambuddho, sallakatho anuttaro.")**

The Buddha's surgery is to pull out the stakes and spikes that are there in the minds of men. On another occasion, He addressed the Bhikkhus this way:

> **"O Monks, there is no medicine as effective as the medicine of Dhamma. Please drink that." ("Dhammosadha samaṃ natthi - etaṃ pibata Bhikkhavo.")**

"O Monks, doctors administer

laxatives to cure illnesses that have arisen due to the bile, due to the phlegm, and due to the wind. O Monks, I too administer noble medicines. Due to that medicine, beings who are given to being born become free of birth. Beings who are given to decay and old age become free of decay and old age. They become free of death. Those beings who are prone to sorrowing, weeping, wailing, privation and unhappiness, become free of these.

*(Anguttara Nikāya- Dasama Nipāta Saññā vagga)*

"O Monks, doctors administer emetics for illnesses caused by bile, phlegm and wind, and make the patients vomit. Monks, I too administer Aryan emetics. Due to these, beings who suffer from birth, decay, old age, death, sorrow, wailing, suffering unhappiness and weeping become free of those."

**Tikicchakā bhikkhave vamanaṃ denti pitta semha samuṭṭhanampi ābādhānaṃ patighātāya. Ahaṃ ceva kho bhikkhave Ariyaṃ vamane dessāmi.**

*(Anguttara Nikāya- Dasama Nipāta - Saññā Vagga)*

Earlier, it was pointed out that the Buddha was presented as a surgeon who pulled stakes and spikes out of the minds of men. It was also said that He cured such illnesses as birth, decay, old age, death, sorrowing, wailing, unhappiness and suffering through laxatives and emetics.

In yet another place, the Buddha addressed a Brahmin this way: "I am an expert surgeon bearing the last body, with permanently washed hands ready to present the Doctrine in response to all requests to preach the Dhamma - a surgeon pulling out stakes and spikes of roots of sense desires.

**Ahamsmi bhikkhave Brāhmano yāca yogo sadā payata pāni antima dehadharo bhisakko sallakattā.**

"O Monks, I am always ready with stretched hands to present the Doctrine whenever a request is made. I bear a last body. I am a great physician as I treat the diseases described as illnesses of the cycle of existence.

I am also a great surgeon as I take out such stakes and spikes as sense-desire, anger and ignorance. As I have got rid of sins, I am also a Brahmin.

O Monks, you are born of my Words - that is, from my mouth. You are born of Dhamma, you are made up of Dhamma, you are the receivers of Dhamma, your material is Dhamma. You are my well-born sons."

The above statement makes it clear that just as Brahmins are said to be born from the mouth of **Mahā Brahma**, the Bhikkhus are born from the Dhamma - mouth of the Buddha.

It also makes it clear that He, the Buddha, is a great physician because He cures the illness of blemishes, and that the greatest legacy the Bhikkhus have is not the material rituals, but the gift of Dhamma.

**In Sallekha Sutta the Buddha refers to forty-four of the numerous illnesses that afflict the human mind. The following are those forty-four mental illnesses, and the cures for those forty-four illnesses.**

*One day, the Buddha placed a few grains of sand on his thumb nail. He asked the monks: "What quantity of sand is greater - the quantity on my thumb nail, or the quantity on earth?" The monks said: "The quantity on earth is greater." The Buddha said: "In the same way, Monks, those beings who will be born as human beings are as few as the grains of sand on my thumb. Those who are born as other beings than human beings are as great as the sand on earth."*

*see page 100*

1. Torturing and hurting others
2. Killing beings
3. Taking things that belong to others
4. Sexual misconduct
5. Uttering falsehoods
6. Bearing tales
7. Using harsh words
8. Uttering futile words
9. Love ot things that belong to others
10. Corrupt minds
11. Wrong views
12. Wrong evil thoughts
13. Uttering wrong words
14. Wrong activities
15. Wrong livelihood
16. Wrong effort
17. Wrong mindfulness
18. Wrong concentration
19. Doing wrong and saying it is right
20. Wrong liberation
21. Oppressed by slothfulness
22. Pride
23. Doubt
24. Short temper
25. Implacable hatred
26. Hypocrisy
27. Duality of mind
28. Jealousy
29. Miserliness
30. Deceit
31. Pretension
32. Stubbornness
33. Egotism
34. Disobedience
35. Having evil friends
36. Reluctance
37. Lack of devotion
38. Lack of shame
39. Lack of fear to sin
40. Lack of knowledge
41. Lethargy
42. Lack of mental alertness
43. Foolishness
44. Holding to one's own view

1. Non-violence
2. Not killing beings
3. Not taking things that belong to others
4. Not indulging in sexual misconduct
5. Telling the Truth
6. Not bearing tales
7. not using harsh words
8. Not uttering futile words
9. Not desiring things , belong to others
10. Not having corrupt minds
11. Correct views
12. Right virtuous thoughts
13. Uttering good words
14. Right activities
15. Right livelihood
16. Right effort
17. Right mindfulness
18. Right concentration
19. Right wisdom
20. Right liberation
21. Eradicated slothfulness
22. Humility
23. Doubtlessness
24. Not being angered
25. Being devoid of implacable hatred
26. Not being hypocritical
27. Lack of duality of mind
28. Lack of jealousy
29. Lack of miserliness
30. Not being deceitful
31. Lack of pretention
32. Lack of stubbornness
33. Lack of egotism
34. Obedience
35. Having good friends
36. Diligence
37. Possessing devotion
38. Shamefulness
39. Fearing sin
40. Possession of knowledge
41. Effort
42. Mental alertness
43. Being full of wisdom
44. Not holding to one's own view

These forty-four forms of illnesses, or blemishes, are primarily mental. There are weaknesses that occur because people get enslaved by their minds. They occur because they have not been able to control and restrain their minds. The best medicine for any of these mental illnesses is Buddhism. The physician who discovered those therapies is the Buddha.

"O great King, there are many medicines discovered by the Buddha. He administers these to cure the illnesses of both men and gods. The following are those medicines:-

a) Four Foundations of Mindfulness (**Cattāro Satipaṭṭhāna**);

b) Four Right Exertions (Catt**ā**ro **Sammappadhāna**);

c) Four Roads to Power (**Iddhi-pāda**);

d) The Five Organs (**Pañcindriya**);

e) The Five Powers (**Pañca bala**);

f) The Seven Factors of Enlightenment (**Satta Bojjhanga**)

g) The Eight-Fold Noble Path (**Ariyatthingika Magga**).

With these forms of medicine the Buddha flushes out wrong views and wrong concepts, and administers an emetic to all blemishes. **Osadhāni, Mahārāja, Bhagavatā akkhātāni yehi osadhehi so Bhagavā deva manusse tikicchati. Seyyathidaṃ cattāro satipaṭṭhānā, cattāro samappadhānā; cattāro iddhipāda; pañcindrīyāni; pañcabalāni; satta bojjhangā; ariyo aṭṭhangiko maggo etehi osadhehi Bhagavā micchādiṭṭhaṃ virecati. Micchā saṁkappaṃ virecati sabba kilesa vananaṃ karoti.**

When **Kisā Gotami'**s son - her only child - died, she consulted all the prominent physicians, but she was not able to bring back her child to life. At last, she went to the Buddha, the greatest of all physicians. She was not able to find the handful of mustard as prescribed by the Buddha. The Buddha had asked her to bring a medicine that is not at all available. The mother who tried to bring back her dead son to life was a patient. She had that expectation because she was ill mentally. Therefore, the Buddha treated not the dead body, but her who was alive. He administered to her the proper therapy, and cured her fully, so that she will not get back that state of mind again.

Modern physicians say that even for many bodily illnesses, the cause is the mind. The Buddha discovered more than 2,500 years ago, that mind is the forerunner of everything. When we consider the long descriptions provided by the Buddha, about the mind and mental phenomena, it is quite evident that the Buddha was not only a psychiatrist, but He was a psychologist, too.

Enlightenment is the highest state a man can achieve in mind cultivation. **Nibbāna** (Liberation) is the highest supra-mundane status a person who has cultivated his mind, can attain. Of all the psychiatrists who flourished in mankind, the Buddha was the mind-Doctor who treated the largest number of mental patients. He was the psychiatrist who cured the largest number of mentally ill patients.

The medicines prescribed by the Buddha for the physical illnesses of the Bhikkhus, too, are found in '**Bhesajjakkhandhaka**'

*"In extending loving-kindness, He included all beings of all levels.I extend my loving-kindness to such beings as serpents that have no feet. I extend my loving-kindness to beings with two feet. I extend my loving-kindness to such beings as cent pedes that have many feet."*

*see page 29*

in '**Mahāvagga Pali**'. The Bhikkhus who lived in forest hermitages were endangered by poisonous serpents, quite frequently. The Buddha prescribed the four **Mahā Vikatas** (The Four Primary Forms of Filth) against snake-bite. The four are:- a) **Mala** (faeces); b) **Mutta** (urine); c) **Carika** (hot ashes) and d) **Mattika** (clay).

For jaundice the aralu nut in cattle-urine was prescribed; for stomach aches, was salt sediment; and pot roast was prescribed for emaciation. When a person had swallowed poison he was made to drink faeces diluted in water. A mustard plaster was placed over a wound. Unguents were applied for eye diseases. Bark shavings and cow-dung were boiled together and applied for itching. Various forms of herbs, varieties of salts, yams and roots were prescribed.

The Buddha presented many varieties of therapies for the illnesses of the Bhikkhus when the Buddha travelled around in villages market cities and forests with large numbers of monks as retinue. In such journeys, medicines were not taken along. Nor did physicians accompany them. If a monk fell ill he was treated in terms of the occasion. This way, the Buddha can be thought of not only as a psychiatrist, but as a physician, too.

# Soul

## Belief in soul is the cause of all the trouble

*Buddhism stands unique in the history of human thought in denying the existence of such a Soul. Self, or Atman. According to the teaching of the Buddha, the idea of self is an imaginary, false belief which has no corresponding reality, and it produces harmful thoughts or 'me' and 'mine', selfish desire, craving, attachment, hatred, ill-will, conceit, pride, egoism, and other defilements, impurities and problems. It is the source of all the troubles in the world from personal; conflicts to wars between nations. In short, to this false view can be traced all the evils in the world.*

***Ven. Dr. W. Rahula, "What the Buddha Taught"***

## CHAPTER 19

# THE BUDDHA - PERSON OF INCOMPARABLE BEAUTY

If in this world anyone possessed a human form that attracted, that pleased everybody who saw him or met him, it was that of the Supreme Buddha. Of all the statues and images of the famous people and leaders who have passed away from time to time, there is hardly any statue or image as popular as a statue or an image of the Buddha.

From this we can glean an idea about the Buddha's incomparable physical presence. Millions of people who were not overwhelmed by statues of great emperors with their crowns and stunning royal splendour, or by the image of a great queen, resplendent in all her feminine glory, have been moved to serene joy by the calm, pleasant and restrained ascetic figure, the robed figure, the figure of the Buddha.

Today, too, this takes place. Anyone who has seen Swami Vivekananda in person - an individual born in an ordinary family in North India - can imagine how **Prince Siddhārtha**, born in a North Indian **Sākyan** royal family, would have appeared.

The Buddha, a long time after He became Buddha, told the monks briefly how He lived in luxury when He was young.

> "O Monks, I was very delicate when I was young - exceedingly delicate. Monks, in my father's palace comely ponds had been made for me. One of these was full of blue lotus. The second was full of white lotus. The third had red lotus. They were there solely for my delight. Monks, I never wore a costume that was not extremely fine. My turban cloth, made of Kasi silk, was extremely fine. All my clothes were extremely fine. My shawl was extremely fine. Day and night, a white umbrella was held over me so that I will not be affected by the cold, the heat, the dew and the dust. Monks, I had three palaces. One befitted the winter. One was for summer. The third was for the rainy season. During the four rainy months I was entertained in the palace fit for that season by an all-female orchestra, without a single male. I never stepped down to the ground floor from the upper storey. In other households the servants are given rice bran and a coarse soup. But, in my father's palace, they were served meat with savoury rice. I lived in that kind of luxury when I was sixteen."

In the above passage Buddha has stated in His own Words, after He became the Buddha, that as **Prince Siddhārtha**, He enjoyed the highest luxury a man could have. There is hardly anything that could be said about the physical appearance of a fortunate young man who enjoyed such privileges. One day, when **Prince**

*"Sāriputta, I who was an ascetic in the quest for purity, spent the whole night in the forest during winter when the snow fell heavily, shivering in the cold".*

*see page 32*

**Siddhārtha** was returning home from the park, a princess named **Kisā Gotami**, who was looking out of the upper floor of a city palace, spoke thus:

> **"The parents of such a young man as this would be the happiest parents. If a young woman were to get a young man like this as husband, she would be exceedingly fortunate." (Nibbutā nūna sā mātā - Nibbutā nūne so pitā -Nibbutā nūna sā nāri- Yassānaṃ īdiso pati)**

These 'Happy Words' ('**Nibbuta Pada**') bear testimony to **Prince Siddhārtha**'s great physical beauty.

Even as an ascetic He had an appearance that hypnotized those who saw Him. When He was going round for alms in the streets of **Rajagaha** all the citizens were overwhelmed by His presence. The city was agitated like Rajagaha when the King Elepdhant entered it. The city was totally disturbed like Heaven, when the King of **Asuras** entered it. King's men informed the King: "Your Majesty, a strange being who cannot be identified either as a god, or as a man, or a **Nāga**, or a **supanna** (mythical bird), is going on alms-round in the city."

The King saw Him from the upper storey of his palace and ordered his men to bring Him along, saying that He is a strange person. ***(Jātakaṭṭha Kathā - Nidāna Kathā)***

When the Buddha was travelling to **Benares** after attaining Enlightenment at **Buddh-Gayā**, an ascetic named **Upaka** saw Him on the road.

He said to the Buddha: "O fortunate One, your bodily features are quite serene. Your complexion is quite clear - exceedingly fair. Under whom have you become an ascetic?" **"Vippasannāni kho avuso indriyāni parisuddho chavi vanno: pari yodāto kaṃsi tvaṃ āvuso uddissa pabbajito?"**

***(Mahā Vagga - Mahā Bandhaka)***

Even this ascetic was especially impressed by the Buddha's physical presence. Once, the Buddha dwelt in the domed Assembly Hall at the Great Forest in the city of **Vesāli**. At that time, about five-hundred **Licchavis** attended upon Him. Some of them were blue. They wore blue costumes, blue accessories. Some were yellow. They wore yellow costumes with yellow accessories. Some were red. They wore red costumes, with red accessories. Some were white. They wore white costumes with white accessories. The Buddha shone in complexion and glory, above all of them.

***(Anguttara Nikāya - Pañcaka Nikāya Catuttha Pannasāka )***

It is clear even from this that the Buddha was of more compelling complexion, even than the Licchavi royals who were considered the comeliest clan in India of that day.

A youth, by the name of **Vakkali**, saw the Buddha one day. He was so overwhelmed by the Buddha's appearance that he kept on gazing upon Him. He decided that the only thing he could do to keep on gazing at the Buddha's incomparable physical presence was getting ordained under Him. He did not become a monk either because he was disillusioned with lay life or because he wanted to achieve **Nibbāna**.

His only concern was to keep on gazing upon the Buddha's physical presence. He would go to any place where the Buddha was, and from a place he could see the Buddha, he would go on gazing upon Him.

He did this as a daily routine. The Buddha noted this behaviour of **Vakkali's**, who would gaze on without meditating. The Buddha told him:]

> "**Apehi Vakkali, apehi Vakkali kiṃ tuyhimina pūti kāyena**?"
> "Vekkali, get out! **Vekkali**, get out! What is the use of this impure body to you?"

When chased out that way he concentrated on his religious life, and became an Arahant.

**Saddhammaratnāvalī** describes this way the attempt of Brahmin **Māgandhi** to give his beautiful daughter in marriage to the Buddha: "She was the daughter of Brahmin **Māgandhi** of **Kuru** country. Her mother, too, was called **Māgandhi**. Her uncle, too, was named **Māgandhi**. That Brahmin woman **Māgandhi** was exceedingly beautiful. As charming as a divine maiden."

However much he tried, her father the Brahmin could not find a husband who was suitable for her. Proposals were sent from very affluent families with vast retinues to take her as bride. But, the Brahmin would insult them and send them away, saying that "You are not fit for my daughter."

One morning, the Buddha was contemplating the world with His vision of great compassion. He realized that Brahmin **Māgandhi** and his wife had the potential to become Non-Returners. The Buddha took His robes and bowl Himself, and visited the place where the Brahmin **Māgandhi** was making offerings to Fire God, outside his house. The Bramin saw the thirty-two marks of an exceptionally great person: on the Buddha's body, and the Buddha's eighty bodily features. Seeing this great soul the Brahmin thought: "There is no other man in this world similar to this gem of a human being. He is exactly suitable for my daughter. I will give my daughter in marriage to Him."He spoke to the Buddha: "O Monk, I have a daughter. Seeing no man fit to be her husband, I have kept her protected in my home all these days. Now that I have seen your physical presence, she is quite suitable for you. You, too, are quite suitable for her. I will give that daughter of mine as your wife just now. Wait here until I bring her here."

The Buddha said neither good or bad. The Brahmin ran home and told his wife: "O fortunate one, what are you doing? I have just now found a person quite suitable to your daughter. I have asked Him to wait on the road. Dress up your daughter and bring her along soon." He got his daughter dressed up, and brought her along with his wife.

When they saw Brahmin going out, the whole city was all agog like a heavenly city invaded by the Asuras. "What a miracle is this? Earlier, this Brahmin seeing the prosperity quite clearly visible of the noble persons from Anga, Magadha, Kasi, Kosala, Vajji, Malla and other places, observing their affluence, retinues and glory, would not accept their proposals, saying 'You are not suitable for my daughter's beauty.' But today, he hurries on taking his wife, saying 'I found an ascetic fit for my daughter.' We must see what a gem of a man he is." Amazed, those crowds followed the Brahmin.

When he came back with the daughter the Buddha had left the place where the Brahmin wanted the Buddha to stay. The Buddha had wished that His foot-print be seen where He stood earlier, and sat down

*'People experience fear due to several reasons. Beings are likely to feel a sense of fear because of their love of life, or because they do not want to die, or else, because of their attachment to their spouses and children, their attachment to their houses and lands and other property. The Buddha does not have any such possessions to which he wanted to feel attached. As a result He had a surprising fearlessness."*

*see page 40*

at a place near there. When the Buddha wishes only such and such persons should see, only they can see. Others do not see. If He wished that it should last so long, it will last for that time, even if floods that carry away elephants, horses, cattle and buffaloes, should occur. Even if a ferocious whirlwind were to be created by a person with magical power, not even a wee bit of the foot-print can be erased.

The Brahmin's wife asked her husband: "Where is the person you saw?" The Brahmin replied: "I asked Him to stay here." When he looked around to see where the Buddha had gone, he saw the Buddha's sacred foot-print.

The Brahmin's wife calculated the signs as she was an adept in the Three Vedas, and as she knew the secrets of signs, told the husband:

> "What on earth are you saying. This is not the foot-print of a man who will make his chest impure by pressing it on a woman's breast which is a lump of flesh. This is not the foot-print of a passionate man who will touch his face to the impure face of a woman. This is invariably the foot-print of a noble person who has eradicated all the blemishes, and who is an All-Knowing person."

Then the Brahmin said: "You Brahmin woman, you are like a person seeing crocodiles in a plate. Are you seeing bandits hiding in the middle of the house? Do not say useless things. Keep quiet." The Brahmin's wife replied: "You Brahmin, though you are born in a Brahmin clan, you do not know even this much. Do whatever you like. However much you say, this is not the foot-print of a man who will indulge in five-fold sense pleasure." At that, the Brahmin looked around and saw the Buddha seated like a drop of ambrosia. He addressed the Buddha: "O Monk, I have brought along my daughter to be given to you in marriage. This is my daughter. Now take her as your wife." The Buddha, without saying whether his daughter was of use for him or not, spoke to the Brahmin: "O Brahmin, I will tell you one particular thing." "Go ahead and say it," the Brahmin replied.

The Buddha started narrating events from the renunciation on.

> "O Brahmin, due to my fear of the cycle of rebirth I gave up a kingdom like **Kapilavatthu** which was like a heavenly city. I gave up a chief queen like **Yasodharā**, a son like Prince **Rāhula**. I gave up my desire for the universal monarchy which was mine to take. At midnight I left my palace where there were about forty thousand noble maidens like divine beauty. I ran away without caring for it as much as for an ant-hill with a female serpent in it. I ran away without even looking back. Even Death (Māra) who has been pursuing me for six years like my shadow could not even detect the trace of a sensuous hesitation. Disillusioned like a jackal who had been protecting red flowers, mistaking them for flesh, **Māra** fled, exhausted. I made a tremendous effort for six years, sat upon the unconquerable seat, under the **Bodhi Tree,** defeated **Māra**, and attained Enlightenment, making the whole earth tremble. Next came the three daughters of **Māra** to avenge their father's defeat. I directed only **anicca** (impermanence), **dukkha** (suffering), and **anatta** (soul-lessness) to the three

faces of **Aratī**, **Ratī** and **Ragā**, the three daughters of **Māra**. I never generated a sense-desire even when I saw these divine maidens from the sixth heaven which is the highest place in sense-desire. Will such a person desire a pot of impurities like your daughter? ***(Saddhammaratnāvalī)***

One can imagine the glorious plysical presence of the Buddha even from this story.

Once, the Buddha travelled in a market town in **Anguttarāpa** with about 1,250 disciples (**Saddhiṃ aḍḍha telasehi Bhikkhu satehi**). There, a Brahmin teacher named **Sela**, who was adept in the Three Vedas, and was an expert in the features of exceptionally great beings, saw the Buddha with about 300 of his young pupils. The Brahmin saw in the Buddha the 32 signs of the exceptionally great beings written down in the Three Vedas (**Āgaṭāni kho pana asmākaṃ mantesū dvattiṃsa mahā purisa lakkhaṅani**). Seeing these signs Brahmin **Sela** praised the physical presence of the Buddha in front of the Buddha Himself. The great specialist averred that according to his science of human features, He is without doubt, a Buddha.

At the end, Brahmin **Sela**, with his 300 pupils, became monks under the Buddha. Receiving higher ordination, he became an Arahant. This learned Brahmin scholar took the Buddha's refuge not because he had listened to a Discourse by the Buddha, but because the 32 physical features and signs found in the science he studied, existed in the Buddha's body.

In other words, he was pleased by the Buddha's physical presence. The well-known stanzas in **Narasīha Gāthā** - composed as if they were the verses with which Queen **Yasodharā** introduced the Buddha to Prince **Rāhula** - extol the appearance of the Buddha in an incomparable manner. This kind of praise cannot be given to any other person in the human kind. Nor can any other person bear such praise.

**"Samano khalu, Gotamo abhirūpo, dassanīyo, pāsādike, paramāya vanna pokkharatāya samannāgato Brahma vanni Brahma vacchasī, akkuddāva kāso dassanāya."** "O Friends, the Buddha is more handsome than all other human beings. One is not content seeing Him. One wants to see Him more and more. One is pleased just seeing Him. He possesses the beauty of complexion. He is of golden hue. His body gleams like Brahma's body. There is plenty of time to see Him," Brahmin **Sona Daṇḍa** said. *(Dīgha Nikāya - Sona Danḍa Sutta)*

**"Singī nikkasavanno Rajagahaṃ pāvisi Bhagavā."** The Buddha who is of gold hue, has arrived in **Rājagaha**.

*(Mahā Vagga)*

There is no statue as popular as the image of the Buddha. On the table of **Bernard Shaw**, too, there was a Buddha image. The Buddha image, even when it is hewn in stone, has a capacity to inspire serenity in anyone.

**Javaharlāl Nehru**, when he was in prison, acquired tranquillity of mind looking at the photograph of the Buddha statue at **Anurādhapura, Sri Lanka. The unique, pleasing, blemishless, serene, restrained appearance seen in the Buddha image cannot be seen in another image. All this goes to prove that this Buddha possessed an an unparalleled physical comeliness.**

*In rendering service the Buddha never divided the mankind through such usages as 'for the good of the Easterners", "for the good of the Westerners", "for the good of the poor", "for the good of the wealthy", "for the good of the underprivileged castes", "for the good of the Āryans", or "for the good of the non-Āryans" His incomparably great compassion was the same for all.*

*see page 168*

*The Buddha boldly stated that there were great Brahmins in the past, they possessed high Brahmanic qualities, that such Brahmanic qualities are not found in contemporary Brahmins.* *see page 163*

## CHAPTER 20

# THE BUDDHA IS THE GREATEST PSYCHOLOGIST

Before He attained Enlightenment Prince **Siddhārtha** tried His level best to make a thorough study of man and his mind, and to conduct research on those themes. By achieving Enlightenment He realized everything there was to know about man and man's mind. He acquired the ability to know the minds of others (**para-citta vijānāna ñāna**).

The Buddha knew the whole profile of an individual who came to see Him; including his character, his ideas and views, his past birth and his next birth. In consequence, the greatest fortune that His contemporaries could have was to be interviewed by the Buddha.

Most of those persons who were able to meet Him achieved a higher status. They derived successful results. About ninety-nine per cent of the people who were able to meet the Buddha, were very fortunate persons. Some of them did not go back to their homes at all. They gave up all such possessions as houses, lands, spouses and children, forget all those, and became the Buddha's disciples.

The psychologist who understood the human mind most extensively was the Buddha. He Himself has described the surprising awareness He had of the mind.

> "O Monks, I can utilize all the psychic powers I like. I can appear as many though I am just one. I appear as two persons, and then merge into one. I will appear to be seen by all, but I can remain unseen by anyone. I can go through walls, fortresses, rocks, without touching just as moving through the air. I can go inside water and also on water. I can travel through the air like a bird. I can walk in the air as if walking on earth. I can touch the sun and the moon with my hands.
>
> "Monks, I can remember my past births as far back as I want to. I can recall not only one past or two, but hundreds and thousands of past births. I scan recall an aeon. In such and such a community, in such and such a clan, subsisting on such and such food. I lived by such and such a name. After departing that birth I was reborn in such and such a place. There, too, I lived in such and such a clan with such and such a name. I can recall where I was born next. I can extend my divine eye as far as I want, and find out men and women who are born and who die. I can know their status - whether they are high or low, good or evil.
>
> "I can know that such and such a person is born in such and such an evil state because of such and such evil deeds. I can also know that such and such a person has gone

*"O, Monks, travel along, from village to village, from market town to market town, from city to city, for the good of the many, for the well-being of the many, and in compassion for the world - for the good and well-being not only of men but of gods, as well. Two of you must not travel along one road. Declare the Doctrine which is good in the beginning, good in the middle, and good at the end. I, too, will set out for the market town of Senāni to Uruvela to preach the Doctrine.* *see page 168*

to such and such pleasant abode as a result of his such and such meritorious deed."

*(Samyutta Nikaya - Kassapa Samutta)*

The only psychologist who knew the human mind fully and comprehensively is the Buddha.

"O Monks, I just cannot see with my wisdom, any other image than that of a woman which attracts the man's mind so tenaciously," the Buddha said.(**Nāhaṃ Bhikkhave aññaṃ ekarupampi samanupassāmi, yaṃ evaṃ purisessa cittaṃ pariyādāya titthati, yathayi da Bhikkhave purisassa cittaṃ pariyādāya titthati**)

Said the Buddha:

"O Monks, I just cannot see with my wisdom any other sound than that of woman which attracts the man's mind so tenaciously." (**Nāhaṃ Bhikkhave aññaṃ ekasaddampi samanu passāmi yaṃ evaṃ purisassa cittaṃ pariyādāya titthati yathayidaṃ Bhikkhāve itthisaddaṃ. Itthi saddaṃ Bhikkhave purisassa cittaṃ pariyādāya tutthati**")

"Similarly,

"O Bhikkhus, the fragrance of women, the taste of women, the touch of women attract men most. O Monks, I cannot see with my wisdom any other phenomena that is more conducive to destruction than the human mind, that has not been cultivated through meditation, that has not been restrained, and that has not been developed properly. (**"Nāhaṃ Bhikkhave aññaṃ eka dhammapi samanupassāmi yaṃ evaṃ abhāvitaṃ mahato anathāya saṃvattati, yathayidaṃ cittaṃ")**

"O Monks, I cannot see with my wisdom any other phenomenon that is more conducive to tremendous good, tremendous progress and great happiness than the mind cultivated through meditation, than the mind that is restrained and developed." (**"Nāhaṃ Bhikkhave aññaṃ ekadhammaṃpi samanupassāmi, yaṃ evaṃ bhāvitaṃ, bahulīkataṃ mahato atthāya saṃvattati, yathayidaṃ cittaṃ**.")

"O Monks, this subconscious mind is radiant, clear and lucid. It gets contaminated with the blemishes that come from outside." (**"Pabhassara midaṃ Bhikkhave cittaṃ tañca kho āgantukehi upakkilesehi upakkilṭṭhaṃ**.")

*(Anguttara Nikāya - Ekaka Nipāta)*

The Buddha, whose mind was filled with compassion and loving-kindness preached His sermons to the heart of men and women. People accepted that Doctrine with their hearts. If a thousand persons listened to a Sermon preached by the Buddha, each one of those will say: "This is being said specifically to me. This is being said specifically to me."

Hardly any other instance is necessary to ask whether the Buddha could penetrate the minds of all those people He met. There is no one who was not happy after listening to a Sermon by the Buddha. There is no one who said that either an intimate discussion or a sermon or a discourse or a reply to questions by the Buddha, was not satisfactory. The only two persons who went away disciplined with the Buddha's Words were Brahmin **Māgandi** and his daughter. They were dissatisfied because the Buddha refused the marriage proposal brought by Brahmin **Māgandi**.

The Buddha said that in every human action the mind was the fore-runner. (**Mano pubbaṃgamā Dhammā - Mano setthā manomayā**.) The inventions have been brought into being after exercising the mind for days, months and years. New things have been discovered that way. Modern scientists achieve miraculous results by developing the mind, systematically. Man was able to land even on the moon by developing the mind along the line of mechanical constructions.

If we consider the worldly achievements that have been won by developing the mind in the material field, it is quite certain that there is hardly anything that cannot be achieved if the mind is developed subjectively and spiritually towards meditations and **jhanas**. The psychologist who developed the mind subjectively to the highest level is the Buddha.

The noble method of developing the mind subjectively through meditation and **yogas** is gradually disappearing. This implies the erosion of a great achievement that could be won through the mind. This is an unbearable loss to human society. Today's human beings can hardly believe that it was possible for the human mind to win such incomparable victories. Some western people do not still believe those miracles that only the wise people in the East could gain by cultivating the mind.

But anyone who has studied Buddhism deeply will clearly see that there is nothing greater than the power of the mind. In short, **Nibbāna** (Eternal Bliss) is a mental phenomenon. It is a state of the mind. The lightness, the unburdened state that occurs when craving has been totally eradicated from the mind can be experienced only by a person who has eradicated the blemishes. It is no wonder that the body, burdened by the weight of blemishes, will drift away - waft away - like a whiff of air when it obtains recluse from those burdens.

All the wonders and miracles of the world have been performed by living human beings who possess a mind. There is no strange or miraculous act performed by a dead body, or an inanimate phenomenon. It is the human mind that has brought miraculous things into being by controlling inanimate forces.

When the mind departs from a living body, one can see the strange change that occurs in that body. From this we can fathom the power of the mind. There is no other person who analysed the human mind so deeply as the Buddha. There is also no other person who demonstrated the different aspects of the mind, as the Buddha did. Scientists have achieved some victories with the help of the mind. But what they have discovered about the mind itself is peripheral.

The miraculous states that can be reached by **yoga**, meditation, **Jhana** and concentration, have been overlooked by modern scientists, so far. In consequence, their inventions and discoveries have not been conducive to the development of the human mind, and to man's spiritual and subjective progress. Man gains in stature, in proportion of the development of the mind. Buddhas, Pacceka Buddhas (Silent Buddhas), Arahants (Holy Ones) who developed their minds to the highest level,

*Seeing that the king was depressed, the Buddha said to him, "O Great King, some women are great, efficient and wise. Therefore, the daughter born to you by Queen Mallika should be very well looked after. The woman who is wise, virtuous, who treats her parents-in-law as deities, and is chaste, is a noble person. The son of such a woman may even rule a country."* *page 160*

are the persons who possess the greatest minds. Lower the mind, lower the man, too. Those yogis, ascetics who had attained higher mental states, recluses, lost their power the moment a blemished thought occurred to them.

**Sakka**, King of Gods, was pleased with the righteous rule of King **Mahāmandhātu**. The **Sakka** took him to his heavenly abode, and gave the king half of his heavenly kingdom. **Mahāmandhātu**, when he started enjoying heavenly luxury, thought of killing **Sakka** and taking over **Sakka**'s half of the kingdom too, to himself. Immediately that vicious, greedy thought occurred to him, he saw that he was back in his own garden, down on earth. This is good object lesson for all to see how, with a good thought, a person ascends to heaven, and with a bad thought, how a man falls down to earth.

The Buddha experienced the bliss of jhana (Absorption), bliss of **vipassanā** (Insight), and the bliss of **Nibbāna**. He did not consider miracles to be important. He found fault with those who performed miracles to please the populace. The Buddha never wanted to perform miracles and to appear a 'magician' who made the people amazed. He never considered miracles and magic as essential because they were not at all a help for the development of the inner being. He found fault with **Ven. Pindola Bhāradvāja** for performing miracles.

Once, the Buddha dwelt in the mango-grove called **Pāvārika**, in the neighbourhood of **Nālanda**. A householder named **Kevaḍḍha** came to see Him, and, standing on a side, said to the Buddha: "Sir, this city of **Nālanda** is quite developed. It is prosperous. It is full of people. Many people living here admire you very much. If anyone of your disciples could perform a miracle to be seen by the people in this city these citizens will have greater admiration for you. Could you request one of your disciples to do so?"

When he made this appeal the Buddha spoke to **Kevaḍḍha**:

> "**Kevaḍḍha,** I never ask my disciples to perform miracles demonstrating higher human powers for the benefit of ordinary laymen."

The Buddha refused **Kevaḍḍha**'s appeal. He requested three times. The Buddha rejected it three times.

This is yet another story that brings out the Buddha's attitude to miracles. One day, the Buddha stayed by a ford in a river with some of His disciples. The ferryman was coming back after taking a person to the nether bank. At that time, an ascetic emaciated, and with hair and beard grown thick and long, came there and looked at the Buddha with a sarcastic smile, quizzically. Then he started walking on the surface of the water and crossed the river.

Seeing his miracle one of the disciples said: "O Sir, I like very much to see you walk on the water, just as that old ascetic did. " The Buddha smiled slightly. "Monks, what on earth is that? It is not worth anything. But whatever it is, I will show you in a moment the exact worth of that act." The ferryman came over to the near bank. The ferryman, seeing the Buddha, came near Him and worshipped Him. The Buddha spoke to him: "You took a man to the other bank now. How much did he pay you as your fare?" "Sir, he paid me half-a-masaka (**Aḍḍhamasaka** -

that is a coin of very low value)."The Buddha turned to His disciple and said:

> **"Just consider that ascetic's miracle is worth only half-a-masaka. But he would have mortified his body over a long period of time to achieve that yogic power. Why should I waste my valuable time that I have to utilize for the well-being of people, for a task that can be done with half-a-masaka?"**

What troubles most people is their lack of true knowledge about the value of the people around them although they associate them. Parents do not know the mind of their children. Teachers do not know properly the wishes and aspirations of their students. Rulers do not know the thoughts and grievances of their subjects. All the problems arose because of this.

Everybody in the world is not a psychologist. There are only a handful of those who can know the minds of others. In consequence, only a few persons can please others. The only psychologist who was able to please a vast number of persons is the Buddha. **The highest lesson we can learn from Him as a psychologist is that we should be ready to work, knowing the minds of the people, always.**

## Persecution

*Of the great religions of history I prefer Buddhism, especially in its earliest forms, because it has had the smallest element of persecution.*

***Bertrand Russell***

## Religion of Man

*Buddhism will last as long as the sun and moon last and the human race exists upon the earth, for it is the religion of man, of humanity as a whole.*

***Bandaranaike, Former Prime Minister of Sri Lanka***

*"If people tend to get angry quite often, if they harbour enmity, if they are likely to forget good done to them, if they hold harmful views, if they cover up their faults deliberately, if a person were to take a loan, but avoids paying back, if a person does not look after one's parents although he can afford to, if a person, visiting others' homes, eats there well, but does not treat them when they come to his house, such a person is a 'vesala'." (an outcaste).*

*see page 163*

CHAPTER 21

## THE BUDDHA IS A RIGHTEOUS KING WHO BUILT AND RULED A RIGHTEOUS KINGDOM

We describe the Buddha as the Enlightened King (**Buda Rajānan Vahansa** in Sinhala). He renounced a worldly kingdom. He went into the forest and became an ascetic with no other worldly possessions than the robe he wore, and the bowl. Eventually, He built an 'army' of virtuous people who practised a noble discipline and established a Kingdom of Righteousness. He became a king who was totally different from all the other kings of the world '**Dhamma Rāja**' (the Righteous King) is one of His epithets.

One day, a Brahmin named **Sela**, who was adept in the Three Vedas, came to see the Buddha. He observed on the Buddha the characteristic signs of an exceptionally great man. He spoke to the Buddha: "You have on you the signs of an exceptionally great person. Why do you not become a universal monarch (**Cakkavatti**) and rule a kingdom?"

The Buddha responded to him this way: "Brahmin **Sela**, I am a king. A great Righteous King at that. I am conducting a Righteous Kisngdom that no one else can run." ***(Sutta Nipāta - Sela Sutta)***

Brahmin **Sela** enquired: "If you are a king where is your General?" The Buddha turned to **Ven. Sāriputta** who was around, and spoke thus: "**Ven. Sāriputta** bears the responsibility of maintaining the Wheel of Dhamma I turned." In consequence, **Ven. Sāriputta** came to be known as '**Dhamma Senāpati**' (the General of Righteousness). The capital of his Righteous Kingdom of the King of Righteousness was 'the City of Righteousness' (**Dhamma Nagara**).

**Ven. Nāgasena** described the nature of this Righteous City to King **Milinda** in **Milinda Panha** (the Questions of **Milinda**): "O Great King, around the great Righteous City of our Supreme Buddha, there are stone walls that obstruct the approach of bandits called 'blemishes. Around it are muddy moats called 'shame' (**lajjā**). Its portals are called 'wisdom' (**ñāna**). Its ramparts are 'effort' (**viriya**). The strong post (**indakhīla**) securing the portals is 'devotion' (**saddhā**). The portal is 'mindfulness' (**sati**). The great palaces of the city are described as 'insight' (**paññā**).

"The Discourses and Sermons (**Suttānta Dhamma**) are the royal court yard. Metaphysical Knowledge (**Abhidhamma**) forms the four-way junction. The courts are the Codes of Discipline (**Vinaya Dhamma**). The four main streets are the Four Foundations of Mindfulness (**Sati Paṭṭhana**)."O great King, in these four main streets, there are flower shops selling all kinds of flowers. There are fruit shops. There are shops selling perfumes. There are shops selling medicines that counter the effects of poisons. There are pharmacies. There are shops selling ambrosia. There are shops selling jewellery, precious metals, and gems. There are shops that sell a multiplicity of goods. Of these shops there are eight.

One of these is a flower shop. In these there is a kind of flower called 'those who have focussed their attention on the attainment of the status of **Arahants** (Holy Ones)'. These 'flowers' are keen to eradicate lust (**rāga**), hatred (**dosa**) and ignorance (**moha**). To achieve this end, they concentrate on impermanence (**anicca**), suffering (**dukkha**), soul-lessness (**anatta**), impurities (**asubha**), misery (**ādīnava**), full understanding (**pahāna**), detachment (**virāga**), extinction (**nirodha**), disinterestedness regarding the whole world (**sabbaloke anabhirata**), the impermanence of all formations (**sabba saṃkhāresu anicca**), concentration on breathing (**ānāpānasati**), a swollen, bloated corpse (**uddhu mātaka**) a discoloured corpse (**vinīlaka**), a festering corpse (**vipubbaka**), a fissured corpse (**vicchidaka**), a mangled corpse (**vikkhāyitaka**, a dismembered corpse (**vikkittha**), a cut and dismembered corpse (**hata vikkhittaka**), a bleeding corpse (**lohitaka**), a corpse infested with worms (**pulavaka**), a skeleton (**atsika**), loving-kindness (**metta**), contemplation on Death (**maranānussati**), mindfulness with regard to the body (**kāyagatāsati**).

"In the stall selling perfumes they have the fragrances called the 'Refuges' (**Sarana Sīla**), the Five Precepts (**Panca Sīla**), the Eight Precepts (**Aṭṭhanga Sīla**), the Ten Precepts (**Dasa Sīla**) and Morality of the Disciplinary Code (**Pātimokkha Saṃvara Sīla**). There you have the moral persons who are the fragrance. This fragrance is wafted in the ten directions.

"In the fruit stall the fruits you have are those who have gained the Fruit of Stream-entry (**Sotāpatti Phala**), the Fruit of Once-returning (**Sakrutāgāmi Phala**), the fruit of non-returning (**Anāgāmi Phala**), the Fruit of being a Holy One (**Arahant Phala**)'.

"In the shop selling medicines that counter poisons you have the medicines that counter the effect of the poison of blemishes. These medicines are the Truth of Suffering (**Dukkha Sacca**), the Truth of the Cause of Suffering (**Samudaya Sacca**), the Truth of the Cessation of Suffering (**Nirodha Sacca**), the Truth of the Path to the Cessation of Suffering (**Dukkha Nirodha Gāmini Ariya Paṭipadā**).

"In the pharmacy you have these medicines - the Four Foundations of Mindfulness (**Catu Satipaṭṭhāna**), the Four Forms of Right Exertion (**Catu Sampappadhāna**), the Four Roads to Power (**Catu Iddhipāda**), the Five Organs of Perception (**Pañandriya**), the Five Forms of Power (**Pañca Bala**), the Seven Factors of Enlightenment (**Satta Bojjhanga**), the Noble Eight-fold Path (**Ariya Aṭṭhangika Magga**).

"In the ambrosia stall you have Mindfulness regarding the Body (**Kāyagatāsati**). According to the Buddha those who would taste Deathlessness (**Amata**) should taste Mindfulness regarding the Body (**Kāyagatāsati**). The Buddha's Words are: "**Amataṃ te Bhikkhave paribhunjanti ye kāyagatāsatiṃ paribhunjanti**." According to the Buddha this Mindfulness regarding Body is the ambrosia (deathless potion) sprinkled to save gods and men from birth (**jāti**), decay and old age (**jarā**), sickness (**vyādhi**), death (**marana**) sorrow (**soka**), wailing (**parideva**), suffering

***The principle of the Five Precepts consists of making people promise to refrain from five wrong deeds that are likely to happen quite often in everyday life.***

***see page 165***

(**dukkha**), unhappiness (**domanassa**) and weeping (**upāyasa**).

"In the gem stall (Ratana) you have such gems as the Gem of Morality (**Sīla Ratana**), the Gem of Concentration (**Samādhi Ratana**), the Gem of Understanding (**Pañña Ratana**), the Gem of Liberation (**Vimutti Ratana**), the Gem of Seeing the Wisdom leading to Liberation (**Vimutti Ṅāna Dassana Ratana**), the Gem of Analytical Knowledge (**Patisambhidā Ratana**), the Gem of the Factors of Enlightenment (**Bojjhanga Ratana**).

"In the stall of miscellaneous things, you have the Teachings of the Buddha with nine features, shrines of the bodily relics and of articles used, and the Brotherhood (**Sangha Ratana).**

"In the Buddha's Righteous City there are many citizens. They are Adepts in the Discourses (**Suttāntikas**), Disciplinarians (**Vinayadharas**), those who are adept in Metaphysics (**Abhidhammadharas**), those adept in the Exposition of the Dhamma (**Dhammakathikas**), those who recite the Birth Tales (**Jātaka Bhānakas**), those who recite the longer Discourses (**Dīgha Nikāya bhānakas**), those who recite the middle-length Discourses (**Majjhima bhānakas**), those who recite Kindred Sayings (**Sanyuttu bhānakas**), those who recite the Graduated Sayings (**Anguttara bhānakas**), those who recite the shorter Discourses (**Khunddaka bhānakas**), those who are morally advanced (**Sīla Sampannas**), those who are advanced in Concentration (**Samadhi Sampannas**), those who are advanced in Insight (**Pañña Sampannas**), those who contemplate the Factors of Enlightenment (**Bojjhanga**), those who practise Insight Meditation (**Vipassanā**), those who interpret (**Attha**), those who dwell in forests (**Ārannakas**), those who prefer the foot of trees (**Rukkhamūlikas**), those who prefer the open air (**Abbhokāsikas**), those who prefer hay-stacks (**Palālapunjakas**), those who prefer cemeteries (**Sosānika**), those who meditate without lying down; those who have attained the Four Paths, those who have attained the Four Fruits, those who are undergoing training (**Sayikkhas**), those who are adept in the three forms of knowledge such as the capacity to recall the past births, those who have the Divine Eye, the Divine Ear, those who know the minds of others, those who possess the six forms of Higher Power (**Abhiññā**). Great **Arahants** (Holy Ones) who have four forms of magical power (**Iddha**) and great **Arahants** capable of various absorptions. These are the citizens who fill that city.

"The Righteous Generals in this city are the great **Arahants** who maintain the Righteous rule, the Counsellors are the great **Arahants** of magical power and of the four-fold analytical powers; the Judges are the great **Arahants** who possess the means of purification, those who brighten the city (**Nagara Jotikas**) are the great **Arahants** who have acquired the Divine Eye through the fulfillment of perfections; the Ministers who protect the Doctrine are the monks who are extensively learned, supports of the Nine-fold Dispensation of the Buddha (**Navanga Sāsanadhara**) adept in the Doctrine and adept in the Discipline; the Protectors of the city are those monks who meditate day and night without sleeping. The Righteous Guild Leaders (**Dhamma Seṭṭhis**) of the City are the monks who possess the gems of the Doctrine, and the gem of learning the wordings of the

Doctrine. O great King, the Righteous City of the King of Righteousness is well created - full of everything - established according to the law and the constitution - well protected. Those enemies who are without morality and devoid of virtue cannot enter this City."

*(Milinda Panha Mahānumāna Panho)*

The manner in which the Buddha appointed the citizens to various offices in His Righteous Kingdom is an example to all the rulers in the world. No such considerations as intimacy, relationship, caste, clan, nationality, province, loyalty, preference, animosity, ignorance or fear will enter into those appointments. After an appointment had been made, there were no gossips and secret comments about those appointments. When He appointed **Ven.Sāriputta** and **Ven. Moggallāna** as the Chief Disciples He said: "I do not appoint a person 'looking at his face' (**Nāhaṃ mukhaṁ oloketvā dammi**)."

Those modern rulers and administrators, Members of Parliament, Ministers, offices, when they appoint people to various offices, must follow the example of the Buddha. In making any appointment, the Buddha gave prominence to the appointee's character. But, He did not accept any testimony or character-certificate from an outsider. The Buddha Himself examined carefully the character, not only in this birth, but in several previous births, as well. Examining that way

He made appointment to various positions strictly according to the efficiency, qualifications and virtues. In this model city those citizens who ranked quite high in virtues and morality never asked for positions. They never competed for posts. They were not greedy of appointments. Never forgot their roots after they received their appointments. They never overlooked the weak and the poor. Never assumed any false airs, as if they had come down from heaven. They fully realized the suffering of the masses. They made an effort to cross over the ocean of becoming, and to make others, too, cross over this ocean of suffering. To bring about the Liberation of the people, they strove hard without sleeping day or night, in cemeteries, in abandoned houses, under trees, in the thick forests, in grasslands, on rock slabs, subsisting on whatever they received, whether it was tasty or coarse, they made a strenuous effort to achieve morality, and to make others moral, to become happy and make others happy.

Of those who received honours and appointments from the Buddha the highest place among the longest standing disciples (**Cirarātragaña**) was given to **Ven. Aññākondanna**. The greatest among the wise was **Ven. Sāriputta**. The greatest disciple in magical power was **Ven. Moggallāna**. The greatest in austere practices (**Dhūtanga dhara**) was **Ven. Mahā Kassapa**. The greatest in the Divine Eye was **Ven. Anurudha**. The disciple with the most sonorous voice was **Ven. Lakuntaka Bhaddiya**. The greatest among those who made the Lion-roar was **Ven. Pindola Bhāradvāja**. The greatest among the exponents of the Doctrine was **Ven. Punna**, son of Brahmin lady **Mantāni**. Greatest among those who could elaborate anything that was said briefly was **Ven. Mahā Kaccāyana**. Greatest among those who could create mental images was **Ven. Cula Panthaka.** The greatest in the absoprtion of the immaterial sphere (Arupajhāna) was **Ven. Mahā Panthaka**. Greatest among those who lead a life totally bereft of blemishes

*"I found an ascetic fit for my daughter." We must see what a gem of a man he is." When he came back with the daughter the Buddha had left the place where the Brahmin wanted the Buddha to stay. The Buddha had wished that His foot-print be seen. He sat down at a place near there .The Brahmin's wife calculated the signs and told the husband: This is invariably the foot-print of a noble person who has eradicated all the blemishes, and who is an All-Knowing person."* *see page 118*

was **Ven. Subhūti**. Greatest among those who deserved offerings was **Ven. Subhūti**. Greatest among forest-dwelling monks was **Ven. Revata**. Greatest among those who were given to absorptions was **Ven. Kankhā Revata.** Greatest among those who made a high effort was **Ven. Sona**. Greatest among those who were pleasant in words was Ven. **Kuṭikanna Sona**. Greatest among those who received the Four Requisites was **Ven. Sīvalī.** Greatest among those who possessed intense devotion was **Ven. Vakkalī**.

Greatest among those who observed discipline was **Ven. Rāhula**. Greatest among those who became a monk due to intense devotion was **Ven. Kundavadhāna**. Greatest among those who can fully realize was **Ven. Vangīsa**. The greatest in arranging places is **Ven. Dabba**, son of the **Malla King**. The greatest among those who were liked by Gods was **Ven. Pilindavaccha**. The quickest person to achieve realization was **Ven. Dārucīriya Bahiya**. Greatest amongst eloquent preachers was **Ven. Kumāra Kassapa**. Greatest among those with analytical knowledge was **Ven. Mahā Koṭṭhita**. The greatest among the well-learned, the possessors of memory-power, the Insightful, those full of effort, and the greatest in attending and caring was **Ven. Ānanda.** Greatest among those who possessed extensive retinues was **Ven. Uruvela Kassapa**. The greatest among those who made clans tranquil was **Ven. Kāludāyi.** Greatest among those recalling past births was **Ven. Sobhita**. Greatest among those who possessed a healthy body was **Ven. Bakkula**. Greatest among disciplinarians was **Ven. Upāli**. Greatest among those who advised nuns (**Bhikkhunīs**) was **Ven. Nandaka**. Greatest among those who had shut the doors of perception was **Ven. Nanda**. Greatest among those who advised the monks was **Ven. Mahā Kappina**. Greatest among those who could attain the Five Absorptions was **Ven. Sāgata**. Greatest among those who could narrate anecdotes to make the Doctrine easier to understand was **Ven. Rādha**. Greatest among those who wore coarse robes was **Ven. Mogharāja**. Those monks received high places.

Greatest among the longest-standing **Bhikkunī** was **Ven. Bhikkunī Mahā Prajāpati Gotami**. Greatest in high Insight was **Ven. Bhikkunī Khemā**. Greatest among the **Bhikkunī** in magical power was Ven. **Bhikkunī Uppalavannā**. Greatest among discipline **Bhikkunī** was Ven. **Bhikkunī Patacāra**. Greatest among the **Bhikkunī** in the exposition of Dhamma was **Ven. Bhikkunī Dhammadinnā**. The greatest among the **Bhikkunī** engaged in absoprtion was **Ven. Bhikkunī Nanda Sāvikā**. The greatest in sustained effort was **Ven. Bhikkunī Sona**. Greatest among those with Higher Power (**Abhiññā**) was **Ven.Bhikkunī Bhadrā Kundalakesi**. Greatest among those with the Divine Eye was **Ven. Bhikkunī Sakulā**. Greatest among those who could recall the past births was Ven. **Bhikkunī Bhadrā Kāpilāni**. Greatest among those who attained Higher Power was **Ven. Bhikkuni Bhaddakaccānā**. The greatest among those who wore coarse robes was **Ven. Bhikkunī Kisā Gotamī**. Greatest among those with intense devotion was **Ven. Bhikkunī Sigāla Māta**. Those are the **Bhikkunī** who had received offices in the Righteous Kingdom. The Buddha conferred offices upon such lay leaders as **Anāta Pinḍika** and **Visākha**. All these offices were conferred in terms of the efficiency in the cultivation of virtues. Given this situation the greatest ruler that should be followed by rulers in ruling kingdoms is the Supreme Buddha - the Righteous King.

During the last 2,500 years all the kingdoms and empires that rose up have disintegrated and broken up after a hundred or two hundred years, due to wars. They became subjected to various forms of change and decay due to conquests and defeats, rises and falls, etc. But, the Righteous Kingdom, established by the Supreme Buddha more than 2,500 years ago, flourished securely.

As long as an uncontaminated Brotherhood (Sangha) exists, this Righteous Kingdom will continue to flourish. The only kingdom that continues to flourish over such a long period as 2,000 years without a king is this Righteous Kingdom established by the Buddha.

## We are impressed by His spirit of reason

*When we read Buddhas's discourses, we are impressed by his spirit of reason. His ethical path has for its first step right views, a rational outlook. He endeavours to brush aside all cobwebs that interfere with mankind's vision of itself and its destiny.*

***Dr. S. Radhakrishnan, "Gautama the Buddha"***

***The Buddha looked down on lazy, effortless, sleepy and reluctant monks. He praised those monks who were progressive, fearless and courageous. Considered this way, the Buddha is a very progressive religious Teacher. The Buddha praised those who made progress.***

***see page 91***

CHAPTER 22

## THE BUDDHA IS THE RELIGIOUS TEACHER WHO SHOWED THE NEXT WORLD AND BROUGHT ABOUT PROGRESS IN THIS WORLD

The Buddha never thought in terms of making everybody in this world either devotees or monks or **Arahants** (Holy Ones). What He wanted to do was to indicate the Path to Liberation (**Nibbāna**) to all those who had the maturity to realize **Nibbāna**, and to eradicate ignorance fully in all the others, and to make them healthy and happy people who would not do wrong, and would lead moral lives.

He wanted them to see the impermanence of life and the value of life, and to make them achieve the highest fruit of their lives. He wanted them to give up lethargy and to make them exert themselves now, immediately. "You must start your exertion today. Who knows whether one would die tomorrow." "**Ajjeva kiccaṃ ātappaṃ ko jaññā maranaṃ suve**."

This was one of the questions He raised. The Buddha exerted Himself all twenty-four hours a day, with the exception of just two hours. He never told anyone that He was tired, He was fatigued, or He was busy. **Emperor Asoka**, who followed the Buddha's Teachings, had it inscribed in his rock inscription **Kālinga** that a ruler who gets tired in ruling is not a great ruler. (**Nītiyanye kilante siyā na te ubhaje**.)

When the Buddha converted a person to Buddhism, He made him take Three Refuges and observe the Five Precepts, not with the intention of sending that convert to heaven. He did so to make him refrain from five forms of wrong doings that can happen in worldly life, and to make him a happy person.

Anyone who observes the Five Precepts will not have to go to courts. He will not have to expose himself to abuse. He will not have to get assaulted. He will invariably be capable of leading a righteous, happy life. He extolled the virtues of generosity to comfort those who suffer mentally without utilizing their wealth properly due to miserliness, and to get part of the wealth of those who are affluent to be donated to such public institutions as temples, schools and hospitals.

He said that those who hoard their wealth and keep it concealed because of their stinginess, will be reborn after their death as ghost-spirits in their house. He stated this to make them frightened of the next birth, and to make them generous during this birth.

He asked the people to observe Precepts with the intention of eradicating the stubborn, foolish and harsh qualities in some human beings, and to make them disciplined, polite and restrained citizens. **He asked the people to meditate, to provide mental calmness, tranquillity and serenity to those human beings**

**who, without any peace of mind, spend all their time for household activities.**

In **Sigālovāda Sutta** (Discourse of Advice to the householder **Sigāla**) and **Vyaggapajja Sutta (Vyaggapajja** Discourse) the Buddha discusses amicably how a layman must conduct himself. He has dealt extensively in these, on such issues as the six ways in which wealth gets squandered, the six evils of taking intoxicating drinks, the six evil results of frequenting streets at ungodly hours, the six evils of frequenting places of entertainment.

The six evils of gambling, the six bad results of slothfulness, good friends, bad friends, friends who should be associated, friends who should be shunned, how parents and teachers should be cared for, how the spouse should be treated, factors conducive to worldly well-being, factors leading to long life, and factors that lead to hell.

In **Parābhava Sutta** (the Discourse on Factors leading to Decline) He has classified twenty-one Factors that bring about ruin. In **Mangala Sutta** (the Discourse on Highest Blessings) He has indicated thirty-eight matters that confer Highest Blessings. In **Karanīyametta Sutta** (the Discourse on the Practice of Loving-kindness) the Buddha has declared what a person wishing progress should do.

These Discourses could be taken as guides that ensure worldly success for human beings. The Buddha has even indicated how a farmer should cultivate his fields.

The Buddha has pointed out that it is essential to establish friendly relations with those who live in the neighbourhood of one's fields, lest they should destroy the fields.

The Buddha instructed laymen to divide one's income into four portions. One of those parts should be set aside for daily expenses - for day-to-day living. Two of these parts should be invested in various enterprises, and one should be saved against possible emergencies. These instructions were given not entirely for the purpose of ensuring **Nibbāna** (Liberation), but also to enable people to live happy lives in this world itself. He pointed out heavenly pleasures to people who did virtuous and meritorious actions in order to encourage them more and more to do good.

By nature, men are tempted to do wrong things. The best method that could be employed to prevent people from yielding to such harmful temptations is to make them see the harmful results that will come to them in the next birth. Without resorting to such a stratagem, it is difficult to prevent them from doing wrong.

Therefore, the Buddha indicated the Evil States (Hells) in which the wrong-doers will have to suffer. To persuade people to do virtuous things the Buddha indicated the Pleasant Abodes (Heavens) they could reach when they did meritorious acts. What the Buddha was keen to do was to make people lead happy and contented lives here, even by pointing out the next world.

This way, the Buddha indicated the next world to people to correct their life here - during this birth - to enable them to lead successful lives. Those who endure suffering in this world will not be able to enjoy comforts in the next birth.

An individual who is not capable of

***The institution called the "Bhikkhu Brotherhood" (Bhikkhu sāsana) which the Buddha constituted through His supreme wisdom, is a universal democratic institution. The pioneer in human history to launch such a methodical and well-organized institution was the Buddha . All members of that institution are identified as the "Sangha" (the Brotherhood). The males are described as "Bhikkhus" (monks), and the females as "Bhikkhunis" (nuns).***

***see page 168***

developing his intellect during this birth will not be able to improve his wisdom in the next birth. It is not possible to surmise that a person who commits bad deeds here will be able to do good during his next birth.

An individual who leads an unfortunate life here cannot be thought of as being able to lead a happy life in the next world. The next birth will be happy only in proportion to the happiness achieved in this world. The Buddha preached His Doctrine to living beings and not to the dead. He was keen to direct living beings along the right path, and not to lead the dead along the correct path. Therefore, the Teachings of the Buddha are solely meant for worldly progress of living beings.

The Buddha is a Teacher who appeared primarily for the purpose of ensuring the worldly well-being of the people.

The best way to live is to lead life according to Buddhism. There is no greater life than that lived according to the Teachings of Buddhism. There is no other way of life that is more righteous, tranquil, calm and correct.

The Buddha preached His Doctrine for the benefit of those who are living today, and also for the good of those who will appear in this world, hundreds and thousands of years later. We who are born 2,500 years after the Buddha can derive all the benefits from His Teachings.

We must never forget the endless suffering the Buddha endured, in quest of Truth. We must remember that frequently. Each one of us should think individually and separately, that "He suffered solely for me - exclusively for me."

If we know properly the endless suffering He endured, His incomparable compassion, and His sole aim, we should sacrifice the whole of our life for Him. The only thing He was concerned with was making us better. His sole concern was to correct those people afflicted with ignorance. His one concern was to make those who suffer feel happy and contented. He was keen to make the whole world live in peaceful co-existence.

He wanted to see that all nations and all people lived in love and unity, like brothers and sisters of one family, with no thought of such differences as high and low, black and white, educated and uneducated, high caste and low caste, rich and poor, and Eastern and Western.

Let anyone lead a Buddhist way of life for one month, as an experiment. Try directing life in the Buddhist way just for one month. Then, one would realize the value of Buddhism - the power of Buddhism, the greatness of Buddhism. Due to what misfortune is it that people do not make the best use of this divine power, divine therapy, this mantram, which brings instant results right in front of your eyes? What disaster is this? Everybody trembles with craving (**Tanhāya tasitā pajā**). Everybody runs after craving. They keep on increasing their craving. The only thing that people do, as individuals, nations, and countries, is chasing after craving.

The primary aim of Buddhism is the elimination of craving. The only force that makes people suffer, that has shackled beings, that destroys man's liberty, that brings about dissension, that leads to conflicts between countries, between nations, and between individuals, is craving. Craving brings about sorrow. It brings about fear. Those who are devoid of craving are free of sorrow. Is it necessary to say that they are free of sorrow as well?

**Tanhāya jāyeti soko**
**Tanhāya jāyati bhayaṃ**
**Tanhāya vippamutthassa**
**Natthi soko kuto bhayaṃ**

The Buddha is the only religious leader who explored over a long period of time the nature of sorrow and fear, and discovered unerringly the cause for it. This was discovered not for the benefit of man in the next birth, but for his benefit in this world. Therefore, Buddhists should do good and acquire merit according to the Teachings of the Buddha, not so much for the well-being in the next birth, but for one's well-being during this birth itself - for the progress of this world. This should be done in order that the world may become happy, contented and healthy.

The Buddha is the Religious Leader who taught the people how best they can organize their life here by showing the people heaven and hell, like an efficient teacher who gives his students a clear understanding by showing them pictures.

## A Plan for Living

*Buddhism is a plan for living in such a way as to derive highest benefit from life. It is a religion of wisdom where knowledge and intelligence predominate. The Buddha did not preach to win converts but to enlighten listeners.*

***A Western Writer***

*Shortly after the Buddha realized Enlightenment His fame spread far and wide in the country. Kings, guild leaders, ministers, courtiers came to see Him and showed their respects to Him. Hundreds of Sakyan princes became monks under the Buddha. Such guild leaders as Anāthapindika began giving alms on a lavish scale. Four requisites began to come in like a great flood.*

*see page 169*

## CHAPTER 23

# THE SUPREME BUDDHA THE BEING OF GREATEST COMPASSION ON EARTH

No one other than a Buddha could have the kind of great compassion that was present within the Buddha. The Buddha, when He wakes up on the morning, considers the beings on earth with His incomparable sense of great compassion.

"What is the service I can render today as the Buddha? How can I relieve the suffering of a person today? How can I save a person who has got into difficulty? How can I correct a person who has taken the wrong path, and make him virtuous? How can I eradicate the blemishes of a person who is fully overwhelmed by blemishes?" The Buddha would contemplate that way.

He would not discriminate between the beggar who goes about begging in the streets, and the kings who lead lives of ultra luxury in great palaces. He would examine all those with His supremely Enlightened eyes and would go to the person, either on foot or through His magical power, to the person who requires His service most.

The Buddha would preach to the selected individual the kind of Sermon or Discourses that would be quite profitable for him from the point of view of both this birth and the next. That way, the Buddha would render him the best possible service and would come back. The first item in the Buddha's daily agenda was the surveying of the world through His great compassionate vision. There was not a single day when He did not perform such an incomparable, supra-mundane, and an immortal service. The greatest period of the Buddha's life consists of the forty-five years of service as the Supreme Buddha. During that period He surveyed the world with His incomparably compassionate vision on 16, 425 mornings. His service to the world, directing His compassionate vision during that period, cannot be properly assessed. That service was endless, unblemished, not worldly.

Men and women of various levels and various strata who lived in India's human society, came within His vision. All those who came within His vision derived a profit. Among them were kings, queens, princes, princesses, great guild leaders, great ministers, generals, Brahmins who were adept in Three Vedas, Brahmin women, householders, cultivators, and men and women of various religious pursuit.

There were also such beings as murderers, thieves, butchers labourers, prostitutes, rakes, and demons (**Ālavaka**), among them. With no regard whatsoever for one's high state or low state, their learning, their aristocracy, their base castes, their violence, their unruliness, or their viciousness, the Buddha extended His compassion to all of them in equal measure.

Good men came to the Buddha and received His compassion. The Buddha went in search of bad men, on foot mostly, and turned his compassion on them, and converted them into good men. He turned murderers into Arahants. He made devotees out of butchers. He turned miserly men of wealth into philanthropists. He turned prostitutes into female devotees. He made patients healthy. Consider the greatness of the Buddha's compassion.

"A certain youth of good family in **Sāvatthi** who was impressed by the Sermons delivered by the Buddha, became a monk and obtained higher ordination. He came to be known as **Ven. Tissa**. In the course of time, he contracted a serious illness which, it seemed, could not be cured by anything short of death. Tiny pimples, the size of mustard seeds, arose in his body. They grew into the size of greengram- grains, later to the size of peas, next into the size of nelli fruits and wood-apples. At that last stage they burst. The whole body seemed a piece of old wood, eaten by white-ants. In a few days the bones, too, got affected. One could hardly look at him. His robes were soaked with blood and pus. His pupils, too, gave him up - unable to look at him. Without any help he was confined to bed.

In the morning, the Buddha surveys the world from the edge of space to his monastery cell. In the evening He surveys the world from His monastery cell to the edge of space. In the Buddha's net of Enlightened vision the monk Putigatta Tissa was caught. He saw that his body was putrid, his merit to achieve Arahanthood was not at all putrid. The Buddha discovered that the potentiality to achieve Sainthood lay deposited within him, like a gem embedded in the mud.

The Buddha thought: "His companions have given him up just because they could no longer cope. I am a physician capable of curing spiritual blemishes. But, I am also a physician capable of attending to bodily diseases. Therefore, he has no help than mine. I cannot treat his mind without treating his body. As there was no one else to do it, at least I should do it."

Thinking that way, He left His monastery cell and went into the kitchen. As He was used to washing pots and pans when He was King **Kusa**, He took out the pot in which water is boiled. He washed it and placed it on fire with water poured into it. He waited until the water was boiled. He tested the water with His hand and found that the water was boiled. He went to the place where the monk was lying. He took hold of one side of the bed to take him out.

Then the other monks came and said, "Sir, please do not exert yourself. We will take it." They took along the bed to the kitchen with the monk in the bed. The Buddha had a wooden trough brought in. He had the hot water poured into it. He got the monks to remove his robes, wash them with hot water and put them in the sun. The Buddha who loathes blemishes of the mind had no loathing for that kind of person. He poured the hot water with His own hands, washed his body and bathed him.

When the bathing was over the robe was dry. He had it brought and had him wear it. Then He had the monk's bathing robe washed in hot water and had it put in the sun. When the water on his body from the bath was dry, the bathing robe was also dry. The monk wore the bathing robe

*Ascetic Gotama has initiated a move to make families childless, to increase widows, and to destroy clans. Jatila ordained a housand. Sanjaya recruited two-hundred and fifty 'paribrājakas'. Members of privileged families from Magadha are becoming onks. There is no knowing who else will be ordained next." This way, people started to abuse with the Buddha, and to reproach Him.*

*see page 169*

and the outer robe. With the discharge washed and light in mind, he lay down in the bed. *(Saddharmaratnāvali)*

If human history records that a person of the Buddha's stature attended upon an afflicted individual of this type, this is the only such instance.

The Buddha spent the rainy season at **Jetavana** Monastery, and at the end of it, the Buddha got ready to set out on a visit to **Dakkhinagiri** with His two Chief Disciples. **King Kosala**, guild leader **Anātha Pinḍika**, **Visākhā** the great female lay devotee, entreated Him to remain. But, they were not able to stop Him. Guild leader went home and went on contemplating in a depressed mood that he was not able to stop the Buddha.

His servant maid **Punnā**, seeing him that way, asked him, "O Sir, why are you in a sad mood today, unlike on other days?" "Yes, **Punnā**, the Buddha is getting ready to go on a visit. I tried to stop Him but I could not." **Punnā** the maid asked him, "Sir, if I stop the Buddha what will you do for me?" The guild leader said, "I will free you from slavery."

**Punnā** ran fast to the Buddha, fell down at His feet and said, "Sir, do not go! Please stay." The Buddha asked her, "Of what use to you is my not going?" **Punnā** said, "O Sir, I am a slave. I am a servant woman. If you stay, I will be freed from slavery. If I am freed from slavery I can take the Three Refuges, and observe the Five Precepts and the Eight Precepts, and acquire merit." The Buddha showed her sympathy. The Buddha considered it important that she should be freed from slavery and should become an **Arahant** later on. The Buddha accepted her plea, stopped His journey, and abruptly turned back to **Jetavana** Monastery.

Hearing this, the people of **Sāvatthi** were overwhelmed with surprise. **King Kosala**, devotee **Visākhā** and guild leader **Anātha Pindika** praised **punnā** for her impressive deed. The Buddha who refused the invitation of the King of the country, an exceedingly rich man in the country, and a great female devotee in the country, agreed to the request made by the servant maid of that great wealthy man's household. Because of that the servant maid achieved freedom from slavery.

Consider the stature of the Buddha's compassion. The King, the guild leader and **Visākhā** were also pleased with the Buddha's gesture - not at all displeased. Servant maid **Punnā** obtained freedom from slavery at the guild leader's house, got ordained in the nunnery, and became an **Arahant**.

*(Manoratha pūrannī - Sattaka Nipata Vannanā).*

The Buddha's compassion was endless. His dedication to service was boundless - so much so that if He met a person who would realize Truth by seeing His heart, He would even take out His heart with His magical power, and will show it to that person. (**Yadi Mahārāja, koci Bhagavato hadayaṃ disvā bujjhaya, tassapi Bhagavā ṭogena hadayaṃ dasseyya.**) *(Milinda Panho).*

These will show the quality of great compassion the Buddha possessed.

> "**Cunda**, I have done to you all that a compassionate religious teacher should do to his disciples. **Cunda**, here are feets of trees (**rukkhamūlāni**). Here are empty houses (**suññāgāra**). **Cunda**, meditate. Do not delay. Do not repent later. This is my advice to

you." *(Majjhima Nikaya - Sallekha Sutta).*

**Angulimāla** killed thousands and cut off fingers of his victims. The fingers that were severed became putrid. He was keen to complete the thousand fingers, and thought, "I will cut off the fingers even of my mother." On that day, in reality, his mother set out into the great forest to see her son.
When the Buddha surveyed the world, He saw **Angulimāla**. The Buddha saw that if He did not visit him that day, he will kill his mother and commit a heinous crime for which there is no reprieve. In compassion for him, He went there on foot and subdued him, ordained him and made him an **Arahant**. The Buddha did not totally dismiss him as a murderer. But He went to him and brought out the good that was concealed within him, and made him an eternally good person. This could be achieved because of the power of the Buddha's great compassion.

A cultivator prepared a field for sowing in a place near the city of **Sāvatthi**. During the previous night a band of robbers had broken into a rich man's house in the city of **Sāvatthi**, and had run away with valuable jewellery and a bundle of thousand gold coins. They entered that cultivator's field to share the booty. They got frightened suddenly and ran away, taking the other stolen goods, but leaving the bag of gold coins behind.

In the morning the Buddha surveyed the world and, seeing that this poor cultivator will get into a difficulty, in compassion for him, the Buddha visited that field with **Ven. Ānanda**. The cultivator saw the Buddha, worshipped Him, and continued his work of preparing the field.

The Buddha saw the bag of thousand gold pieces, which the cultivator had not seen so far, showed it to **Ven. Ānanda** with His hand, and asked, "**Ānanda**, did you see that serpent?" "Yes Sir, I saw," **Ven. Ānanda** replied. The cultivator overheard this conversation. After the Buddha and **Ven. Ānanda** had gone away, the cultivator thought that he will kill the serpent shown to **Ānanda** by the Buddha.

When he went to that spot with a cudgel, he saw not a serpent, but a bag of gold coins. He took it, put it on the ridge and covered it with some earth. The cultivator continued his work. The whole city was astir with the news of the theft that had happened during the previous night. Many people were probing this theft. One of these persons found the gold coins on the field-ridge. They took hold of the cultivator and took him to the King. The King heard what had happened and ordered that he be tortured and killed.

When the King's men took him along, torturing him, the cultivator started crying, saying, "**Ānanda,** did you see the serpent? " "Yes Sir, I saw." The King's men asked him why he was saying this. When the cultivator narrated the incident the King's men took him back to the King and told him what had happened. The King took the cultivator to the Buddha and informed Him the whole story.

The Buddha said that He went to the field where the cultivator was working, seeing the bag of gold coins, He described that as a serpent, and that He did all this because of His compassion for the cultivator. The Buddha also said that had He not gone there with Ven. **Ānanda**, the King would have ordered him to be killed, instead of bringing him to the Buddha. The Buddha established his innocence. The cultivator, whose innocence was proven by

*The Buddha's step-mother Pajāpati Gotami, who raised Prince Siddhārtha from childhood on, once prepared a valuable clothe woven by herself, spinning the thread herself. She presented it to the Buddha, saying, "It is for the Buddha's exclusive use." The Buddha did not accept and told Pajāpati Gotami: "Gotami, give this to the Sangha (the Brotherhood of Bhikkhus). When i is given to the Sangha, it is equivalent to have been given to me. It is as if it was given to the Sangha, too."* *see page 17*

the Buddha's evidence, was freed by the King. (Saddhama ratanāvalī)

The only person who showed compassion to **Paṭacārā** was the Buddha. Demented by the sudden deaths of her husband, her two children, her mother, her father and her bnrother, **Patācārā** ran along the road. When the Buddha was preaching to the four-fold assembly she ran before the Buddha, having lost the clothes she was wearing.

The Buddha showed her compassion. Those who were there, totally unaware of her past and the extremely moving situation she was in, tried to drive her away. The Buddha prevented it. Stopping them, the Buddha told her, "Younger sister, come back to your senses."

Due to those kind words she regained her normal senses. The Buddha was the only person who knew that she was the daughter of a guild leader's family who lived in royal luxury, that she eloped with a servant boy in her household, that she earned her living by pounding rice, that she had suffered vastly, and that she had become demented by the deaths of six persons, namely, her husband, her two children, her parents, and her brother. Therefore, the Buddha focussed His incomparable compassion on her and made her an Arahant.

If you delve into the history of beggar women who walk about city streets, carrying children and taking along some children, how many hundreds of **Patācārās** can one see? Who else but the Buddha would have shown compassion, which is a noble human quality, to one of these woman?

One morning, when the Buddha was surveying the world a Brahmin, holding false views, came into His vision. He was cultivating a field near a river. The Buddha looked on at what the Brahmin was doing. The Brahmin continued to work, taking no notice of the Buddha. The Buddha asked him, "O Brahmin, what are you doing?" The Brahmin said, "Ascetic Gotama, I am cultivating a field. " With that, the Buddha turned back and came to the monastery.

On the second day, too, the Buddha went to the Brahmin's field and asked him, "Brahmin, what are you doing?" The Brahmin said, "Ascetic Gotama, I am sowing seeds." With that, the Buddha came back.

On the day the Brahmin was weeding the field, the Buddha went there and asked, "Brahmin, what are you doing?" "Ascetic Gotama, I am weeding my field," the Brahmin said. With that reply, the Buddha went back to the monastery.

Next, when the Brahmin was looking after his field the Buddha went to him and asked, "Brahmin, what are you doing?" "Ascetic Gotama, I am protecting my field."

The Brahmin thought, "This ascetic has asked me what I was doing when I was ploughing, sowing, weeding and protecting the field. Therefore, when my grains are harvested, I will give Him a portion of it."

The Brahmin addressed the Buddha, "Ascetic Gotama, when the grain is harvested, I will not consume the yield without giving you a portion. From now on, you are my friend." The Buddha listened to him and went back.

Eventually, the grain ripened. But in the night before the day he planned to harvest his field, a heavy rain fell, and the whole field was inundated by the flood and was destroyed. The Brahmin went there and saw the destruction. He thought, "From the day I started cultivation work on this field, the Buddha came to see the field. I promised to give Him half of the yield." Unable to keep the promise he went home and slept, depressed.

The Buddha went to his house directly that day, without going to his field, and enquired, "Where is the Brahmin?" People at his house said that the Brahmin was sleeping, his mind disturbed at the destruction of the field. The Buddha called the Brahmin to Him, and asked him why he was unhappy. The Buddha said that the cause for sorrow was craving (**Tanhāya jāyati soko**). The Buddha also said that the person who has no craving has no sorrow or no fear (**Tanhāya vippamuttassa natthi soko kuto bhayaṃ**). After listening to the Buddha the Brahmin attained Stream-winner status (**Sotāpatti Phala**).

If a person is fortunate enough to come within the Buddha's compassion the Buddha will seek him out, wherever he is. He will visit him not once, but several times - either with His disciples or all alone. **That way, the Buddha always helped them to achieve good. When He focussed His compassion on someone He never considered whether the place was land, water, a mountain peak, a difficult mountain pass, a field, or a swamp. He never thought of His comfort.**

Once, the Buddha traveled a distance of twelve leagues to **Alavi** City with a retinue of five-hundred monks just to help a poor man. The people of that city received the Buddha and the monks with great respect, and prepared the mid-day meal for Him.

A poor man from that village was extremely keen to listen to a Sermon by the Buddha, but, as one of his oxen had gone astray, he had to go in search of that. After a long while he found the ox. Tethering the ox to a tree in his garden, he set out to see the Buddha, thinking that it was all right, even if it was a little late now.

At the end of the meal, the Buddha awaited the arrival of that poor man, without starting His Discourse. The Buddha saw that poor man who came there hungry. He asked one of those persons who organized the alms-giving to give some food to that poor man, if there was any food left. He gave the poor man some food. When the poor man came to the Buddha, after his meal, the Buddha started His Discourse.

Just as many others who listened to Him the poor man, too, achieved the Fruit of Stream-winner (**Sotāpatti Phala**). The disciples who witnessed this gesture on the part of the Buddha were quite surprised. Seeing that they were surprised the Buddha said that it was not a matter for surprise. He came all the way to listen to a sermon.

There is no use preaching to a hungry man without first quelling his hunger. He explained the reason for His action. The greatness of the Buddha's compassion can be gauged from this. There were two monks named **Mahā Panthaka** and **Cūlla Panthaka** who had become monks under the Buddha. Of these two, **Ven. Cūlla Panthaka** was unable to memorize a small stanza for four months due to the result of a previous kamma.

When he memorized the first line he would go to the second. When he

*'en. Channa was found guilty of a wrong doing. But he was not willing to accept that as wrong-doing. The Buddha was informed f this. The Buddha assembled the monks and held and inquiry. The Buddha said that punishment should be imposed on Ven. Channa.*

*see page 172*

memorized the second line he would forget the first. When he went to the third line he would forget the second line. When he went to the fourth line he would forget the third line. His older brother **Mahā Panthaka** became impatient about this. "If you cannot memorize four lines in four months how much time would you take to learn the whole of the Buddha's Word in the **Tipitaka**, where you have hundreds of thousands of things to memorize? Therefor, give up robes." But, **Cūlla Panthaka** liked being a monk. Therefore, he was reluctant to go.

That day, the great physician **Jīvaka** met Ven. **Mahā Panthaka** and asked him how many monks were there with the Buddha. He said there were five-hundred. He invited all the five-hundred monks to his residence for meals. **Ven. Mahā Panthaka** said, "Devotee, **Cūlla Panthaka**'s intellect is low. Therefor, he is not fit to be a monk. Because of that I will invite all but **Cūlla Panthaka**. **Cūlla Panthaka** overheard this. He told himself, "My brother is deeply disgusted with me. " He decided to give up robes early next morning.

The Buddha surveyed the world and saw this incident. He went to **Cūlla Panthaka**'s monastery cell and walked up and down in front of the gate which **Cūlla Panthaka** had to go through, to give up robes. The Buddha asked him what the matter was, and told him in kind words to say on. The Buddha stroked **Cūlla Panthaka**'s head with His hand which was as soft as His words, and took him along. "The Buddha came. He put His hand on my head. Took me by the hand and conducted me into the monastery."

**Bhagavā tatha āgañci**
**Sīsaṃ mayahaṃ parāmasī**
**Bāhāya maṃ gahethvāna**
**Sanghārāmaṃ pavesayī**

(*Apadāna pāli*).

This Stanza is a statement made by **Ven. Cūlla Panthaka**. The Buddha showed the kind of compassion an affectionate father will show a son. He treated an innocent novice monk that way. The elder brother, who is **Ven. Mahā Panthaka**, drove out the younger brother **Cūlla Panthaka** because he was unable to memorize a stanza.

The Buddha showed him kindness and compassion. He took him along and gave him a piece of clean white cloth. The Buddha asked him to look in the direction of the rising sun, and to rub the piece of cloth, repeating, '**rajo haranaṃ**', '**rajo haranaṃ**'.

After instructing him that way, the Buddha went to **Jīvaka**'s residence for meals. Before long, the Buddha had **Ven. Cūlla Panthaka** to the alms-giving as an **Arahant**, though he was only a novice monk a little earlier. Consider the great compassion of the Supreme Buddha.

A friendship started between **King Bimbisāra** of **Rajagaha** and **King Pukkusāti** of **Taxila**. This friendship was brought about by traders of the two countries. While sending his friend various gifts, **King Bimbisāra** sent his friend **King Pukkusāti** a letter written on a sheet of gold in which he said, "In this country we have Three Jewels, named 'Buddha', 'Dhamma' and 'Sangha'."

The moment he heard this, **King Pukkusāti** too gave up all his royal luxury like Prince **Siddhārtha**, and set out to see the Buddha. He came away wearing a yellow robe, while his subjects were weeping and wailing.

As a long distance journey cannot be done all alone he followed a caravan of trading carts. In a few days, travelling a distance of 192 yojanas, he came to the city of **Rajagaha**. He asked where the Buddha was. People said that he has travelled 45 yojanas, passing the city of **Sāvatthi** where the Buddha was residing. As it was not possible to go back the same night, he tried to find out whether there was a place where monks could take shelter in the night. Hearing that there was the potter's shed, he took the potter's permission and was resting there.

The Buddha at that time was looking for a person on whom He could focus His compassion that day. He noted that King **Pukkusāti** had given up royal luxury just as He has done, and that he was coming to see Him. He also saw that the next morning he will die by an accident.

The Buddha, disguised as an ascetic wandering forth, left **Sāvatthi** and came to the city of **Rajagaha**. He came to the potter's shed where Pukkusāti was resting and asked the potter whether he could rest for the night there. The potter said the ascetic who came earlier was resting and that if he liked, he too may rest there.

The Buddha went to the potter's shed and approached the ascetic who was there, and said, "If you like, I too can rest here for the night." When he said so, the Buddha sat on the floor filled with dirt and dust.On this dirty floor are now seated two strange ascetics who had given up royal luxury. One was **Sākya Muni Siddhārtha Gotama**. The other was **King Pukkusāti** who had become a monk, giving up a kingdom more than 100 yojanas in extent, and royal luxuries. Both these were tired as they had both walked a long distance. They spoke thus, and entered into a state of deep concentration.

The Buddha;

"Who are you? From where have you come?"

Pukkusāti:

"I am **King Pukkusāti**, King of **Taxila**."

The Buddha:

"Under whom have you become a monk? Why have you come here?"

**Pukkasāti**:

"My friend **King Bimbisāra** wrote to me on a sheet of gold that the Three Gems - Buddha, Dhamma and Sangha are found in the city of **Rajagaha**. The moment I heard it, I gave up my kingdom, bought yellow robes from a shop, wore them, and came in search of the noble Buddha. I heard here that He resides at **Sāvatthi**. I rested here because it is late in the night. I am going to see Him tomorrow morning."

**The Buddha**:

"Have you never seen the Buddha?"

**Pukkusāti**:

"No."

**The Buddha**:

"Can you recognize Him, if you saw Him?"

**Pukkusāti**:

"No."

That was the only conversation. Both became silent. In the early hours of the morning the Buddha preached the Doctrine to ascetic **Pukkusāti**. Hearing the Sermon, **Pukkusāti** realized that the ascetic who was with him last night was the Buddha. Asking the Buddha to pardon him for calling him **Āyusmat** (Friend), ascetic **Pakkusāti** requested to be ordained, and to be given higher

*A Brahmin who was exceedingly happy after listening to the Buddha behaves this way. "Then Brahmin Brahmāyu got up from his seat. adjusted his shawl properly. He worshipped the Buddha, placing his face on the feet of the Buddha. He kisses the Buddha feet with his lips. He strokes the Buddha's feet with his hands. He spoke thus to the Buddha: 'Sir, I am Brahmin Brahmāyu. Thu he introduces himself by his name.*

*see page 9*

ordination.

The Buddha asked him to find robes and a bowl. Ascetic **Pakkusāti** left the potter's shed and went in search of a rag in a garbage heap. At that time the Buddha reached **Jetavana** Monastery. A young cow that was roused butted **Pakkusāti** with both horns while he was looking for a rag in the garbage heap. He died there instantly. The ascetic who had already attained the Non-returner status (**Anāgāmi**) was born in **Aviha** Brahma World where he attained Arahanthood. **King Bimbisāra** heard this, and he cremated the body with great solemnity. He built a cetiya, enshrining his relics. This story, too, enables us to realize the quality of the Buddha's compassion.

## Buddhist Idea of Sin

*Its idea of sin differs somewhat from the Christian idea. Sin to the Buddhist is mere ignorance or stupidity. The wicked man is an ignorant man. He doesn't need punishment and condemnation so much as he needs instruction. He is not regarded as 'violating God's commands' or as one who must beg for divine mercy and forgiveness. Rather it is necessary for the sinner's friends to make him reason in the human way. The Buddhist does not believe the sinner can escape the consequences in prayerful attempts to bargain with God.*

***John Walters, "Mind unshaken"***

CHAPTER 24

## BUDDHA THE GREATEST SOCIAL REFORMER

India is like a museum that preserves intact such phenomena as traditional customs and manners, thoughts and philosophies, cults, creeds, beliefs and religions, and caste systems, over a long period of time. Prince **Siddhārtha** appeared in such a land at such a time. During that day almost the totality of Indian society was built on Brahmanic thinking.

There was no one to examine what was right or wrong in that system. There was no one brave enough, powerful enough, or wise enough to point out the right or wrong of those Brahmanic systems. All kings received counsel from Brahmans. In consequence, from the king down, every body in society respected Brahmanic beliefs. A universal hero had to appear to cleanse the Indian society of its fallacies, superstitions and corruption. He had also to be a member of a royal family. Going counter to those fallacies that had got entrenched in society, that had taken deep root in society, was a hazardous task. This is because when a powerful society becomes antagonistic it can weaken or cripple any strong person.

The Supreme Buddha, who was born in a royal family, made a very high sacrifice and had discarded selfishness fully, accepted this great challenge serenely and non-violently. He presented himself not as a dictator or a totalitarian or a politician, but as a great Ascetic who was the symbol of compassion and loving-kindness. But, just as all the social reformers of history, the Buddha too faced both bouquets and brickbats. On the one hand, millions rallied round Him and began to venerate Him; and on the other, some even made attempts on His life. Charges of abusing women and murder were levelled against Him. But He was protected by His exemplary life and His noble thoughts and aspirations.

The Buddha initially started attacking Brahmins who were in the highest rungs of contemporary society. He started attacking their rites and rituals and their system. He preached against the animal sacrifices of the day, showing that taking life for whatever reason was a serious sin. He liberated women who did not have even human freedom. "What is wrong in being a female, if that person is wise?" the Buddha asked.

Once, when **King Kosala** was in conversation with the Buddha a royal courier came and whispered in the king's ear. The secret he communicated was that Queen **Mallikā** had given birth to a daughter. The king became distressed at this news. Seeing that the king was depressed, the Buddha said to him,

> "O Great King, some women are great, efficient and wise. Therefore, the daughter born to you by Queen **Mallika** should be very well looked after. **The woman who is wise,**

*The Buddha surveyed the world and saw this incident. He went to Cūlla Panthaka's monastery cell and walked up and down in front of the gate which Cūlla Panthaka had to go through, to give up robes. The Buddha asked him what the matter was, and showed him kindness and compassion. He took him along and gave him a piece of clean, white cloth. The Buddha asked him to look in the direction of the rising sun, and to rub the piece of cloth, repeating, 'rajo haranaṃ', 'rajo haranaṃ'.* *see page 156*

**virtuous, who treats her parents-in-law as deities, and is chaste, is a noble person. The son of such a woman may even rule a country."**

It was then that the king's displeasure disappeared.

The Buddha said that the monopoly the Brahmins had on the development of the intellect, on teaching, on learning, on practising various specialities, and on counselling, should be put an end to, and that these should be made freely available, like air, water and sunlight.

The first Indian, the first public speaker, and the first social reformer to agitate against entrenched Brahmanic views, was the Buddha. The more He spoke against entrenched Brahmanic views those wise Brahmins who respected truth began to venerate Him.

Some became monks under Him. Even His two chief disciples were the two Brahmanic youths **Sāriputta** and **Moggallāna**. Some Brahmins rose against the Buddha. They abused Him as "the Shaveling One" (**mundake**) and the outcaste (**vasalo**).

The Buddha did not recognize those social divisions which had existed even before He was born. The Buddha asserted fearlessly that the measure of assessing the value or the nobility of a human being was not His caste, clan or birth, but his words and deeds.

The Buddha did not approve of the caste system which was like a wall that separated man from man.

One day, the Buddha had a dialogue with **Ven. Vāseṭṭha** who was a Buddhist monk from a Brahmanic family.

**The Buddha**:

"**Vaseṭṭha,** you became a Buddhist monk, coming from a Brahmanic family."

**Vaseṭṭha:**

"Yes, Sir. They abuse me and insult me when they meet me."

**The Buddha**:

"How do they abuse you, insult you?"

**Vāseṭṭha**:

"Only Brahmins are great - only they are noble - only they are pure - only the Brahmins are born from **Mahā Brahma**'s mouth. All the others, except Brahmins, are impure - all the others are low. They abuse me and tell me that I have given up the noble Brahmanic clan, and I have gone to associate with a group of shaven monks who are born from the foot of **Mahā Brahma**."

"People in India describe one caste as Brahmin. They say that however base, violent, vile and evil may be the things they do, those acts are not a blemish to their nobility. But, according to the real meaning of the word Brahmin, and in terms of the noble ethics and virtuous behaviour of the Brahmins of old, many of the contemporary Brahmins are not Brahmins." The Buddha analyzed the caste concept this way:

"One does not become a Brahmin from the turban round one's head. Nor does one become a Brahmin by one's birth, or by one's clan. If someone has Truth and virtuous behaviour within one, such a person is pure. He is a real Brahmin."

"If one does not do evil, either by one's mind or by one's words or by one's body, such a person whose three doors of perception are pure, is a Brahmin."

"If one is not given to bad ways, if a person endures abuse, attacks and tortures patiently, and if that person has made patience his power and his army, I call such a man a Brahmin."

"The person who lives like a friend among enemies, like a peaceful individual among violent ones, and like a desireless individual among the greedy, I call such a person a Brahmin."

The Buddha never described as "**vasalas**" those in Indian society who had been discriminated against, characterizing them as outcastes, base, **vasala** and **candāla**. He never accepted that categorization. He admitted them even to the order of monks.
He characterized the following as '**vasalas**'(outcastes)."

"If people tend to get angry quite often, if they harbour enmity, if they are likely to forget good done to them, if they hold harmful views, if they cover up their faults deliberately, such persons should be known as '**vasalas**'(outcastes)."

"If a person were to take a loan, and when the creditor asks him to pay it back, avoids paying back, such a person is a '**vasala**'."

"If a person does not look after one's parents although he can afford to, such a person is a '**vasala**'."

"If a person, visiting others' homes, eats there well, but does not treat them when they come to his house, such a person is a '**vasala**'.

That is the way in which the Buddha desccribed the '**Vasalas**' in society. The Buddha boldly stated that there were great Brahmins in the past, they possessed high Brahmanic qualities, that such Brahmanic qualities are not found in contemporary Brahmins.

We mentioned earlier that in ancient Indian society women had not been given any freedom. It was the Brahmins who denied women their freedom. Brahmins said that the women must obey and be protected by their parents at home, by their husbands after marriage, and by their sons whey they grew old. They limited her freedom to the four walls of the house. At such a time, the Buddha ordained them and gave offices to outstanding nuns. He allowed them to move freely, within the rules of the Code of Discipline.

Brief biographies of many ancient Indian women are found in **Theri Gāthās** (Psalms of the Nuns). When we read them these biographies reveal the paeans of joy uttered by nuns who, by being ordained, received freedom, escaping from pounding rice, from hewing fire-wood, from fetching water, from cooking, from slavery, from masters, from mistresses, from husbands, from mothers-in-law, from fathers-in-law, from co-husband, and from co-wives. The best evidence of the freedom achieved by some Indian women because of the Buddha, is this collection of paeans by the nuns (**Theri Gāthās**).

The Supreme Buddha was the first hero to shatter the shackles of conservative Brahmanic thought of ancient India, that kept women in bondage. The Buddha reformed a good part of the North Indian society through His Teachings of Three Refuges, and the Five precepts. The

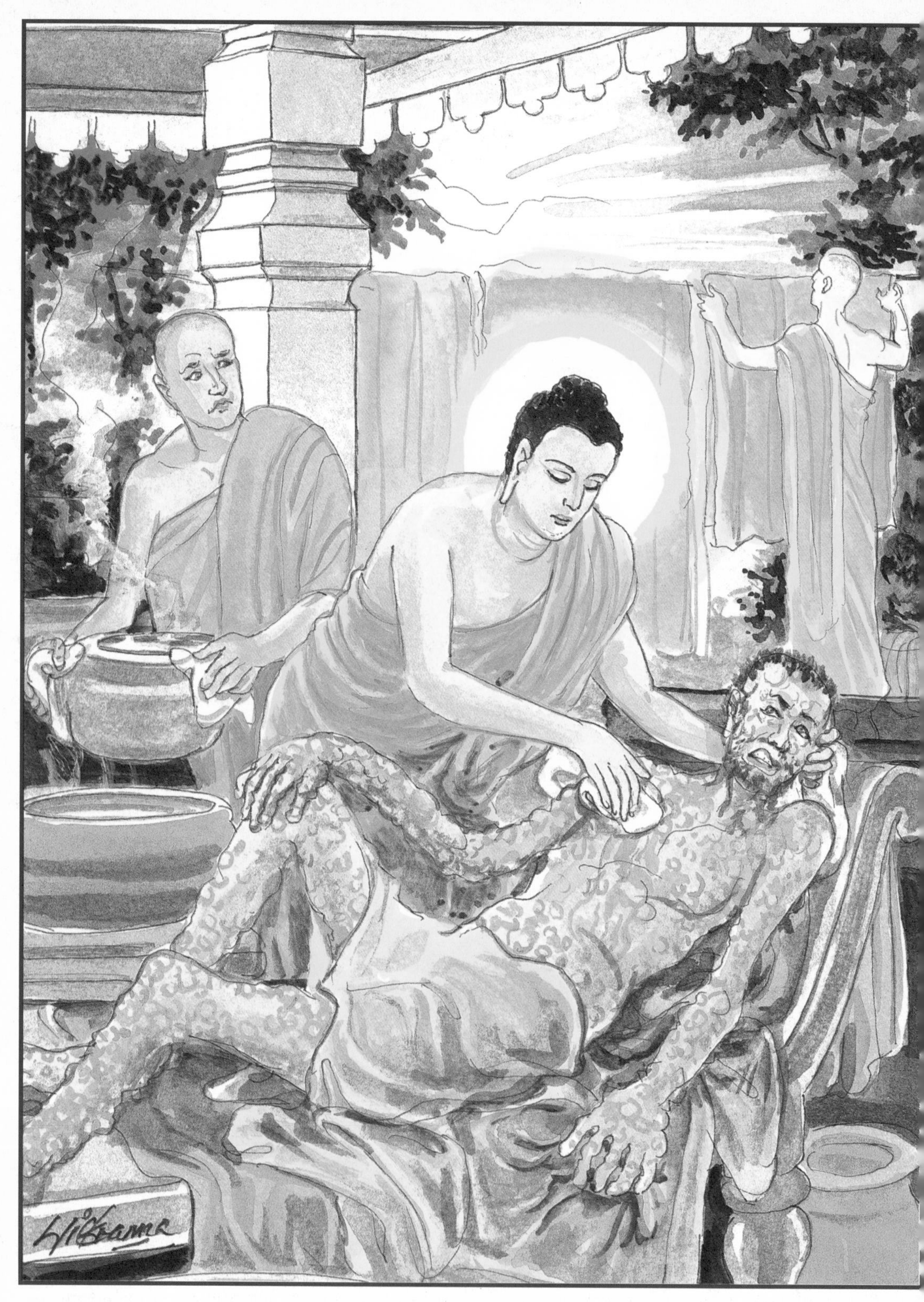

*The Buddha thought: "His companions have given him up just because they could no longer cope. I am a physician capable of curing spiritual blemishes. But, I am also a physician capable of attending to bodily diseases. Therefore, he has no help than mine. I cannot treat his mind without treating his body. As there was no one else to do it, at least I should do it."* *see page 148*

principle of the Five Precepts consists of making people promise to refrain from five wrong deeds that are likely to happen quite often in everyday life.

Those people who became Buddhists at that time, taking refuge in the Triple Gem, and observing the Five Precepts, kept their five promises to the letter. There is no other society that rose to the highest rung of civilized life than the society that observed the Five Precepts so scrupulously. This noble society created by the Buddha is a model for the whole world.

In truth, the Buddha did not expect to ordain the whole world, or all the citizens of a country, or to make all of them realize **Nibbāna**. His intention was to build a righteous society - righteous world - founded on the principle of Five Precepts. During the Buddha's day, and even for a long time after that, in many countries in Asia, there were many individuals who scrupulously observed the Five Precepts.

What we find in some countries today is obtaining Five Precepts and not observing Five Precepts. Some Buddhists have got used to the idea of merely repeating verbally some principles that should be implemented to the letter. Taking Five Precepts has become a mere custom. It is a grave fault to promise to do something that one will not at all do. The only result, that we get today is the daily breaking of five religious promiss.

There is a deep chasm - a wide gap - between the great noble society established by the Buddha and the social system of our day. As long as this wide gap exists people could not be considered to be followers of the Buddha.

The Supreme Buddha is the greatest social reformer of mankind over and above all others, due to the synthesis of a series of virtuous qualities. He was an exemplary leader. When He pointed out any shortcoming in others, He ensured that He is devoid of that shortcoming. He disregarded both bouquets and brickbats from society. He did not yearn for glory, praise or profit, even in His dreams. He had compassion foremost in His mind. He eschewed selfishness fully and totally. And, above all, He was the symbol of compassion and loving-kindness.

## Challenge to other religions

*It is Buddhism as we find it actually recorded, not a hypothetical primitive system, which still forms a challenge to other religions.*

***Bishop Gore, "Buddha and the Christ"***

*No political philosopher has uttered, to-date, so noble, so wide-ranging in implication, so great, so democratic, and so socialist a slogan as "may all beings be free of suffering", "may all beings be healthy", and "may all beings be happy". He wished the well-being of all beings with the expression "may all beings be happy" "sabbe sattā bhavantu sukhitattā".* *see page 168*

*The Buddha said: “O Monks, I just cannot see with my wisdom any other sound than that of a woman which attracts the man’s mind so tenaciously.” (Nāhaṃ Bhikkhave aññaṃ ekasaddampi samanu passāmi yaṃ evaṃ purisassa cittaṃ pariyādāya titthati vathayidaṃ Bhikkhāve itthisaddaṃ. Itthi saddaṃ Bhikkhave purisassa cittaṃ pariyādāya tutthati”)* *see page 126*

CHAPTER 25

## THE SUPREME BUDDHA
## PIONEER IN SOCIALISM AND DEMOCRACY

Addressing the first sixty Arahants (Holy Ones), the Supreme Buddha spoke thus, for the well- being of the world

> "O, Monks, travel along, from village to village, from market town to market town, from city to city, for the good of the many, for the well-being of the many, and in compassion for the world - for the good and well-being not only of men but of gods as well. Two of you must not travel along one road. Declare the Doctrine which is good in the beginning, good in the middle, and good at the end. I, too, will set out for the market town of **Senāni** in **Uruvela** to preach the Doctrine.

No formula as socialist and as democratic as the above three expressions - namely, "for the good of the many" (**bahujana hitāya**), "for the well being of the many" (**bahujana sukhāya**), and "in compassion for the world" (**lokānukampāya**) - has escaped the lips of any other person in human history.

In rendering service the Buddha never divided mankind through such usages as 'for the good of the Easterners", "for the good of the Westerners", "for the good of the poor", "for the good of the wealthy", "for the good of the underprivileged castes", "for the good of the **Āryans"**, or "for the good of the non-**Āryans"**. In such expressions as "for the good of the many", "for the well-being of the majority", "for the good of all", and "in compassion for the whole world", what is found embodied is a total commonality. His incomparably great compassion was the same for all.

No political philosopher has uttered, to-date, so noble, so wide-ranging in implication, so great, so democratic, and so socialist a slogan as **"may all beings be free of suffering", "may all beings be healthy",** and **"may all beings be happy".** He wished the well-being of all beings with the expression **"may all beings be happy"** "**sabbe sattā bhavantu sukhitattā**". Most politicians and political philosophers wished only economic well-being of the people. But the Supreme Buddha wished not only the economic well-being of all beings, but also the mental, physical well-being, and their well-being both here and hereafter. He also pointed out how these could be obtained through righteousness and non-violence.

The institution called the "Bhikkhu Brotherhood" (**Bhikkhu Sāsana**) which the Buddha constituted through His supreme wisdom, is a universal democratic institution. The pioneer in human history to launch such a methodical and well-organized institution was the Buddha . All members of that institution are identified as the "**Sangha**" (the Brotherhood). The males are described as "**Bhikkhus**" (monks), and the females as "**Bhikkhunīs**" (nuns). Any one from any country, from any nationality, from any caste can gain entry into this institution.

Shortly after the Buddha realized Enlightenment His fame spread far and wide in the country. Kings, guild leaders, ministers, courtiers came to see Him and showed their respects to Him. Hundreds of Sakyan princes became monks under the Buddha.

Such guild leaders as **Anātha Pindika** began giving alms on a lavish scale. Four requisites began to come in like a great flood. Some people who saw these extensive offerings wanted to become monks on that account. The chief physician of that day Physician **Jīvaka** was under obligation to attend to the king, those in the harem, and to the monks. In consequence, other ordinary people could not get medical attention from him. Some patients became monks, got medical attention, and left robes when they were cured.

Some parents ordained their five-, six-year old sons so that they could eat and drink freely and lavishly. Hundreds of such children started crying in the night when they became hungry. When the Buddha heard them cry He made enquiries and prohibited the ordaining of little children. Notorious thieves and criminals became monks to save their lives. This way, the number of people getting ordained began to increase by thousands. A public concern occurred lest the number of lay people would decline when the ranks of monks began to burgeon.

"Ascetic Gotama has initiated a move to make families childless, to increase widows, and to destroy clans. **Jatilas** ordained a thousand. **Sañjaya** recruited two-hundred and fifty "**paribrājakas**". Members of privileged families from **Magadha** are becoming monks. There is no knowing who else will be ordained next." This way, people started to accuse the Buddha, and to reproach Him.

*(Mahāvagga Pāli - Sāriputta Moggallāna Pabbajjā).*

As a result of a number of such causes it became necessary to impose conditions on those to be ordained. When emphatic defects were found in the persons who were ordained, those early monks became a group of popular representatives. They became the focal point of popular attention. Their costumes were different in colour. The style of wearing the robe was unprecedented. It was quite a change from how the lay people wore their clothes. Yellow is a colour that repels flies and mosquitoes. It befitted the climate. The colour is attractive to the eye and communicates a sense of serenity.

With heads is shaven, they became a group apart from lay people. Shaving takes away the sense of pride, and gives them an appearance of humility. They became a tranquil, harmless, non-violent community. All members of this community had to have a simple way of life. They should be attuned to the idea of service to others. They should have a sense of community.

Such a monk is fully and completely a member of a common group. Everything he has belongs to the whole Sangha community. The temple He resides in, does not belong to him personally. It belongs to the Brotherhood (the **Sangha**).

***Those who possess wealth should not think of hoarding, adding more and more to one's wealth. Instead, they must give to those who do not have. They must exert for the well-being of others. They must think of others. They must work for others.***

***see page 38***

Monks have no attachments, bondages and links. He has no dependents. There are no persons awaiting his return. There are no people who will be hungry if he did not get back. There is no one who will cry for him. He does not belong to anyone. Therefore, "A monk never laments" ("**Nahi socati Bhikkhu Kadāci**" *(Saṁyutta Nikāya).*

He has dedicated his whole to the institution called the Dispensation (**Sāsana**). He has gifted his life to it. If there is a group of people who have dedicated their lives for a noble cause that group is the Bhikkhu community. "**Sangha**" means "Group", "Community"."**Sānghika**"means belonging to the Group - the Community. The founder of this community - the Buddha Himself - honoured this community.

The Buddha's step-mother **Pajāpati Gotamī,** who raised Prince **Siddhārtha** from childhood on, once prepared a valuable clothe, woven by herself, spinning the thread herself. She presented it to the Buddha, saying, "It is for the Buddha's exclusive use." The Buddha did not accept and told **Pajāpati Gotamī**:

"**Gotamī**, gived this to the **Sangha** (the Brotherhood of Bhikkhus). When it is given to the **Sangha**, it is equivalent to have been given to me. It is, as if, it was given to the **Sangha**, too." "**Sanghe Gotamī dehi. Sanghe dinne ahaṃ ceva pūjito bhavissāmi sanghoca**." So saying, He offered it to the **Sangha**.

In the same way, the Buddha extolled the virtues of the **Sangha**. Recounting the virtues of the **Sangha**, the Buddha Himself said:

"The Sangha Brotherhood has excellent principles **(supaṭipanno).** Their attributes are straight **(ujupaṭipanno).** They are bent towards **Nibbāna (ñāyapaṭipanno).** They have pleasant words **(sāmicipaṭipanno).** They are worthy of honour, worshipping and veneration **(āhuneyyo, pāhuneyyo, dakkhineyyo, añjalikaraniyo).** They are like a fertile field for the people to sow seeds of merit **(anuttaraṃ puññakkhettaṃ lokassa)**.

In India, at that time, there was no other group of ascetics or monks that was organized with that kind of strict discipline as the Bhikkhus - the disciples of the Buddha. The ways of such other recluses as **ājīvakas, jaṭilas, acelakas, paribbājakas** of the Buddha's day, and the attitude those others adopted towards the Buddhist monks can be observed from their own descriptions.

One day, **Ven. Ānanda** visited a place called **Devakata Sobbha** with a group of monks. At that time, an ascetic named **Sandaka**, who resided there, and his large group of followers sat there laughing aloud, guffawing, indulging in all kinds of unseemly talks. Ascetic **Sandaka** saw Ven. **Ānanda** in the distance. He quietened his followers, saying,

"Don't shout; don't shout; don't guffaw. There is Ven. **Ānanda** - a disciple of Ascetic **Gautama.**He is coming this way. They esteem silence, quietness, serenity, discipline. Therefore, all of you must remain silent - absolutely silent. Remain calm and quiet."

At this, the whole group of ascetics became silent and still. The **Sangha** Order

(Bhikkhu Brotherhood) has been able to reach the highest rung from the point of view discipline obtained through codes of conduct. All postures - eating, drinking, coming and going, sitting and standing - all these have to be done strictly in terms of the code of conduct.

When building a society, well organized and fit for people to dedicate their lives to, codes of conduct are needed embodying the rules of discipline which the members of this Brotherhood should adhere to, setting down all such details and codifying the punishments for the breach of rules. The great Theras who held religious councils, compiled Buddhist codes of law in such works as **Mahā Vagga** and **Cūlla Vagga**. Monks held these codes of conduct in the highest esteem.

The index to that esteem is the statement to the effect that "Discipline is the life-span of the Dispensation (**Vinayo nāma sāsanassa āyu**). Those who are adept at law are described as lawyers. In the same way, monks adept in rules of **Vinaya** (Discipline) are described as **Vinayadhara** (Experts in Laws of Discipline).

All disciplinary action relating to monks are done through the code described as the "four prior notices" (**ñatti catuttha**). **Ñatti** implies the due prior notice that has been given fully and comprehensively about the intended disciplinary action. It is very much similar to the presentation of the "Draft Ordinance" or "Draft Bill" to a modern parliament. Next, the **Kamma Vākya** (the Charge) should be read out three times.

In the **Sangha** parliament described as "**Sangha Sabhā**" (the Assembly of Monks) only those above twenty have the right to vote at a hearing of a disciplinary action on a monk. In other words, only monks who have acquired higher ordination possess the right to vote. Of those monks who have been found guilty on some count, have no right to vote.

Just as the postal vote can be cast today, at these disciplinary actions a monk could vote by proxy. A monk who cannot attend can send his vote through a monk who attends. When a monk reaches the age of twenty, and is being given the right to vote, that is, when he is given the higher ordination, the Assembly of Monks questions him on the certain matter to find out whether there are disqualifying factors (**antarāyika dhamma**).

The Order of the **Sangha** was a system, of the **Sangha**, by the **Sangha**, and for the **Sangha**. The punishment imposed on a monk who was proven guilty was quite in keeping with the law. It was democratic, humane and just. When a monk does something wrong the Assembly of Monks is summoned. The monk who is considered guilty is brought before the Assembly. The charge (complaint) against him is presented. He is made to understand that he is guilty under such and such Disciplinary Rule. The punishment due to him is read out three times. Next, the approval and unanimity of all the members are obtained for the punishment. Then the punishment is imposed.

**Ven. Channa** was found guilty of a wrong doing. But he was not willing to accept that as wrong-doing. The Buddha was informed of this. The Buddha assembled the monks and held and inquiry. The Buddha said that punishment should be imposed on **Ven. Channa**. This was how the punishment had to be imposed. Firstly, charges should be read against him. He should be reminded of his wrong-doing. After reminding, the complaint should be formally presented. After that formality, a prominent, eloquent monk should announce this way:

> "Sirs, may the monks listen to me. This **Ven. Channa** has committed a wrong deed. But he is not prepared to accept it. If the Assembly of Monks so wishes, the Act of Suspension (**Ukkhepaniya Kamma**) could be imposed on him to prevent him working with other monks (**sambhoga**). This is the notice of that judgement. Sirs, may the monks listen to me. This monk **Channa** has committed a wrong deed. But he is reluctant to admit it. Therefore, the Assembly of Monks imposes suspension (**Ukkhepaniya Kamma**) on the monk named **Channa**, so that he will not be able to work with the other monks. If a member of the Assembly approves this punishment please let him be silent. If a member of the assembly does not approve this punishment, let him state that. I will repeat this for the second time. I will repeat for the third time. If the assembly of Monks approves this punishment, let the monks be silent. If there is someone who disapproves this, let him speak out."

Then he imposed the act of suspension on Monk **Channa**. The Assembly of Monks approved it. Therefore, the monks kept silent. It meant that they approved it.

> "Monks, the Act of Suspension has been imposed on the Monk **Channa** for not recognizing the fact that he has committed a wrong act. This Act of Suspension will prevent him from working with other monks. I will announce this in all residences of monks."

The non-aggressiveness, the civilized quality, the justice, and the democratic flavour of the Buddhist Law can be seen from these developments. Those Buddhists who are aware of the democratic principles of the Buddha offer a newly built monastery to the Brotherhood of Monks, saying that it is for the use of the members of the **Sangha** who arrive from the four directions. When a monastery is offered that way it has no single owner. In the cave-dwellings of ancient Sri Lanka, this legend is inscribed:

> "**Agata anagata catudisa sagasa dine**" (This has been conferred upon the members of the Sangha who arrive from four directions, today and in the future).

The greatness of these few words is difficult to be put into words.

The principal characteristics of a democratic, socialist society should be the absence of private ownership of property. The best formula for that is the phrase "**Agata, anagata catudisa sagasa dine**" (This has been conferred upon the Members of the **Sangha** who arrive from four directions, today and in the future).

When He implemented His socialist and democratic principles, the Buddha did not find fault with such capitalists as guild leader **Anātha Pinḍika**, or guild leader **Mahā Dhana**. He did not abuse them. He did not suggest that their wealth should be distributed among the poor. But, He indicated how best the wealth should be utilized. He stated not once or twice, but thousands of times, the ill-effects of being subjugated by wealth, of being miserly,

*"O Monks, illnesses are of two kinds. They are illnesses of the body and mental illnesses. There are those who live for one year, two years, three years, four years, five years, ten - twenty years, thirty, forty years, fifty years and, in some instances, even hundred years, without being afflicted by physical illnesses. But it is difficult to find those who are free of mental illnesses, even for one moment. The only exception are the Arahants"*

*see page 108*

of being stingy, and of craving. In short, the Buddha preached soul-lessness and pointed out the danger of selfishness and private ownership. He advocated that one should not regard even "Dhamma" with a strong sense of possessiveness, and that "Dhamma" should be utilized as a raft to cross over **saṃsara** (the cylce of becoming). **The Buddha advised that one should treat everybody alike, like the moon, without focussing on such differences as rich and poor, relations and non-relations, knowns and unknowns, friendliness and enmity, supporters and non-supporters, etc.**

**"O Monks, do not discriminate against anyone. Like the moon shining in the sky. Do not think in terms of the body and the mind. Always be fresh in attitude. Do not get excessively involved with families. Approach the houses of supporters with that kind of attitude, without attachment."**

**When we consider the above facts and other matters that occur in the Tipitaka texts, it can be firmly asserted that the earliest religious leader who built a democratic institution, supported by democratic ideas and ideals, two-thousand-five-hundred years ago, is the Supreme Buddha.**

## Joyful religion

*Buddhism is quite opposed to the melancholic, sorrowful, penitent and gloomy attitude of mind which is considered a hindrance to the realization of truth. On the other hand, it is interesting to remember here that joy is one of the seven "Factors of Illumination", the essential qualities to be cultivated for the realization of Nirvana.*

***Ven. Dr. W. Rahula, "What the Buddha Taught"***

## No assumption in Buddhism

*It is a glory of Buddhism that it makes intellectual enlightenment an essential condition of salvation. In Buddhism morality and intellectual enlightenment are inseparable from one another. While morality forms the basis of the higher life, knowledge and wisdom complete it. Without a perfect understanding of the law of causality and transformation (Pratityasamutpāda), no one can even be said to be truly moral if he does not possess the necessary insight and knowledge. In this respect Buddhism differs from all other religions. All monotheistic religions start with certain assumptions are contradicted by the growth of knowledge it increases sorrow. But Buddhism starts with no assumptions. It stands on the firm rock of facts, and can therefore never shun the dry light of knowledge.*

***Prof. Lakshimi Narasu, " The Essence of Buddhism"***

## Vasala Sutta
### The Discourse on Outcastes

The Teachings of the Buddha are distinguished by his initiatives towards unprecedented social changes. The Indian society of the Buddha's day, was uncompromising in its attitude towards caste-divisions.

The hide-bound conservatism at that age, reduced some sections of society to a demeaning and utterly degrading level. In a daring challenge to the strongly entrenched views of his day, the Supreme Buddha upheld the nobility of the human person. This was two-thousand, five-hundred years ago - long centuries before modern thinkers evolved philosophies to safeguard human rights.

The Buddha's concern for those who are down-trodden, harshly exploited and ostracized for no fault of theirs, set him apart as the greatest humanist the world has ever known. In a social context in which the domination of the brahmins who claimed unquestioned superiority because of the reason of birth, the Buddha wrought a revolution of ideas, that echoes down the corridors of time, even to our day. The formula of the Buddha's thought revolution is contained in many of his discourses. But, it is in Vasala Sutta (The Discourse on outcastes) that the Buddha's challenging views are unambiguously articulated. Vasala Sutta (The Discourse on outcastes) derives from the Buddha's response to a caste-proud Brahmin, who insulted the Buddha, for daring to appear at the site of a fire-ritual he was getting ready to perform.

## VASALA SUTTA

**Evaṃ me sutaṃ: Ekaṃ samayaṃ Bhagavā Sāvatthiyaṃ viharati Jetavane Anāthapiṇḍikassa ārāme. Atha kho, Bhagavā pubbanhasamayaṃ, nivāsetvā pattacīvaram-ādāya Sāvatthiyaṃ piṇḍāya pāvisi.Tena kho pana samayena, Aggikabhāradvājassa brāhamanassa nivesane aggi pajjalito hoti āhuti paggahitā. Atha kho, Bhagavā, Sāvatthiyaṃ sapadānam piṇḍāya caramāno yena Aggikabhāradvāja brāhmanassa nivesanaṃ, ten'upasankami. Addasā kho Aggikabhāradvājo brāhmano Bhagavantaṃ dūrato va āgacchantaṃ. Disvāna Bhagavantaṃ etad-avoca. "Tatr'eva muṇḍaka, tatr'eva samanaka, tatr'eva vasalaka, tiṭṭhāhi'ti. Evam vutte, Bhagavā Aggikabhāradvajaṃ brāhmanaṃ etadavoca: "Janasi pana tvam brāhmana vasalaṃ vā vasalakarane vā dhamme?" ti. "Na khvāhaṃ bho Gotama jānāmi, vasalam vā vasalakarane vā dhamme. Sadhu me bhavaṃ Gotamo tathā dhammaṃ desetu yathāham jāneyyaṃ vasalaṃ vā vasalakarane vā dhamme'ti. "Tena hi brāhmana sunāhi sādhukaṃ manasikarohi. Bhāsissamū'ti. "Evam-bho'tiAggikabhāradvajo brāhmano Bhagavato paccassosi. Bhagavā etad-avoca:**

## THE DISCOURSE ON OUTCASTES.

Thus have I heard: On one occasion, the Supreme Buddha was residing at Jeta-Grove Monastery of **Anātha Pindika**, near the city of Savatthi. One morning the Supreme Buddha, put on his robes with decorum, entered the city of **Sāvatthi** for alms, bearing his bowl and robe. Just at this time Brahmin Aggika **Bhāradvāja** kindled a fire and was getting ready for a ritual-offering. The Supreme Buddha, going from house to house on his alms round, reached the house of Brahmin **Aggika Bhāradvāja**, seeing the Buddha approaching his house, the Brahmin was quite perturbed. He spoke to the Buddha harshly, "Stay there O shaveling, stop there, O miserable monk, stay there O, wretched outcaste." Unperturbed, the Buddha spoke to the Brahmin. "O, Brahmin, do you know who the outcaste is - or do you know what makes one an outcaste?" "No, I do not know those Venerable Gotama. I do not know who an outcaste is - or what makes one an outcaste. Will venerable Gotama be good enough tell me the law that explains who an outcaste is and what makes an outcaste?" "All right, Brahmin. Please listen and keep it well in mind. I will tell you.

| | | |
|---|---|---|
| 1. | **Kodhano, upanāhi ca**<br>**Pāpamakkhi ca yo naro**<br>**Vipannadiṭṭhi māyāvi**<br>**Taṃ jaññā vasalo iti** | If a person tends to get angry, if a person growls and grumbles, if one is vicious, if one's views are awry, and if one is deceitful, know such a person as an outcaste |
| 2. | **Ekajaṃ vā dvijam vā'pi**<br>**Yo'dha, pānāni himdsati**<br>**Yassa pāne dayā natthi**<br>**Tam jaññā vasalo iti** | If a person hurts a living being whether once-born or twice-born, if, in a person there is no love of living beings-know such a person as an outcaste. |
| 3. | **Yo hanti parirundhati**<br>**Gāmāni nigamāni ca**<br>**Niggahāko samaññāto**<br>**Taṃ jaññā vasalo iti** | If a person is given to destroying, if one besieges villages and market-towns intimidating those who live there, if one earns a notoriety as a terrorist, know such a person as an outcaste. |
| 4. | **Gāme vā yadi vāraññe**<br>**Yaṃ paresaṃ mamāyitaṃ**<br>**Theyyā adinnaṃ ādiyati**<br>**Taṃ jaññā vasalo iti** | Whether in the village or in the forest, if someone steals what belongs to others or if one takes what is not given - know him to be an outcaste. |
| 5. | **Yo have, inam-ādāya**<br>**cujjamāno palāyati**<br>**'Na hi te inam-atthī'ti**<br>**Taṃ jaññā vasalo iti** | If a person were to take a loan, but were to evade when asked to repay, saying "I am not indebted to you," - know such a person to be an outcaste. |
| 6. | **Yo ve kiñcikkhakamyatā**<br>**Panthasmiṃ vajataṃ janaṃ**<br>**Hantvā kiñcikkham-ādeti**<br>**Taṃ jaññā vasalo iti** | If a person needing some little thing kills a man walking along a road, and takes some trivial thing - know such a person to be an outcaste. |
| 7. | **Yo, attahetu parahetu**<br>**Dhanahetu ca, yo naro,**<br>**Sakkhīputtho musā brūti**<br>**Taṃ jaññā vasalo iti** | If an individual, when asked to give evidence, utters lies either for his own sake or for the sake of another or for the sake of money - know such a person to be an outcaste. |
| 8. | **Yo, nātinaṃ sakhānam va**<br>**Dāresu patidissati'**<br>**Sahasā sampiyena vā**<br>**Taṃ jaññā vasalo iti.** | If a person, whether by force or by mutual consent is seen among the wives of relatives or of friends, - know such a person to be an outcaste. |
| 9. | **Yo mātaraṃ vā pitaraṃ vā**<br>**Jinnakaṃ gatayobbanaṃ**<br>**Pahu santo na bharati**<br>**Taṃ jaññā vasalo iti** | If a person while being rich, possessing considerable wealth - does not look after one's aged mother or father who is decrepit and whose youth is gone - know such a person to be an outcaste. |

| | | |
|---|---|---|
| 10. | **Yo mātaraṃ vā pītaram vā**<br>**Bhātaraṃ bhaginiṃ, sasuṃ**<br>**Hanti roseti vācāya**<br>**Taṃ jaññā vasalo iti** | If a person were to strike physically or by harsh speech one's mother, father, brother, sister or one's parents -in-law - know such a person to be an outcaste. |
| 11. | **Yo, atthaṃ pucchito santo**<br>**Anattham-anusāsati**<br>**Paṭicchannena manteti**<br>**Taṃ jaññā vasalo iti** | If an individual were to give veiled advise to a person to do harm, when that person seeks advise about moral virtues - know such a person to be an outcaste. |
| 12. | **Yo, katvā pāpakaṃ kammaṃ**<br>**'Mā maṃjaññā'ti icchati,**<br>**Yo paṭicchannakammanto**<br>**Taṃ jaññā vasalo iti** | If an individual, having done a wrong deed, desires not be known as the doer of that crime, and is secretive in his actions - know such a person to be an outcaste. |
| 13. | **Yo ve parakulaṃ gantvā**<br>**Bhutvāna sucībhojanam**<br>**Āgataṃ na paṭipūjeti**<br>**Taṃ jaññā vasalo iti** | If a person, who had partaken of delicious food at another's house, does not treat that other person well, when he comes to his house - know such a person to be an outcaste. |
| 14. | **Yo brāhmanam vā samanaṁ vā**<br>**Aññaṃ vāpī vanibbakaṃ**<br>**Musāvādena vañceti**<br>**Taṃ jaññā vasalo iti** | If a person were to deceive by lies, a brahman, an ascetic or any other wandering monk - know such a person to be an outcaste. |
| 15. | **Yo brāhmanam vā samanam vā**<br>**Bhattakāle upaṭṭhite**<br>**Roseti vācā na ca deti**<br>**Taṃ jaññā vasalo iti** | If a person were to scold a brahmin, or an ascetic who comes when meal-time is at hand and does not give him alms - know such a person to be an outcaste. |
| 16. | **Asataṃ yo'dha pabrūti**<br>**Mohena paliguntito**<br>**Kiñcikkham nijigiṃsāno**<br>**Taṃ jaññā vasalo iti** | If a person, shrouded in ignorance and desiring trivial profits, speaks untruths - know such a person to be an outcaste. |
| 17. | **Yo c'attātanaā samukkaṃse**<br>**Paraṃ cam-avajānati**<br>**Nīhīno sena manena**<br>**Tam jaññā vasalo iti** | If an individual while praising one's own self were to denigrate others, being of a lowly mind because of undue pride - know such a person to be an outcaste. |
| 18. | **Rosako kadariyo ca,**<br>**Papiccho, macchari Satho**<br>**Ahiriko, anottāpī**<br>**Taṃ jaññā vasalo iti** | If a person is angry, miserly, given to evil desires, avaricious, sly, shameless, unafraid to do wrong - know such a person to be an outcaste. |

19. **Yo Buddhaṃ paribhāsati**
**Atha vā tassa sāvakaṃ**
**Paribbājaṃ gahaṭṭhaṃ vā**
**Taṃ jaññā vasalo iti**

If a person were to denounce the Buddha or his disciples, or a wandering ascetic or a householder - know such a person to be an outcaste.

20. **Yo ve, anarahā santo**
**Arahaṃ paṭijānati**
**Coro sabrahmake loke**
**Esa kho, vasalādhamo**
**Ete kho vasalā vuttā**
**Mayā vo ye pakāsita**

If, an individual, while not being a holy, perfected saint, were to claim to a saint, he is a cheat of the whole universe, including the world of the Brahmas. Indeed, he is the worst of outcastes. Such persons are indeed characterized as outcastes. Let me tell you, they are the worst outcastes.

21. **Na jaccā vasalo hoti**
**Na jaccā hoti brāhmano**
**Kammanā vasalo hoti**
**Kammanā hoti brāhmano**

One does not become an outcaste by birth. One does not become a brahmin by birth. One becomes an outcaste due to deeds. One becomes a brahman due to deeds.

22. **Tad-aminā pi vijānātha**
**Yatha me'dam nidassanam**
**Candālaputto Sopāko**
**Mātango iti vissuto**

**So yasaṃ paramaṃ patto**
**Mātango yaṃ sudūllabhaṃ**
**Āgañchuṃ, tass'upaṭṭānaṃ**
**Khattiyā brāhmanā bahu**

**So devayānaṃ-āruyha**
**Virajaṃ so mahāpatham**
**Kāmarāgaṃ virājetvā**
**Brahmalokūpago ahu**

Know that, by this example I will give you. **Sopāka**, the son of an outcaste, became famous as **Mātanga**. He attained the highest glory that is rare to come by. Khattiyas (Royal Warriors) and many brahmins attended upon him. Ascending the celestial chariot, discarding desire and passion he took the noble path of passionlessness and was gone to the world of the Brahmas.

23. **Na naṃ jāti nivāresi**
**Brahmalokūpapattiyā**
**Ajjhāyakākule jātā**
**Brāhmanā, mantabandhuno**

**Te, ca pāpesu kammesu**
**Abhinham-upadissare**
**Ditth'eva dhamme gārayhā**
**Samparāye ca duggatiṃ**
**Na te jāti nivāreti**
**Duggaccā garāhāya vā**

His birth did not prove an obstacle to be born in the world of the Brahmas. Even those privileged Brahmins, born into the class of brahmanic scholars, in whose blood the sacred texts run, are frequently seen doing evil. They are found fault with, in this birth itself. After death they are reborn in woeful states. Birth cannot protect them from being born in woeful states or from being blamed.

24. **Na jaccā vasalo hoti**
**Na jaccā hoti brāhmano**
**Kammanā vasalo hoti**
**Kammanā hoti brāhmano**

One does not become an outcaste by birth. One does not become a brahmin by birth. One becomes an outcaste due to deeds. One becomes a brahman due to deeds.

***On one occasion, the Supreme Buddha was residing at Jeta-Grove Monastery of Anātha Pindika, near the city of Sāvatthi. One morning the Supreme Buddha, put on his robes with decorum, entered the city of Savatthi for alms, bearing his bowl and robe.***

*ust at this time Brahmin Aggika Bharadvaja kindled a fire and was getting ready for a ritual-offering. The Supreme Buddha, oing from house to house on his alms round, reached the house of Brahmin Aggjika Bhāradvāja.*

***On seeing the Buddha approaching his house, the Brahmin was quite perturbed. He spoke to the Buddha harshly, "Stay there O shaveling, stop there, O miserable monk, stay there O, wretched outcaste."***

*'nperturbed, the Buddha spoke to the Brahmin. "O, Brahmin, do you know who the outcaste is - or do you what makes one an utcaste?" "No, I do not know those Venerable Gotama. I do not know who an outcaste is- or what makes one an outcaste. Will 'enerable Gotama be good enough to tell me the law that explains who an outcaste is and what makes an outcaste?""All right, rahmin. Please listen and keep it well in mind." The Supreme Buddha went on:*

***If a person tends to get angry, if a person growls and grumbles, if one is vicious, if one's views are awry, and if one is deceitful, know such a person as an outcaste.***

*f a person hurts a living being whether once-born or twice-born, if, in a person there is no love of living beings-know such a person s an outcaste.*

***If a person is given to destroying, if one besieges villages and market-towns intimidating those who live there, if one earns a notoriety as a terrorist, know such a person as an outcaste.***

***Whether in the village or in the forest, if someone steals what belongs to others or if one takes what is not given - know him to be an outcaste.***

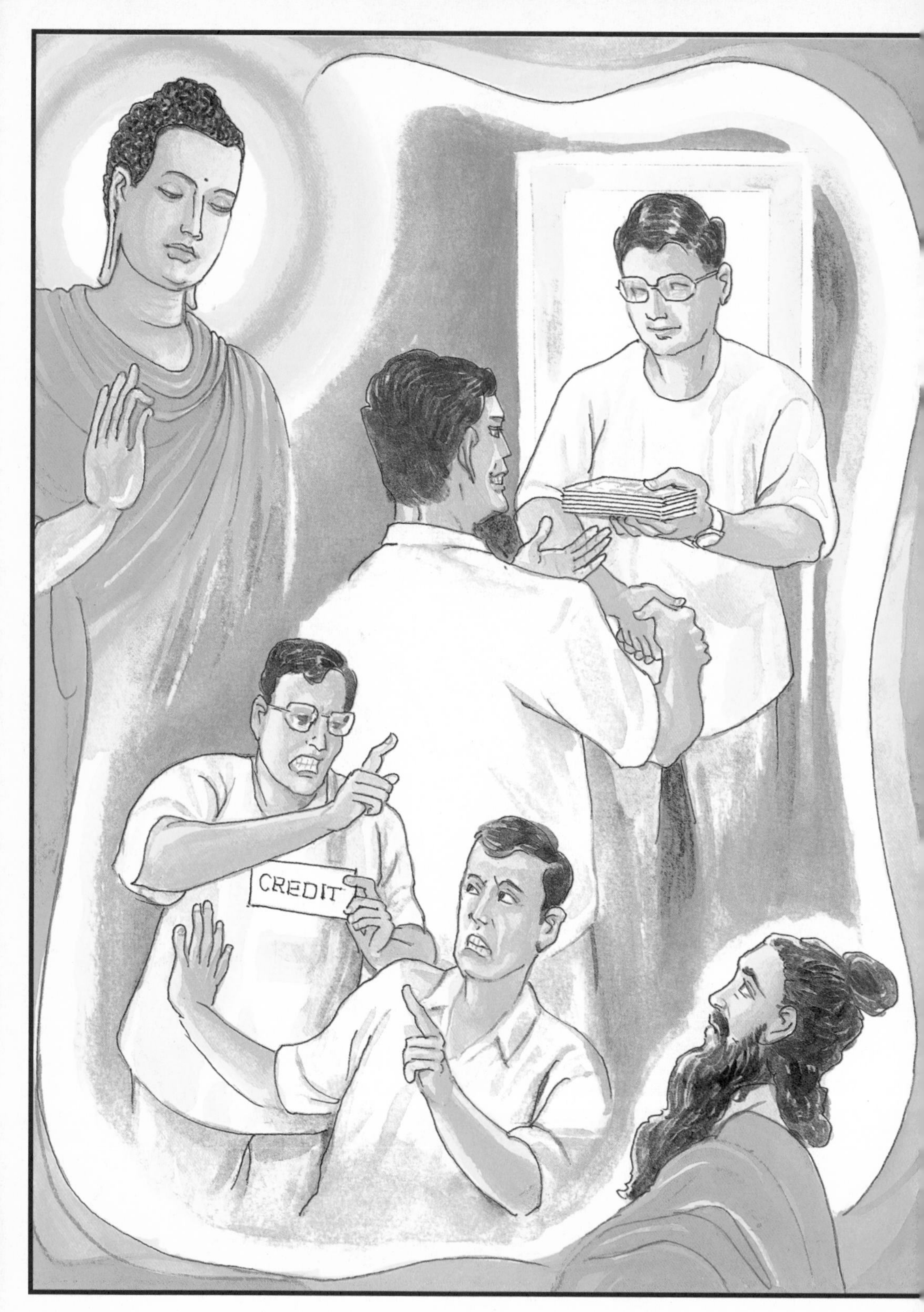


***If a person were to take a loan, but were to evade when asked to repay, saying "I am not indebted to you," - know such a person to be an outcaste.***

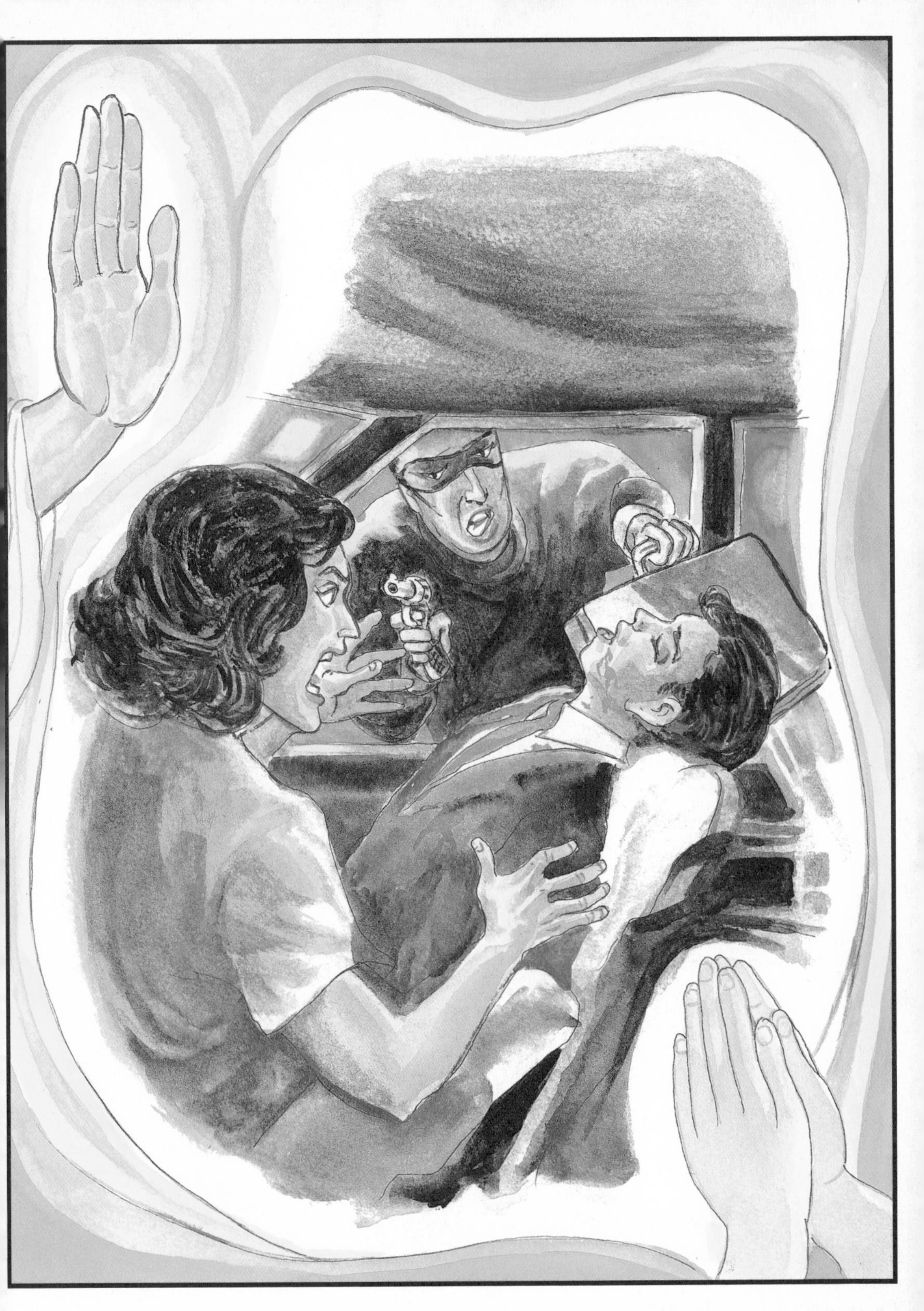

***If a person needing some little thing kills a man walking along a road, and takes some trivial thing - know such a person to be an outcaste.***

***If an individual, when asked to give evidence, utters lies either for his own sake or for the sake of another or for the sake of money - know such a person to be an outcaste.***

*If a person, whether by force or by mutual consent is seen among the wives of relatives or of friends, - know such a person to be a outcaste.*

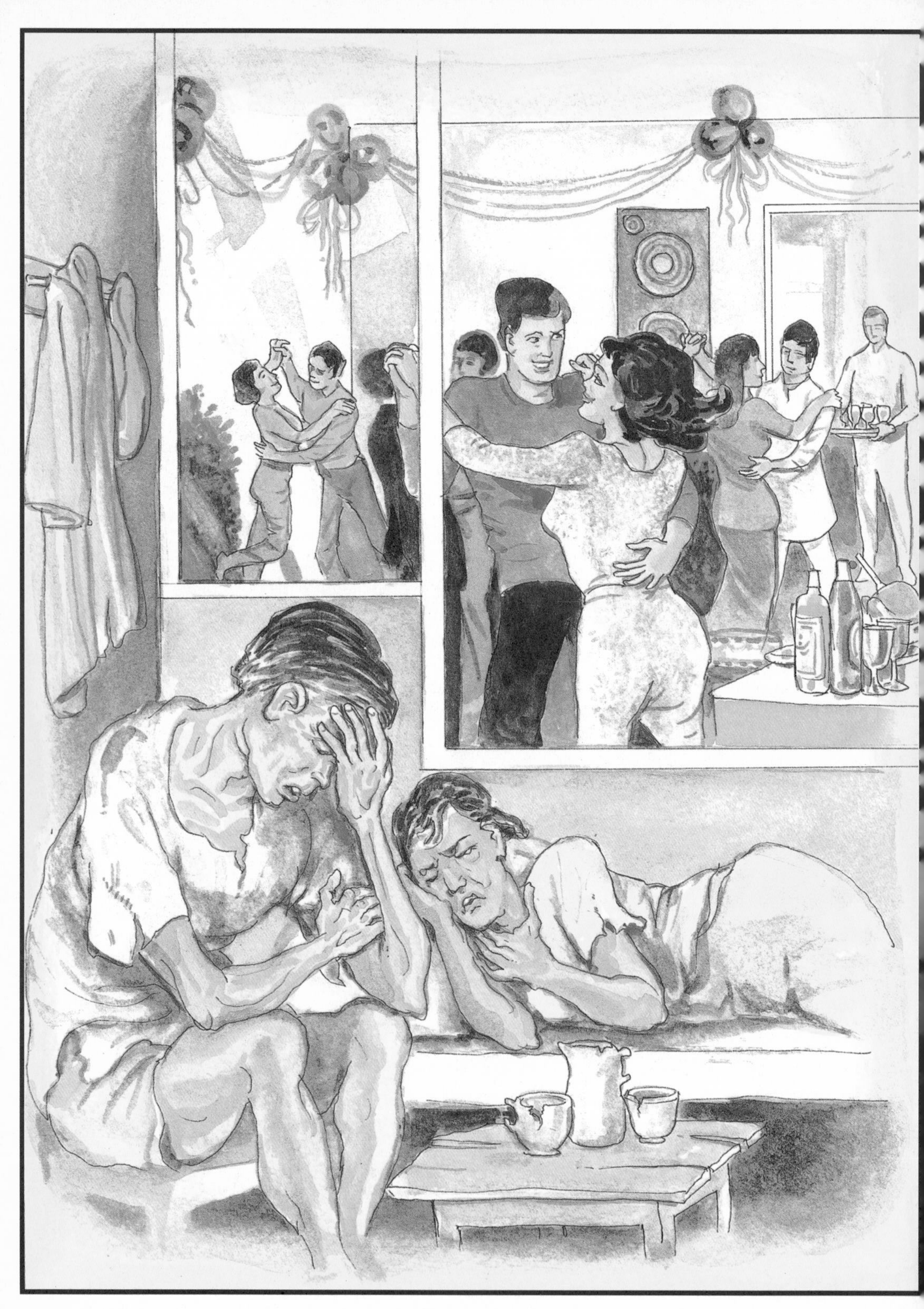

***If a person while being rich, possessing considerable wealth - does not look after one's aged mother or father who is decrepit and whose youth is gone - know such a person to be an outcaste.***

***If a person were to strike physically or by harsh speech, one's mother, father, brother, sister or one's parents-in-law - know such a person to be an outcaste.***

***If an individual were to give veiled advise to a person to do harm, when that person seeks advise about moral virtues - know such person to be an outcaste.***

*f an individual, having done a wrong deed, desires not be known as the doer of that crime, and is secretive in his actions - know uch a person to be an outcaste.*

***If a person, who had partaken of delicious food at another's house, does not treat that other person well, when he comes to his house - know such a person to be outcaste.***

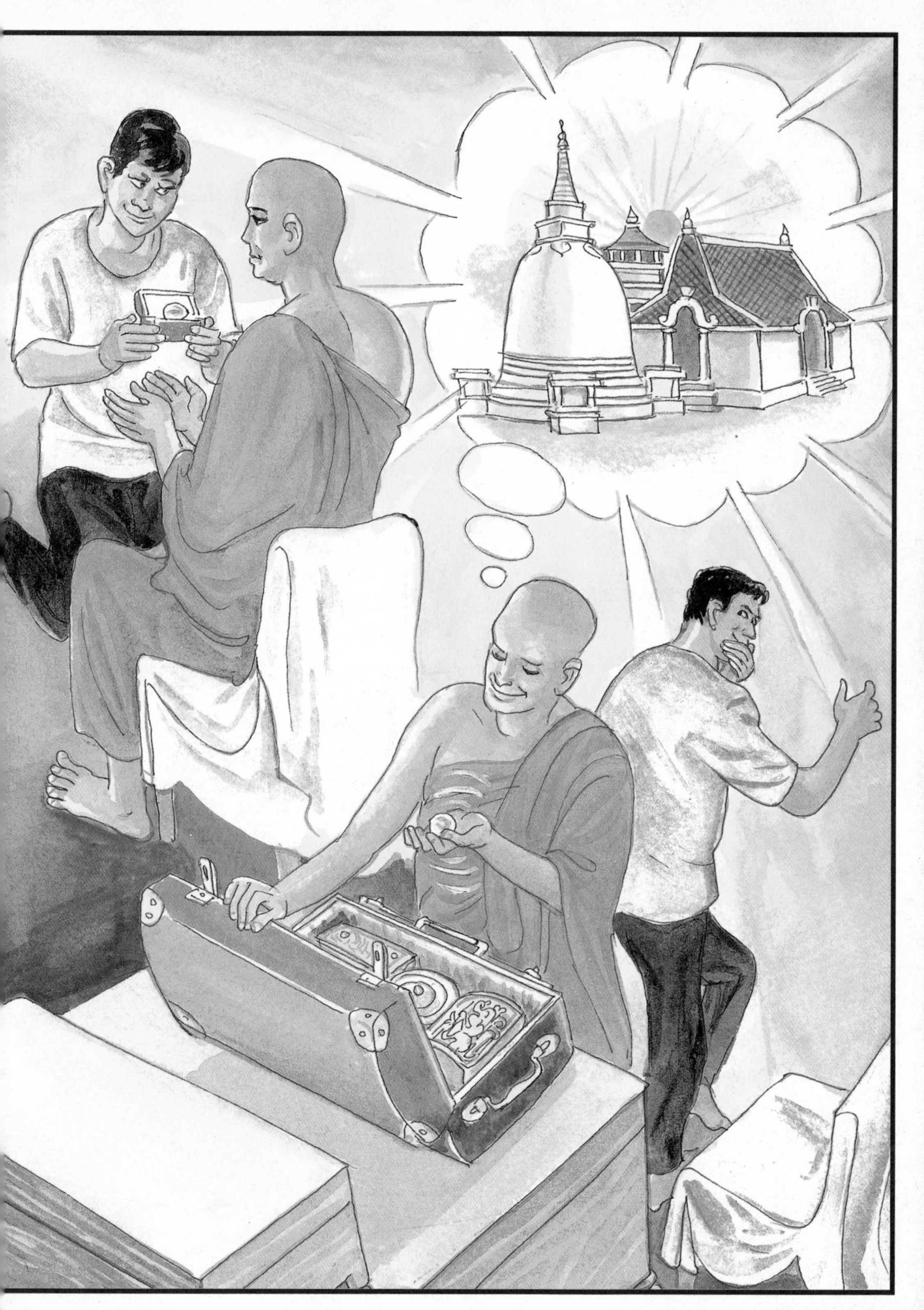

*f a person were to deceive by lies, a brahman, an ascetic or any other wandering monk - know such a person to be an outcaste.*

***If a person were to scold a brahmin, or an ascetic who comes when meal-time is at hand and does not give him alms - know such person to be an outcaste.***

*a person, shrouded in ignorance and desiring trivial profits, speaks untruths - know such a person to be an outcaste.*

***If an individual while praising one's own self were to denigrate others, being of a lowly mind because of undue pride - know such person to be an outcaste.***

*f a person is angry, miserly, given to evil desires, avaricious, sly, shameless, unafraid to do wrong - know such a person to be an utcaste.*

***If a person were to denounce the Buddha or his disciples, or a wandering ascetic or a household - know such a person to be an outcaste.***

*; an individual, while not being a holy, perfected saint, were to claim to a saint, he is a cheat of the whole universe, including the orld of the Brahmas. Indeed, he is the worst of outcaste. Such persons are indeed characterized as outcastes. Let me tell you, they e the worst outcastes.*

***One does not become an outcaste by birth. One does not become a brahmin by birth. One becomes an outcaste due to deeds. One becomes a brahman due to deeds.***

***Know that, by this example I will give you. Sopaka, the son of an outcaste, became famous as Matana. He attained the highest glory, that is rare to come by.***

***Khattiyas (Royal Warriors) and many brahminsattended upon him. They all cconsidered him a great person, in spite of his lowly birth.***

*Ascending the celestial chariot, discarding desire and passion he took noble path of passionlessness and was gone to the world of the Brahmas. His birth did not prove an obstacle to be born in the world of the Brahmas.*

*Even those priviledged Brahmins, born into the class of brahmanic scholars, in whose blood the sacred texts run, are frequently seen doing evil. They are found fault with in this birth itself. After death they are reborn in woeful states. Birth cannot protect them from being born in woeful states or from being blamed.*

## SACRED RELICS OF THE SUPREME BUDDHA

The long and glorious sweep of the history of mankind is replete with spectacular monuments erected to the memory of outstanding personalities. The Pyramids of Egypt, Taj Mahal of India are remarkable among structures built in the name of prestigious rulers of ancient times.

But there has never been anything at all in the whole of human history, to parallel the story of endless monuments, stupas, pagodas and cetiyas that were erected with great devotion and dedication to preserve the relics of the Supreme Buddha.

Most of the other monuments have their glory only for a brief period. But in the instance of the relics of the Buddha they are a living reality everyday, every moment. The relics of the Supreme Buddha are venerated with undiminishing respect, ardour and devotion all over the Buddhist world, even today.

The most impressive instance is the royal reception recently accorded to the Tooth Relic of the Enlightened One, donated by an Indian monk to the Kingdom of Taiwan. When this sacred relic passed through Bangkok, Thailand, on its way to Taiwan, the honour and adoration provided was right royal.

The adoration of the relics of the Supreme Buddha, throughout a period spanning over twenty-five centuries, is a story of epic proportions. As ages pass the glory of the Buddha's relics continues to grow, enhanced and enriched by the increasing dissemination of Buddha-knowledge on a global scale.

The Buddha's relics are classified into three groups. They are:

1) **Sārīrika** (bodily) relics. These are sacred relics from the body of the Buddha.
2) **Pāribhogika** (belonging to the category of .personal use) relics. These are objects used by the Supreme Buddha - the Alms-bowl, Robes and the Bodhi Tree that sheltered Him when He attained Enlightenment.
3) **Uddesika** (memorial) relics. The innumerable statues of the Buddha created in various cultures of the world come within this category.

Of these three categories of the Buddha's relics, the bodily (**Sārīrika**) relics are very widely spread in the Buddhist world.

Their story is, in a way, high spiritual drama, as events and episodes relating to these relics have a tremendous capacity to inspire a deep sense of devotion.

The history of the relics of the Buddha can move even those who may not be Buddhists because of their significance in the spiritual annals of man.

## The Beginning of the Story of the Buddha's Relics

Strangely enough, the great story of the Buddha's bodily relics begins almost from the time He achieved Supreme Enlightenment. The Buddha had just emerged from His deep contemplation of the Bliss of Enlightenment. At this time, two merchant brothers - **Tapassu** and **Bhallika** - were travelling from Ukkala in Orissa, toward where the Buddha was residing. At the request of a deity the two brothers met the Buddha and offered Him food (according to records, dough and honey).

It was so early in the Buddha's spiritual career that He did not even have a bowl to receive the offered food. The scripture says that the four guardian gods offered the Buddha four bowls. The Buddha accepted the meal. The two merchant brothers became His first lay disciples, taking refuge only in the Buddha and the Dhamma, since the Third Refuge (the *Sangha*) had not come into being yet.

The Buddha, pleased at their devotion, presented the two merchant brothers some hair-relics from His head. According to the history of Buddhism this is the earliest reference to the Buddha's body-relics. It is said that the two brothers, **Tapassu** and **Bhallika**, built a *stupa* enshrining these hair-relics in Orissa. Later on, these relics are said to have found their way to Burma (Myanmar) where the Stupa Shwedagon was built enshrining these hair-relics.

The formal history of the Buddha's bodily relics has its beginning in **Mahā Parinibbāna Sutta**. In that Discourse on the Great Demise of the Buddha, the Enlightened One Himself provided a description of the manner in which His bodily remains should be treated.

**Ven. Ānanda**, in his deep respect and affection for the Buddha, was quite earnest about how the funeral rites of the **Tathāgata** should be performed. With this in mind he asked the Buddha: "Venerable Sir, how should we act in respect of the **Tathāgata**'s mortal remains?"

"**Ānanda**, you may not worry about paying honour to the mortal remains of the **Tathāgata**. **Ānanda**, strive for your own well-being. Direct your efforts towards your own good. Be diligent, zealous and intent on your own good. There are, **Ānanda**, wise **khattiyas**, wise **brahmanas** and wise **gahapatis** who are greatly devoted to the **Tathāgata**. They would render due honour to the **Tathāgata**'s body."

"Venerable Sir, how should the **Tathāgata**'s body be treated?"

"**Ānanda**, the **Tathāgata**'s body should be treated in the same manner as a **cakkavatti** king's body is treated." "Venerable Sir, how is a **cakkavatti** king's body treated?" "**Ānanda**, a ***cakkavatti*** king's body is firstly wrapped with new cloth. Having so wrapped, it is then wrapped with teased cotton wool. So wrapped, it is wrapped again with new cloth."

"In this manner, the body of a **cakkavatti** king is wrapped alternatively in five hundred layers of new cloth and teased cotton. Then the body is placed in a metal coffin containing oil and is covered with a metal lid. Then a funeral pyre is erected containing all kinds of fragrant wood, and the body of the **cakkavatti** king is consigned to the flames of the pyre. And at the meeting place of four cross-roads, they erect a *stupa* in honour of the **cakkavattii** king. This Ananda, is how they attend towards the body of a **cakkavatti** king. So should the **Tathāgata**'s body be treated. And a **stupa** should be erected for the **Tathāgata** at the cross-roads of four ways. And whosoever shall offer flowers, incense, fragrant powder, pay reverence to it, and are pleased in mind at its sight, are blessed with well-being and happiness for a long time "Ānanda, there are these four persons worthy of a **stupa**. Who are the four? The **Tathāgata**, the **arahant**, the All-Enlightened Buddha is worthy of a **stupa**; the **pacceka-Buddha** is worthy of a *stupa*; the disciple of the **Tathāgata** is worthy of a *stupa*, and the **cakkavatti** king is worthy of a *stupa*.

"For what reason, **Ānanda**, is the **Tathāgata**, the *arahant*, the All-Enlightened Buddha worthy of a **stupa**? **Ānanda**, the hearts of many people would be pleased saying, 'this is the **stupa** of that **Bhagavā**, the ***arahant***, the All-Enlightened Buddha'. Being so pleased in heart therein, they become reborn in a pleasant birth in the heavenly abode, at the dissolution of their bodies. Ananda, this fact itself makes the **Tathāgata**, the **arahant**, the all-Enlightened Buddha worthy of a *stupa*.

"**Ānanda**, for what reason is a **pacceka-Buddha** worthy of a ***stupa***? Ānanda, the hearts of many people would be pleased saying, 'this is the **stupa** of that **Bhagavā**, the **pacceka Buddha**'. They, with their hearts so pleased, become reborn in a pleasant birth in the heavenly abode at the dissolution of their bodies. **Ānanda,** this fact itself makes a ***pacceka-Buddha*** worthy of a ***stupa***.

"**Ānanda**, for what reason is a disciple of the **Tathāgata** worthy of a **stupa**? **Ānanda**, the hearts of many people would be pleased saying, 'this is the **stupa** of the disciple of that **Bhagavā**, the **arahant**, the All-Enlightened Buddha'. They, with their hearts so pleased become reborn in a pleasant abode in the heavenly region at the dissolution of their bodies. **Ānanda**, this fact itself makes a disciple of the **Tathāgata** worthy of a **stupa**. "**Ānanda**, for what reason is a *cakkavatti* king worthy of a ***stupa***? **Ananda**, the hearts of many people would be pleased at its sight, saying, 'this is the *stupa* of that righteous monarch who ruled righteously'. They, with their hearts so pleased thereat, become reborn in a pleasant abode in the heavenly region at the dissolution of their bodies. Ananda, this fact itself makes a *cakkavatti* king worthy of a *stupa*. "These, **Ānanda**, are the four persons worthy of a stupa". The Buddha's words in response to the questions asked by Ven. **Ananda** prove, beyond any doubt, that the veneration and respect to the relics of the Buddha are quite in keeping with the pristine and original Teachings of the Buddha.

The long and still unfinished, ever-renewing epic of the bodily relics of the Supreme Buddha originated immediately after the sacred last rites were performed for the Buddha on His Great Demise. **Mahā Parinibbāna Sutta** (the Discourse on the Great Demise) narrates the last days of the Supreme Buddha, with due attention to all the details that centrally matter.

In the last segment of **Mahā Parinibbāna Sutta** the persons and events relating to the story of the Buddha's bodily relics are referred to extensively. The miraculous was present at almost all stages of the story of the Buddha's bodily relics.

Although **Malla** chiefs were ready to set fire to the Funeral Pyre of the Enlightened One, it did not happen exactly as they planned. Ven. **Kassapa**, who arrived late, paid homage to the Buddha circumambulating the Pyre three times. Ven. **Kassapa** touched the Supreme Buddha's feet with his head and paid his last respects. Immediately he performed these rites the Funeral Pyre ignited of itself. The flames of the Pyre made only the bones of the Buddha remain - not even ashes or dust remained.

The initial custodians of the Buddha's bodily relics were the **Mallas** of **Kusinara**. The **Mallas** arranged for the bodily relics of the Buddha to lie-in-state in their Assembly Hall (parliament) for a week. A guard-of-honour kept a vigil. This enabled crowds of mourners to pay their respects to the Buddha's bodily relics. This first-ever exposition of the Buddha's relics, took place to the accompaniment of music, singing and dancing. Flowers and garlands were offered.

After this started the phase of distributing the Buddha's bodily relics. There were several claimants to a share of the Buddha's bodily relics. They were:

1) King **Ajatasatta Vedehiputta**, the ruler of **Magadha**, sent word to the **Mallas** of **Kusānara** na indicated that he needs a share of the Buddha's bodily relics. Making this claim, King **Ajatasatta** argued: "The Buddha was a **Khattiya** - I too am a **Khattiya**. Therefore, I should receive a share of the relics.
2) The **Licchavis** of **Vesali** made an identical claim.
3) The **Sakyas** of **Kapilavatthu** argued: "The Buddha was the Chief of our clan. We must have a share of the relics."
4) The **Bulayas** of **Allakappa made** a similar claim.
5) The **Koliyas** of **Ramagrama** requested a share of the relics on the same grounds.
6) Brahmin **Vethadipa** said that he deserves a share of the Buddha's relics.
7) The **Mallas** of **Pava** had the same arguments: "We are **Khattiyas**; so was the Buddha. Therefore, we need a share of the relics."
8) On hearing all these claims, the **Mallas** of **Kusinara** adopted an aggressive attitude. The Buddha passed away in our territory - in our land. In consequence, we will not give away any share to any claimant."

With all these arguments and cross-arguments an impasse ensued.
It was then that Brahmin **Drona** intervened in the role of peace-maker between contending parties. He said: "It is not at all proper that there should be this kind of unseemly confrontation about sharing the relics of the best of men. Patience and compassion are the Teachings of the Buddha. Let us therefore through patience and understanding this dispute.

The contending parties were convinced that Brahmin **Drona**'s proposal was the right approach. The parties said: "Why, friend Brahmin **Drona**, you yourself could divide the relics justly." Consenting to the request he divided the relics into eight parts. Since he did not get a share he requested the leaders assembled there to give him the urn that was used by him as the measure to divide the relics.

Although that is how it is stated in **Mahā Parinibbāna Sutta** there is a slightly different tradition. According to this version, recorded in the Sri Lanka classic ***Thupawamsa*** (The Chronicle of the Shrine), this is what took place: Brahmin Drona opened the Casket in which all the relics were kept. Immediately it was opened the kings, ministers, courtiers and others were so emotionally moved, there was general wailing, weeping and lamentation. In this commotion Brahmin **Drona**, unseen by others, took the right tooth of the Buddha and concealed it in his hair-knot. **Sakka**, the Chief of Gods, seeing what Brahmin **Drona** had done found through his divine vision, that Brahmin **Drona** was not able to honour the Buddha's tooth relic as it deserved. Therefore, **Sakka** took it from his hair-knot and conveyed it to heaven in a golden casket placed on his head. This tooth-relic was enshrined in **Silumini** Cetiya in Heaven.

According to this version, Brahmin **Drona** did not claim a share of the relics for himself because he had already taken the tooth-relic unknown to others. At the end of the dividing of the relics he checked and found that the tooth-relic, he had concealed was gone. That, in terms of this version, is the reason why he hurriedly settled for the urn used in the dividing of the relics.

To come back to the **Mahā Parinibbāna** Sutta, there emerged another claimant to a share of the relics. They were the Moriyas of **Phippalivana**. Their arguments, too, ran along familiar lines: "The Buddha was a **Khattiya**. So are we. Therefore, we have a right to a share of the relics." By this time all the relics had been given away.The eight other kings told them: "You have come late. There are no relics left now. If you so wish you can take cinders from the site of the Buddha's Funeral Pyre. Seeing that it was futile to challenge eight kings, the **Moriyas** of **Pipphalirama** settled for the cinders.

## History of Buddha's Relics in India

In the first stage of the diffusion of the bodily relics of the Buddha ten **stupas** were erected in the following fashion:

1) **Stupa** built by King **Ajatasattu** at **Rajagaha**;
2) **Stupa** built by the **Licchavis** at **Vesali**;
3) **Stupa** built by the **Sakyas** at **Kapilavattu**;
4) **Stupa** built by the **Balayas** at **Allakappa**;
5) **Stupa** built by the **Koliyas** at **Ramagama**;
6) **Stupa** built by **Brahmin** of **Vethadipa** at **Vethadipa**;
7) **Stupa** built by the **Mallas** at **Pava**;
8) **Stupa** built by the **Mallas** at **Kusinara**;
9) **Stupa** built by Brahmin **Drona** for the urn;
10) **Stupa** built by the **Moriyas** for the cinders.

The tradition of holding Relics Festivals began immediately after these ten *stupas* were built. Kings and leaders who extended patronage to the building of *stupas* enshrining relics were also the patrons of these early Relics Festivals.

In the ancient Indian traditions relating to the relics of the Buddha the most spectacular pageant to celebrate the Buddha's relics was held by King **Ajatasattu** of **Magadha** kingdom. He conducted his share of the sacred relics in a grand procession from **Kusinara** to **Rajagaha**, his capital, hundred leagues away.

The grand procession he organized was so elaborate that, it is said, it took seven years, seven months and seven days for the procession to reach **Rajagaha**.

At the request of Arahant **Maha Kassapa**, King **Ajatasattu** enshrined a large quantity of relics in a specially protected *Cetiya*. Tradition has it that king **Ajatasattu** had a precious gem enshrined there to enable less affluent kings of the future to perform relics festivals. In this spectacular **stupa** King **Ajatasattu** had mechanical figures installed.

According to tradition the king had images of the eighty disciples, King **Suddhodana**, Queen **Mahā Māyā**, the Bodhi Tree, Queen **Yasodhara**, minister of **Kāliudaī**, Minister **Channa**, and others installed inside the Relics *Cetiya*.

It is also said that **Arahant Maha Kassapa** foresaw that Emperor **Asoka** will appear in later centuries and build **stupas** throughout the length and breadth of India to enshrine the bodily relics of the Buddha.

Just as foreseen, eventually, Emperor **Piyadassi Asoka** arose. Earlier, he was a ferocious ruler who ruthlessly destroyed all his enemies. Seeing the subdued ways of novice Bhikkhu **Nyagrodha**, he embraced Buddhism with an unprecedented ardour, and came to be known as **Asoka** the Righteous. At the behest of Emperor **Asoka** eighty-four thousand *stupas* were built to represent the eighty-four thousand segments of the Buddha's Dispensation.

Once the **stupas** were built the Emperor came up against the problem of finding Buddha's relics to enshrine in those **stupas**. He was led to the secret *stupa* that had been erected at **Rajagaha** by King **Ajatasattu,** instructed by **Arahant Maha Kassapa**. He discovered the site and found that the mechanical guardian figures that whirled around fast, bearing weapons, were still active. After removing that barrier he entered into the chamber where the relics were preserved. He divided these relics into eighty-four thousand portions and had each portion enshrined in one of the eighty-four thousand **stupas** he built.

**The *stupas* erected by Emperor Asoka bear eloquent testimony to the fact that during his reign Buddhism had spread to almost all parts of India, and into countries beyond its borders. Arahant Moggaliputtatissa Thero, who supervised Emperor Asoka's missionary programmes, had monks sent to several countries in the neighbourhood of India.**

Emperor **Asoka**'s fervour to dedicate his reign to the spread of Buddhism was determined to a great extent by his discovery of the treasure house of relics enshrined by King **Ajatasattu** of **Magadha** Kingdom. When he entered this shrine with the help of experts in mechanical devices, who stopped the whirling figures, he found the key to the shrine. Immediately he opened the door he came upon a precious gem of great value. Beside it was the message scrawled during King **Ajatasattu'**s days. The message said: "Those less affluent kings who will appear in later times can take this invaluable gem and raise the funds needed for the performance of Relics Festivals.

Emperor **Asoka** was slightly perturbed, it is said, that he should have been characterized as "less affluent king". He said to himself: "I am not poor at all," and stepped inside the relics-shrine. There, he was delighted to discover a sheet of gold on which **Arahant Maha Kassapa** had inscribed this message: "In the future a king named **Piyadassa** will become emperor of India by the name **Dharmāsoka**. He will acquire these relics and will erect eight-four thousand **stupas** in all parts of India to enshrine them." He was elated and overjoyed to read this. In his great joy he clapped his hands, saying: "**Arahant Maha Kassapa** had foreseen me when this *stupa* was originally built."

All these provided the Emperor Asoka the impetus to launch his efforts to spread Buddhism in his empire and outside its boundaries. As a zealous follower of the Buddha he decided that it was his sacred duty to make the Buddha's Teachings known to the world.

He extended his patronage to a **Dhamma**

**Sangayana** (Religious Council) to cleanse the Teachings of the Buddha that had, in some instances, been sullied by the corrupt doctrines that had begun to creep in. **Arahant Moggaliputtatissa** presided over this Buddhist Council. At the end of the Council, Buddhist missionaries were sent to various lands. According to literary sources missionaries were sent to such far countries as the land of the Yavanas (Ionian Greeks). Among other places that received the missionaries sent by Emperor **Asoka** were **Gandhara**, **Kashmi**r, the **Himalayan** Region **Aparantaka**, **Vanavasi** and Mysore. It is assumed that **Asokan** Buddhist missionaries were sent to Malaya (present Malaysia), and Indonesia. These lands are referred to in Buddhist literature as **Swanabhumi** (the Land of Gold).

It is surmised that Emperor **Asoka**'s Buddhist missionaries established links with King Antiochus II of Syria, Ptolemy of Egypt, Antigonus of Macedonia, Alexander (Alikasundara) of Epirus, and Magas of Cyrenia in North Africa.

It can be safely assumed that the missionaries who were sent to these various countries from Emperor **Asoka**'s India, took along the Buddha's relics with them. This assumption becomes all the more logical when we compare what took place in Sri Lanka. **Arahant Mahinda** and his retinue who brought Buddhism to Sri Lanka, organized the enshrining of relics in Sri Lankan **stupas**.

The occasional discovery of relics in China and in some places in India, leads to the belief that these are, in fact, re-discoveries of relics originally enshrined during Emperor Asoka's campaign to erect **stupas** and spread Buddhist thoughts far and wide. With increasing sophistication of the techniques of archaeology and the revelation of hitherto unknown centres of ancient Buddhist cultures, relics are quite likely to turn up in least suspected places.

## The Story of the Buddha's Relics in Sri Lanka

The history of Buddhist relics in Sri Lanka forms an extremely fascinating narrative. The history dates back to the time of Emperor **Asoka**'s missionary campaign. In his missionary activities Sri Lanka had been given a special place.

He was an unseen friend of the ruler of Sri Lanka. Emperor **Asoka** and King **Devanam Piyatissa** of Sri Lanka exchanged messages and gifts. Emperor **Asoka** had informed early in their exchanges of friendly gifts, that he had discovered the greatness of Buddhism. Emperor **Asoka** sent gifts to King **Devanam Piyatissa** on the occasion of the Sri Lankan king's coronation. Among the gifts sent were the five auspicious objects needed for the coronation. This way, their friendship stood on a very firm footing.

The Emperor's son, **Arahant Mahinda**, came over to Sri Lanka bearing the message of the Enlightened One. Emperor **Asoka**'s grandson, **Sumana** the novice **Bhikkhu**, was part of **Arahant Mahinda**'s group. When King **Devanam Piyatissa** decided to build a **stupa (cetiya)**, it was novice **Sumana** who went to see Emperor Asoka, his grandfather, for Buddha's relics to enshrine in the *stupa* that was being built by the King.

Novice **Sumana** brought along not only the relics given to him by Emperor **Asoka**, but also the right collar-bone of the Buddha, which was gifted by the **Sakka**. These relics were enshrined in Thuparama which was the first Buddhist *cetiya* to be built in Sri Lanka. According to one tradition the Buddha's alms-bowl, too, was brought to Sri Lanka by novice **Sumana**.

In the monumental *stupa* called "**Ratnamali Cetiya**", built by King **Dutthagamini**, the relics that were enshrined are considered to have been brought from the land of the Nagas. The relics in the possession of the Nagas came from the portion given originally to the **Koliyas** of **Ramagama**. The **stupa** built by them was swept away by the sea. The casket containing the relics was rescued by the Nagas who built a **cetiya** for them. When **Ratnamali Cetiya** was being built, novice, **Sonuttara** went to the land of the Nagas and brought them to **Anuradhapura** to be enshrined in **Ratnamali Cetiya**, built by King **Dutthagamini**.

From those early days on, the story of the Buddha's relics in Sri Lanka evolved through various impressive stages. **An outstanding episode in the history of Buddha's relics in Sri Lanka is the arrival of the Buddha's left eye-tooth in Sri Lanka. It was brought to Sri Lanka in 71 A.D. during the reign of King Meghavarna, by Prince Datta and Princess Hemamala who had the relic concealed in her hair.**

From the time this relic was introduced to Sri Lanka it became a national palladium. The possession of the tooth-relic became the symbol of the power of a ruler. Those who had rival claims to the throne, at times, tried to wrest the tooth-relic from the person who possessed it.

## Relics at the Present Exposition

The Sri Lankan relics at the present exposition come from several ancient and prestigious monasteries. One of the monasteries from which relics have been brought for this exposition is **Mahiyangana** Monastery. This is quite a sacred place for several reasons. It marks the spot where the Buddha arrived in Sri Lanka during His first visit there.

The Supreme Buddha's first visit to Sri Lanka occurred in the ninth month after His attainment of Enlightenment. The Buddha's mission was to dispel the threat to the island from demons. After the Buddha quelled the evil spirits, an Assembly was held by divine beings to listen to the Buddha.

A deity, by the name of **Sumana**, achieved stream-winning status, and requested the Buddha for a memento for him to worship and honour. The Buddha presented him a handful of hair from his head. A **stupa** was built at **Mahiyangana** to enshrine those hair-relics. This was when the Supreme Buddha was alive.

According to tradition another sacred relic was enshrined here. That was the Buddha's neck-bone It is said that a monk named **Sarabhu** took this bone out of the Buddha's funeral pyre, while the pyre was still burning.

Some relics at the present exposition come from a very ancient monastery named **Tissamaharama**, in the deep south of Sri Lanka. It is a widely renowned shrine that has existed for 2,226 years.

The builder of this *stupa* was King **Kavantissa** of Southern Sri Lanka. This place is hallowed by the Buddha's presence here, as He visited this site during His third visit to Sri Lanka. He spent a few moments in deep meditation at the spot where **Tissamaharama** would be erected 315 years after His demise.

The main Buddha-relic enshrined in Tissamaharama is the temple-bone of the Buddha. According to tradition, inside the *stupa* an image of the Buddha in gold is enshrined. The Buddha's temple-bone is enshrined behind the forehead of this golden statue. This monastery had been the centre of Buddhist learning for several centuries. In its early days it was the place where the monks from all over congregated to discuss matters regarding the Doctrine.

There is something miraculous about the neem trees around this monastery. Leaves of the neem tree are bitter in taste. But the leaves of neem branches, turning towards the monastery, are not bitter. Some Buddha-relics at this exposition come from the ancient temple at **Telwatta**. This, too, is located in the South of Sri Lanka. The ancient name for this monastery is "**Rampath Vihara**" (the Monastery with Golden Tiles).

The reputation and the renown of this temple depend, to a very large extent, on the erudite monk who resided and worked in this monastery in the 15th Century. His learning was fabulous.

He was well-versed in six languages. Because of his royal origins he enjoyed exceptional privileges. But, towards his last days, he became the victim of court intrigues. This learned monk named Ven. **Totagamuwe Sri Rāhula** had super-human powers, according to legend. He was able to tame demons and evil spirits to do his bidding.

Just before he passed away he drank a special medical potion, to ensure that his body will remain without decaying. It is popularly believed that even after about a century, his body did not decay. It even bled, it was said. His body lay in a cave called the Cave of **Indurugallena**.

This monastery was a flourishing centre of learning in the days of that learned monk. Some of its ancient glory is still intact. The monastery still possesses Buddha's relics that have been deposited in that place, centuries ago.

## Ultimate fact of reality

*Here it is necessary to draw attention to another unique feature of the religion of the Buddha, namely, that it is the only religion of any religious teacher, which is the outcome of a consistent philosophy, which claims to tell us about the ultimate facts of existence and reality. The religion of the Buddha is a way of life resulting from the acceptance of a view of life, which is said to be factual. His philosophy is not without an account of the nature of knowledge.*

***Dr. K. N. Jayatilleke, "Buddhism and Peace"***

## MAHĀ PARINIBBĀNA SUTTA

### How The Relics were Distributed

At that time venerable**Mahakassapa** was journeying along the highway from **Pāva** to **Kusinārā** accompanied with a large company of **bhikkhus** amounting to about five hundred. The venerable **Mahakassapa** steeped out from the road and sat at the foot of a certain tree. Then a certain **ajivaka** who had picked up a **mandār** flower in **Kusinara**, was travelling along the high-road leading to Pava. Venerable **Mahakassapa** saw the **ajivaka** coming in the distance, and spoke to him thus. "Friend, do you know our teacher?" "Yes, friend I know. Today is the seventh day from the **parinibbana** of **samana Gotama**. This **mandara** flower was picked up by me from there." Then of the **bhikkhus** there were not some yet freed from the passions, some threw up their arms and wept. Some flung themselves on the ground, rolled about to and fro bewailing, 'the Buddha has passed into **parinibbana** too soon, the **Sugata** has passed into **parinibbana** too soon, the eye of the world has disappeared too soon.' And those bhikkhus who were freed from passion, being mindful and composed, they endured reflecting, 'component things are impermanent. How could it be otherwise?'

Then at that time, a certain **Subhadda**, who had entered the Order in his old age was in the group. Then **Subhadda**, the old entrant to the **sangha**, spoke thus to the **bhikkhu**. 'Enough friends, do not weep, do not lament. We have been well-freed from the great **samana**. We were oppressed by his saying, 'this is proper for you, this is not proper for you.' Now we can do what we like, and do not do what we like not.' Then venerable **Mahakassapa** spoke to the bhikkhus. "Enough friends, do not weep, do not lament. Has it not been declared by the Buddha, friends, in advance, itself, that it is the nature of all things that we hold pleasant and dear, that we move out, leave and sever ourselves from what we hold dear. Where could you get a situation where what is brought into being, put together land subject to dissolution would not break ;up? Such a situation does not occur. And there could not be such a situation as to wish that the body of the **Tathagata** may not come to dissolution."

Then at that time, four **Malla** chieftains, having bathed their heads, and wearing new clothes, thinking, 'we will set fire to the Buddha's pyre,' strived to set fire to it, but were unable to do so. Then the Mallas of **Kusinara** said thus to venerable **Anuruddha**. "Venerable sir, **Anuruddha**, what is the reason, what is the cause that these four **Malla** chieftains, who, having bathed their heads, and wearing new garments, attempting to set fire to the Buddha's pyre, have not been successful in doing so?" "**Vasitthas**, the desire of the deities is different." "Venerable sir, what is the desire of the deities?" **"Vasittthas**, the desire of the deities is that venerable **Mahā kassap**a being on his way from Pava to Kusinara with a large company of bhikkhus numbering five hundred, and so long as the venerable **Mahā kassapa** does not salute the feet of the Buddha with bended head, the pyre of the Buddha shall not set alight." "Venerable sir, let it be so as the deities wish."

## Arrival of Mahā kassapa

Then venerable **Mahā kassapa** arrived at where the pyre of the Buddha was, near the **Makutabandhan**a **cetiya** of the **Mallas** of **Kusinara**. Having arrived, he wore his robe covering one shoulder, and with folded hands walked three times round the pyre with his right hand towards it in veneration, and opening the feet to sight saluted the feet of the Buddha with bended head. And the five hundred bhikhus too, with their robes covering one shoulder, and with folded hands walked round the pyre, keeping their right turned towards it in veneration, and worshipped the feet of the Buddha with bended heads. And as the venerbale **Mahā kassapa** and the five hundred bhikkhus completed their homage, the pyre of the Buddha burst into flames by itself.

As the body of the Buddha was burnt, neither ash particles remained of whatever had been of the skin, the integument, flesh, sinews and the fluid of the joints, neither soot nor ash was seen. Only bodily relics remained. Just as there remains no soot or ash when ghee or oil is burnt, in the same way as the body of the Buddha was burnt, whatever there was of skin, integument, flesh, sinews, and the fluid of the joints, neither soot nor ash was seen. Only bodily relics remained.And of the five hundred pairs of cloth, the cloth that was at the bottom of all, and the cloth that was at the top of all were not burnt. When the body of the Buddha had been burnt, torrents of water fell from the sky, exinguished the pyre of the Buddha. And water from the sala trees too poured forth, and extinguished the pyre of the Buddha. The **Mallas** of **Kusinara** also extinguished the pyre of the Buddha with water scented with many perfumes.

**Then the Mallas of Kusinara laid the bodily relics of the Buddha inside a lattice work constructed with spears within the Council Hall land surrounding it with a rampart of bows, honoured, respected, venerated and reverenced them with dance, song, music, garlands and perfumes for seven days.**

## Requests for Relics

The **Magadhan** king **Ajatasattu**, son of Vedehi heard that the Buddha had passed into **parinibbāna** at **Kusinara**. Then the

*Ven. Maha Kassapa , arrived at the funeral pyre of the Supreme Buddha. Joining his hands together in worship he went round th pyre three times. Ven. Maha Kassapa, uncovered the feet of the Supreme Buddha and paid his last respects to the Enlightened On touching the feet of the Supreme Buddha, with his head. Once his homage was done, the funeral Pyre, lighted by itself .*

**Magadhan** king **Ajatasattu**, son of **Vedehi** sent a messenger to the **Mallas** of **Kusinara** saying, "the Buddha was a **khattiya**. I too am a **khattiya**. I too am worthy to receive a portion of the bodily relics of the Buddha. I too shall build a **stupa** for the relics of the **Uddha** and hold a fitting festival in their honour."
The **Licchavis** of **Vesali** too heard the news that the Buddhda had passed into parinibbana at **Kusinara**. Then the **Licchavis** of **Vesali** sent a messenger to the **Mallas** of **Kusinara**. "The Buddha was a **khattiya**. We too are **khattiyas**. We too are worthy to receive a portion of the bodily relics of the Buddha. We too shall build a thupa for the bodily relics of the Buddha, and holding a fitting festival in their honour."

The **Sakyas** of **Kapilavatthu** heard the news that the Buddha had passed into **parinibbāna** at **Kusinara**. Then the **Sakyas** of **Kapilavatthu** sent a messenger to the **Mallas** of **Kusinara** saying, "the Buddha is our noblest kinsman. We too are worthy of receiving a portion of the bodily relics of the Budddha. ;We too shall erect a thupa for the bodily relics and hold a festival in their honour."

The **Bulis** of **Allakappa** heard the news that the Budddha had passed into **parinibbāna** in **Kusinara** saying, "the Buddha was a **khattiya**. We are also **khattiyas**. We too are worthy of receiving a portion of the bodily relics of the Buddha. We also shall erect a **stupa** to the relics of the Buddha and hold a festival in their honour."

The **Koliyas** of **Ramagama** heard the news that the Buddha had passed into **parinibbāna** in **Kusinara**. Then the **Koliyas** of **Ramagama** sent a messenger to the **Mallas** of **Kusinara** saying "the Buddha was a **khattiya**. We too are **khattiyas**. We too are worthy of receiving a portion of the bodily relics of the Buddha. We also shall erect a **stupa** to the relics of the Buddha, and hold a festival in their honour.

The brahmana of **Vethadipa** heard the news that the Buddha had passed into **parinibbāna** in **Kusinara**. Then the **brahmana** of **Vethadipa** sent a messenger to the **Malas** of **Kusinara** saying, "the Buddha is a **khattiya**. I am a **brahmana**. I am also worthy to receive a portion of the bodily relics of the Buddha. I shall also erect a stupa to the relics of the Buddha and hold a festival in their honour."
The **Mallas** of **Pava** heard the news that the Buddha passed into **parinibbāna** in **Kusinara**. Then the **Mallas** of **Pava** sent a messenger to the **Mallas** of **Kusinara** saying, "the Buddha is a **Khattiya**. We too are **khattiyas**. We are also worthy of receiving a portion of the bodily relics of the Budddha. We too shall erect a stupa to the relics of the Buddha, and hold a festival in their honour."
When this was said, the **Mallas** of **Kusinara** said thus to the assembled gathering. "The Buddha has passed into **parinibbāna** within our village region. We shall not give away portions of the relics of the Buddha."

## Intervention of Brahmana Drona

When this was said, the **Brāhmana Drona** said thus to the assembled crowd:
"Good ones, listen to this one word of mine. Our Buddha advocated forbearance. It would be unseemly if there arises strife over the bodily remains of such a noble person.
"Good ones, let us all with one accord, and in peace, and joyous heart divide the remains into eight portions. There shall be stupas spread in all directions. Many are those who are delighted with the All-seing One."
"In that case **Brāhmana**, many you yourself divide well, the bodily relics of the Buddha into eight equal portions." **Drona**, the **Brāhmana** replying to the assembled

*The Malla Rulers of Kusinagar kept the relics in their council Hall (Parliament ) for one week. While the relics lay in state in the Assembly hall, armed guards kept a vigil over them. This was the first ever Exposition of the sacred Relics of the Buddha.*

gathering said, "good ones, let it be so," and divided well,the bodily relics of the Buddha into eight equal portions.

Then he said thus to the assembled gathering. "Good ones, may you give me this measure. I shall also erect a stupa over the measure and hold a festival in its honour. " They handed over the measure to the **Brāhmana Drona.** The **Moriyas** of **Pipphalivana** heard the news that the Buddha had passed into **parinibbāna** in **Kusinara**. Then the **Moriyas** of **Pipphalivana** sent a messenger to the **Mallas** of **Kusinara**. "The Buddha was a **khattiya**. We too are **khattiyas**.' We too are worthy to receive a portion of the bodily relics of the Buddha. We shall also erect a stupa over the relics of the Buddha and hold a festival in their honour." There are no more portions of the bodily relics of the Buddha. All the bodily relics have been divided. You may take the cinders." Then they removed the embers from there.

## Erection of Stupas

Then **Ajatasattu**, the king of **Magadha**, son of **Vedehi** erected a stupa in **Rajagaha**, over the bodily relics of the Buddha, and held a festival in their honour. The **Licchavis** of **Vesali** erected a **stupa** in **Vesali** over the bodily relics of the Buddha, and held a festival in their honour. The **Sakyas** of **Kapilavatthu** erected a stupa over the bodily relics of the Budddha in **Kapilavatthu** and held a festival in their honour. The **Bulis** of **Allakappa** erected a stupa in **Allakappa** over the bodily relics of the Buddha, and held a festival in their honour. The **Koliyas** of **Ramagama** erected a stupa in **Ramagama** over the bodily relics of the Buddha and held a festival in their honour. The **brāhmana** of **Vethadipa** erected a stupa in **Vethadipa** over the bodily relics of the Buddha, and held a festival in their honour. The **Mallas** of **Pava** erected a stupa in **Pava** over the bodily relics of Buddha, and held a festival in their honour. The **Mallas** of **Kusinara** built a **stupa** in **Kusinara** over the bodily relics of the Buddha, and held a festival in their honour. **Drona**, the **brāhmana** too, built a stupa over the measure, and held a festival its honour. The **Moriyas** of **Pipphiivana** built a stupa in **Pipphalivana** over the cinders, and held a festival in their honour. Thus there were eight stupas over the bodily relics, the ninth, the stupa built over the measure, and the tenth, the stupa built over the cinders. Thus were they erected in the past.

The bodily relics of the All-seeing One are eight dronas in all.

Seven dronas are venerated in **Jambudipa**. One drona of the noblest of men, is honoured by the naga king of **Ramagama**. One tooth-relic is worshipped in the Tavatimsa heaven. One is honoured in the city of **Gandhara**. Another in the territory of the king of **Kalinga**. And another is worshipped by the naga kings.

By their glory, this earth is bedecked with noblest offerings. Thus the bodily relics of the All-seeing One are greatly venerated by those who are honoured.

They are thus honoured by the chief of the gods, **nagas** and men, similarly by noblest of human beings. May you worship him with folded hands. The Buddha is indeed a rare being rarely met for hundreds of kappas.

Forty tooth-rlics, hair relics, and hair-relics of the body, were separately removed by the gods to the series of world systems.

**BOOKS BY THE SAME AUTHOR**

**Treasury of Truth - Illustrated Dhammapada**
**Life of the Buddha in Pictures**
**Parents & Children - Key to Happiness**
**The Highest Blessing - Maha Mangala Sutta**
**Morals of the Young**
**Nature of Life and Death (In Print)**
**Buddhist Way of Meditation**
**Reflection on Death**
**Buddha Word**
**Meditation on Loving Kindness**
**Life of the Buddha for Children**
**Vision of the Buddha - (Publisher)**
**Light of Asia - (Publisher)**

---

**COVER**

*In the whole of Human History, the Supreme Buddha is the Greatest Ever Embodiment of Loving-Kindness - the Greatest ever Personification of Compassion.*

*The painting that forms the Cover-Art of this work depicts a single drop from the vast ocean of the Buddha's Supreme compassion.*

*Once, the Buddha was walking along serenely past a group of Brahmins getting ready to perform a fire-sacrifice. A new - born lamb, in milk-white purity, was held in the harsh hand of a brahmin, awaiting the signal to sever its head and spill its innocent blood. The helpless, frightened lamb was caught in the net of the Buddha's supreme compassion. The compassionate Buddha took the little lamb in his hands before the sword could fall to destroy that little drop of life. The tiny lamb became the symbol of millions of lives the Buddha would save from the grip of Mara.*

*The Artist has caught that eternal moment of compassion in the cover drawing.*

**With bad advisors forever left behind,**
**From paths of evil he departs for eternity,**
**Soon to see the Buddha of Limitless Light**
**And perfect Samantabhadra's Supreme Vows.**

**The supreme and endless blessings of Samantabhadra's deeds,**
**I now universally transfer.**
**May every living being, drowning and adrift,**
**Soon return to the Pure Land of Limitless Light!**

**I vow that when my life approaches its end,**
**All obstructions will be swept away;**
**I will see Amitabha Buddha, and be born in**
**His Western Pure Land of Ultimate Bliss and Peace.**

**When reborn in the Western Pure Land,**
**I will perfect and completely fulfill**
**Without exception these Great Vows,**
**To delight and benefit all beings.**

**~ The Vows of Samantabhadra, Avatamsaka Sutra ~**

Ven. Weragoda Sarada Maha Thero presents in this profoundly significant book entitled "The Greatest Man Who Ever Lived - The Supreme Buddha," a fresh view of the life of the Enlightened One. With this work, which in fact is a multiple-book, the publications of the SBMC, are rapidly moving towards the 200th title. Several publications are accommodated together, within the covers of this present work.

This publication also marks an unprecedented religious collaboration between SBMC and Phor Kark See Temple, for the organization of a Joint Exposition of the Relics of the Buddha. In consequence, the present work has a segment on the history of the Buddha's bodily relics.

The Venerable Author of this publication is now recognized world-wide as a Buddhist monk who has contributed a series of outstanding books to world literature on issues relating to Buddhism and to problems linked to human ethics.Millions of his books have been distributed world-wide, free. His unerring recognition of the reading habits of the moderns has resulted in the production of high quality works lavishly illustrated with colour art.

This Venerable author began his sacred mission of spreading the Word of the Buddha, world-wide, quite a long while ago. Born in Sri Lanka in 1941, he was ordained a Buddhist monk in 1953, when he was just 12. He pursued his higher education at Sri Jayawardhanepura University, Sri Lanka, and obtained his First Degree in 1964. He functioned as Principal, Indurupathvila University College, Sri Lanka, from 1965 -1967, and from 1967 - 1969, he was Principal, Sudharma University College.

He dedicated himself fully and with missionary zeal to the spreading of the Word of the Buddha abroad, beginning his service in this field in Penang, Malaysia. There, he was Principal, Mahindarama Sunday Pali School until 1979. In that year, he came over to Singapore and founded The Singapore Buddhist Meditation Centre (SBMC). The Centre has always been supported by a highly dynamic and enthusiastic group of devotees.

The Venerable Author, currently the Chief Monk at SBMC, pioneered in the founding of the American-Sri Lanka Buddhist Association of which he is still the Director. In addition, he is the current General Secretary of Japan-Sri Lanka Buddhist Centre of which he was the Founder-President. He is the Chief Incumbent Monk of Jayanthi Vihara, Weragoda, Sri Lanka.

His unique publications programme is distinguished for a whole body of works which have established a series of records. His monumental work **'Treasury of Truth - Illustrated Dhammapada'** is unparalleled for the thousands of responses it evoked just in one day. This was followed by a series of outstanding publications **'Parents and Children - key to Happiness' 'Morals of the Young' 'The Highest Blessing - Maha Mangala Sutta'.** His works appear in Sinhala, Japanese, Korean, Chinese and in English. His magnum-opus to-date, **'Treasury of Truth - Illustrated Dhammapada'**, was recently brought out in a Chinese version. His **'Illustrated Jataka Tales**, work on which is in progress, will have especially commissioned illustrations to adorn its text. Blessed with a fertile imagination the Venerable Author has already lined up an impressive array of publishing projects to spread the Word of the Buddha for the good of the many, for the well-being of the many.

**Edwin Ariyadasa**

ISBN: 981-04-0282 -1

# DEDICATION OF MERIT

May the merit and virtue
accrued from this work
adorn Amitabha Buddha's Pure Land,
repay the four great kindnesses above,
and relieve the suffering of
those on the three paths below.

May those who see or hear of these efforts
generate Bodhi-mind,
spend their lives devoted to the Buddha Dharma,
and finally be reborn together in
the Land of Ultimate Bliss.
Homage to Amita Buddha!

**NAMO AMITABHA**

**南無阿彌陀佛**


**財團法人佛陀教育基金會 印贈**

台北市杭州南路一段五十五號十一樓

Reprinted and donated for free distribution by

**The Corporate Body of the Buddha Educational Foundation**

11F., 55 Hang Chow South Road Sec 1, Taipei, Taiwan, R.O.C.

Tel: 886-2-23951198 , Fax: 886-2-23913415

Email: overseas@budaedu.org.tw

Website:http://www.budaedu.org.tw

**This book is strictly for free distribution, it is not for sale.**

Printed in Taiwan

40,000 copies; MAY 2002

EN128-2761